Assessment in Online and Blended Learning Environments

Assessment in Online and Blended Learning Environments

edited by

Selma Koç
Cleveland State University

Xiongyi Liu
Cleveland State University

Patrick Wachira
Cleveland State University

INFORMATION AGE PUBLISHING, INC.
Charlotte, NC • www.infoagepub.com

Library of Congress Cataloging-in-Publication Data

A CIP record for this book is available from the Library of Congress
http://www.loc.gov

ISBN: 978-1-68123-044-3 (Paperback)
       978-1-68123-045-0 (Hardcover)
       978-1-68123-046-7 (ebook)

CONTENTS

SECTION II

BLENDED LEARNING AND ASSESSMENT

PREFACE

Online and blended learning requires the reconstruction of instructor and learner roles, relations, and practices in many aspects. Assessment becomes an important issue in non-traditional learning environments. Assessment literacy, that is, understanding assessment and assessment strategies, is critical for both instructors and students in creating online and blended environments that are effective for teaching and learning. Instructors need to identify and implement assessment strategies and methods appropriate to online or blended learning. This includes an understanding of the potential of a variety of technology tools for monitoring student learning and improving their teaching effectiveness. From the students' perspective, good assessment practices can show them what is important to learn and how they should approach learning; hence, engaging them in goal oriented and self-regulatory cognitions and behaviors.

The book targets instructors, instructional designers, and educational leaders who are interested in understanding and implementing either summative or formative assessment in online and blended learning environments. This book will assist the relevant audience in the theory and practice of assessment in online and blended learning environments. Providing both a research and a practice perspective, this book can help instructors make the connection between pedagogy and technology tools to maximize their teaching and student learning. Among the questions addressed in this book are:

- What assessment strategies can be used in online or blended learning?

Assessment in Online and Blended Learning Environments, pages vii–x
Copyright © 2015 by Information Age Publishing
All rights of reproduction in any form reserved.

- How can instructors design effective formative assessment strategies?
- What methods or technology tools can be used for assessment in online or blended learning?
- How does peer assessment work in online or blended learning environments?

The book is divided into two parts: assessment in online learning and assessment in blended learning environments. The chapters discuss various topics such as formative assessment strategies and methods, technology tools utilized, peer assessment, Web-based assessment tools, and a framework for assessment from an institutional perspective.

PART I: ONLINE LEARNING AND ASSESSMENT

In Chapter 1, Michelle Bakerson, Tracey Trottier, and Malinda Mansfield discuss formative assessment providing a practical overview with specific examples and resources with respect to the design and use of formative embedded assessment in online learning environments.

Jennifer V. Lock and Petrea Redmond in Chapter 2 discuss an assessment practice that utilized an authentic learning activity for assessment. The assessment required students to identify their best contributions in the learning activity. This shift in assessment required students to reflect on their learning, identify evidence of their learning, and foster the development of further metacognition skills.

In Chapter 3, Philip Bonanno proposes a process-oriented model advocating an "assessment design approach" that integrates the assessment of the product with the assessment of the process—assessment "of" with assessment "for" technology-enhanced learning. The model assesses interactions along three dimensions (domain, technology, and community) and three pedagogical levels (acquisition, participatory, and contributory).

In the fourth chapter, Gail Casey uses action research to explore the unique qualities of social and participatory media within the face-to-face classroom. It was found that while redesigning the curriculum programs, the teacher also needed to rethink the assessment process to better align with the online interactions that now existed within class projects. A student-centered assessment process was explored that focused on student self-assessment, peer assessment, and teacher observations.

Shijuan Liu, in Chapter 5, reports on a qualitative study that examines the assessment methods used in online courses at the graduate level. Twenty instructors teaching online courses at five master's programs at a large public university in the United States were interviewed on a one-on-one basis. The assessment methods used in 22 online courses taught by these instructors were analyzed.

In Chapter 6, Marius Boboc discusses various formative assessment techniques aimed to increase student interactivity supporting a dynamic, ongoing course design. The course design is dynamic because it balances various opportunities online students have to interact with the content, peers, and the instructor with specific ways in which the curriculum accommodates emerging learner needs and interests.

In Chapter 7, Larisa A. Olesava and Luciana C. de Oliveira describe how embedded audio feedback was provided in students' case study reports and discuss the observed changes in students' reports when feedback was provided. The chapter also provides pedagogical implications and suggestions for instructors and designers in providing feedback on assessments in asynchronous online courses.

Chapter 8, by Barbara E. Rowan and Walter D. Way, introduces a self-paced online learning assessment system called Propero. The assessment strategy used in Propero includes formative material to keep students engaged in the course and motivated to finish while also providing summative measures of student learning. Additional services are provided to Propero students, including such as tutoring, counseling, and direct intervention, in an attempt to assist students with the learning process.

PART II: ASSESSMENT
IN BLENDED LEARNING ENVIRONMENTS

In Chapter 9, Norman Vaughan presents a research study on how blended learning and digital technologies can be used to support a triad approach to student assessment. This triad approach consists of integrating self-reflection, peer feedback, and teacher assessment practices in a blended pre-service teacher education program at a Canadian university.

Chapter 10, by Norman Herr and his colleagues, describes the continuous formative assessment (CFA) model for utilizing cloud-based collaborative document technology to instantly collect responses from multiple students, groups, and class sections.

In Chapter 11, Kay Stables and Dan Davies outlineoutlines an approach that uses dynamic Web-based performance portfolios as developed through an e-scape project (e-solutions for creative assessment in portfolio environments). Three case studies tell a collective story of how they work in practice: (a) as "controlled" summative assessment that could be used for national assessments at age 16 in design and technology, (b) as classroom assessment of scientific enquiry with primary-age learners, and (c) as formative and summative assessment in project-based learning across a range of school subjects in junior and senior high schools.

Chapter 12, by Anupama Aurora and her colleagues, presents findings from a 3-year grant project on blended learning and assessment practices. The chapter includes three case studies that describe strategies for integrating online tools into the classroom to further assessment practices demonstrating how technology facilitated a multipronged approach to formative assessment in the blended classroom. Faculty who participated in the project reported that their understanding of assessment and assessment practices changed.

In Chapter 13, David S. Stein and Constance E. Wanstreet present a rubric to assess higher-order thinking in synchronous, learner-led discussions. The rubric is designed to be used by peers to assess how content is generated, how interactions help produce content, and evidence of democratic discussion processes and critical reflective thinking. The rubric can provide students with concrete, immediate feedback on the results of their discussion process and product as well as a path to improving their performance.

Malec Wojciech, in Chapter 14, discusses the theoretical underpinnings of criterion-referenced testing in web-based and blended learning environments, and describes the development of a web-based system, WebClass, that enables the construction, administration, and test analysis of criterion-referenced language tests. Compared to traditional paper and pencil language tests, tests via WebClass offer more efficiency and practicality for teachers and promote student learning by allowing peer correction and self-assessment in addition to teacher feedback.

The final chapter, by Jean-Marc Wise and Tami Im, introduces a framework that defines six core dimensions of assessment, each forming the intersection of an agent (student, instructor, and institution) with an area of performance (education, academia, and economy) and includes selected variables for each dimension. Institutions of higher education may find the framework helpful to guide their design and implementation of a comprehensive, 21st-century assessment strategy.

SECTION I

ONLINE LEARNING AND ASSESSMENT

CHAPTER 1

THE VALUE OF EMBEDDED FORMATIVE ASSESSMENT

An Integral Process in Online Learning Environments Implemented Through Advances in Technology

Michelle Bakerson
Indiana University South Bend

Tracey Trottier
Springfield Technical Community College

Malinda Mansfield
Ivy Tech Community College

INTRODUCTION

With the explosion of online learning environments and the simultaneous continued demand for accountability, the need to identify and implement best assessment practices in online learning environments surges. In this age of accountability, priority is given to educational achievement of students at all levels; however, what worked to promote accountability in face-to-face settings in the past does not necessarily work in online environments

Assessment in Online and Blended Learning Environments, pages 3–20
Copyright © 2015 by Information Age Publishing
All rights of reproduction in any form reserved.

(Goldstein & Behuniak, 2012). The pedagogical theory is the same; however, the implementation varies across learning environments.

Assessment is the systematic process of documenting learning through measurable evidence. It is used to measure knowledge, skills, dispositions, or beliefs gleaned through instructional sequences, with an aim to improve all aspects of student learning. The two main types of assessment are formative and summative. While each is used for different purposes, both inform decisions regarding student learning. Summative assessment happens at the end of a learning sequence and typically consists of culminating projects or standardized tests. Formative assessment, on the other hand, can be thought of as a process that happens throughout the learning sequence. "The entire process involves decisions about when to test and what to test, selection or construction of suitable assessment procedures, judgments about whether assessment-elicited evidence should lead to adjustments, and choices about the nature of any adjustments" (Popham, 2011, p. 2).

Differentiating between these two forms of assessment, Michael Scriven (1967) suggested that evaluation of students for "the on-going improvement of the curriculum" (p. 41) was formative, whereas evaluation "to decide whether the entire finished curriculum...represents a sufficiently significant advance on the available alternatives to justify the expense" (pp. 41–42) was summative. Like its namesake, formative embedded assessment is an ongoing process, but its focus is much more on the assessment of student learning, rather than on the curriculum itself. Formative embedded assessment is similar to assessment FOR learning. "Students partner with their teacher to continuously monitor their current level of attainment in relation to agreed-upon expectations so they can set goals for what to learn next and thus play a role in managing their own progress" (Stiggins, 2005, p. 327). In short, formative embedded assessment is continuous information provided by instructors to students intended to improve student learning. Formative embedded assessment is strongly encouraged as it has immediate effects on student learning. All types of assessment happen in various learning environments, be it a face-to-face, a blended, or an online learning environment. The difference is in the delivery method.

The online learning delivery method offers opportunities unique to that learning environment. Technology plays a positive role on student learning, offering an engaged learning environment (Bakerson & Rodriguez-Campos, 2006). Done correctly, online learning can "provide student and instructor with richer, more immediate feedback" (Bajzek et al., 2008, p. 1) increasing student learning. Assessment in this environment benefits students and instructors (Dewald, Scholz-Crane, Booth, & Levine, 2000). It also is a practical necessity, considering that at all levels of education, from Pre-K to higher education, the demand for accountability has a firm grip that is not going to loosen anytime soon.

DESIGNING AN ONLINE LEARNING ENVIRONMENT

The first step in designing an online learning environment using best practice, as with any course and setting, is to identify the learning objectives. Establishing exactly what students are expected to learn is pivotal. Once the objectives are established, all learning activities and assessments are derived from them. Along with information regarding all assignments, teaching strategies, and assessments, learning objectives must be listed on the syllabus (Sewell, Frith, & Colvin, 2010). Ideally, each learning activity, assignment, and assessment listed will indicate which objective it is intended to meet; a model syllabus will include artifacts linked to program goals and objectives. Most instructors follow Bloom's (1956) taxonomy, but many also follow Anderson and Krathwohl (Krathwohl, 2002). Regardless of the taxonomy used, in designing objectives, it is important to understand what the students are learning and how evidence will be gathered to assess whether students have met the established learning objectives. Before preparing assessments for the semester, an instructor should answer the following questions: What needs to be submitted/collected, or how should a given lesson be administered, to provide evidence that students have achieved the course learning objectives? How will feedback be communicated to provide information on a student's progress? What does proficiency mean to students? Thinking through these questions will prepare instructors to consider how to tailor the specific tasks to an online learning environment.

CRITICAL DIFFERENCES IN LEARNING ENVIRONMENTS

One key difference in an online environment is the inability for the instructor to read the student's body language. Instructors in online learning environments are at a disadvantage, missing nonverbal cues—expressions of confusion on a student's face, for example, or distracted doodling in a notebook—that could help them gauge understanding. Lacking such real-time information to guide their continuing assessment, online instructors need to take extra care to assess students from the beginning. They can begin by establishing a baseline assessment of each student's skill level and ability to meet the technology requirements of the online learning environment. Students need to be able to demonstrate their ability to complete tasks in an online environment before learning the content itself. In other words, formative assessment needs to be used as an "early detection" device. If students feel frustrated or lost in the early part of an online course, they will most likely continue to feel lost for the remainder of the course and miss out on important learning opportunities. Early detection begins with an assessment before the course starts and then continues as embedded formative assessment along the way. It allows the instructor to make immediate, needed changes to the course so students can work at mastering the subject material and meeting the course objectives. Instructors can use commercial programs or tests that measure technology skills, such as SmarterMeasure Assessment, The Accuplacer Computer Skills Placement Test, and the Kentucky Community & Technical College System (KCTCS) Computer Literacy Exam, or they can create embedded assessments for that purpose, such as mock assignments asking students to post coursework or answers, send an email, send an instant message, or complete "get to know you" assignments. This is when the instructor can intervene if needed.

Another fundamental difference—and sometimes the cause of failure in online learning environments—is the lack of community. The sense of community comprises four distinct but interconnected elements: membership, influence of the student on the community, meeting of personal student fulfillment/needs, and a sense of personal connection (McMillan & Chavis, 1986). Creating a sense of community and engagement in an online learning environment can be a challenge, but it can be accomplished by incorporating techniques into the instructional design. One way to do so is through the use of asynchronous collaboration tools, such as Adobe Connect or Blackboard Collaborate. With such tools, an instructor can load PowerPoint presentations for the class that the students view live, together, on the Internet, following a short introduction by the instructor. The instructor can narrate the presentation live or through a recording. Simply making the event an experience shared in real time can help establish a sense of classroom community.

An online instructor can assess the sense of community by observing who is participating in the group, who is presenting, and what has been said in the group reflections. The instructor, however, also must be an integral part of the community. It is becoming more prevalent for instructors in online learning environments to use more engaging, formative approaches to assessment instead of giving traditional tests at the end of chapters (summative) (Tinto, 2009).

ONLINE LEARNING ASSESSMENT TECHNIQUES: GATHERING EVIDENCE

Assessment is vital for the success of any learning environment, but it is imperative in an online learning environment, where threats to reliability and validity are higher. Reliability is defined as "an indication of the consistency of scores across evaluators, [or] over time" (Bond, Herman, & Arter, 1994, p. 23). Regardless of when the assessment takes place or who scores it, the results should be the same. Yet conditions are not the same for each test-taker. In an online learning environment, there are constraints in how assessments can be conducted. Many learning management systems have time limits that can be set to address some of this threat to reliability. Cheating, however, is harder to control. The risk of cheating can be alleviated through proctoring exams or other learning activities; a study conducted by Richardson and North (2013) suggests that exam proctoring can help deter students from cheating.

When students' use of outside materials during a testing situation cannot be controlled, assessments in the form of tests need to be carefully designed using higher-order thinking skills. Students are then required to come up with well-developed answers, instead of answers that can be easily looked up. Another form of cheating, though, is unique to online environments: not being able to verify who is actually taking the course (Christen, 2003) or taking an assessment. This could be mitigated with asynchronous meetings where students meet in a live session with the instructor. One other aspect of cheating that is common to all types of learning environments is plagiarism. The program Turnitin.com can offers an originality check against numerous sources and provides the student and the instructor a detailed report. Besides helping to detect plagiarism, the report can offer students needed feedback to improve their writing, which will enhance their overall learning experience. Betts, Bostock, Elder, and Trueman (2012) found that first-year students "reported a broadly positive experience of using Turnitin and reported that the experience helped to raise awareness of the issues surrounding good practice in academic writing" (p. 78). Finally, feedback that goes unread or is misinterpreted is not valuable to students. In place of or in addition to the more conventional written feedback, instructors have the option of voice feedback. Voice feedback may decrease threats to reliability since there is less chance of misinterpretation. Furthermore, the ability to provide feedback through different modalities is important to teaching diverse students.

Validity is defined as "an indication of how well an assessment actually measures what it is supposed to measure" (Bond et al., 1994, p. 24). When an online learning environment is not designed with embedded formative assessments built in to the course delivery, construct validity takes on added importance. Students can easily misunderstand information, definitions, or meanings. Instructors in face-to-face classrooms have more of an opportunity to pick up on these misunderstandings through nonverbal communication and can provide clarification immediately. In online learning environments, such misunderstandings might go unnoticed. Technology such as automatic assessment programs, which may be designed to assess something outside of the course objectives, further challenges the validity of assessment. Additionally, extraneous factors can interfere with the learning process; these might include personality, physical limitations, the ability to read or write, and, most importantly, in online learning environments, the ability to use technology. Instructors must ensure that assessments assess only what is in the actual course objective, and must exclude from the assessment those things that get in the way of students seeking to demonstrate what they have learned. Well-developed embedded formative assessment meets that standard.

TECHNOLOGIES FOR ONLINE EMBEDDED FORMATIVE ASSESSMENT: USING WHAT IS PRACTICAL

For all aspects of embedded formative assessment, technology can be used to implement and foster enhanced student engagement with the learning experience. Instructors can use discussion postings (Vonderwell, Liang, & Alderman, 2007), 1-minute papers (Angelo & Cross, 1993; Vonderwell, 2004), reflective writing and journaling (Butler, Tatner, & Tierney, 2010; Fink, 2003), embedded quizzes (Lowe & Hasson, 2010), surveys, or authentic learning activities to evaluate how students are learning, then use this evidence to modify lessons.

How can technology assist instructors in determining whether, and how well, students are learning? How can instructors decide what is best assessment to use in a particular online learning environment? How can these technologies be used while ensuring they are both reliable and valid? When should these technologies be used? Of the many technologies available, how can it be determined which will meet the needs of instructors? To look at these sorts of questions, Leahy, Lyon, Thompson, and Wiliam (2005) present five approaches for assessment, approaches that define what assessment could look like in any classroom:

1. Clarifying and sharing learning intentions and criteria for success
2. Engineering effective classroom discussions, questions, and learning tasks
3. Providing feedback that moves learners forward
4. Activating students as the owners of their own learning
5. Activating students as instructional resources for one another. (p. 20)

In his book Embedded Formative Assessment, Dylan Wiliam (2011) gives suggestions how these strategies can be used in face-to-face classes. In an online or blended learning environment in which instructors and students do not necessarily meet face-to-face, technology may be required to implement these approaches. This section highlights some technologies that can be used, including online authoring tools, rubrics, feedback tools, and several features of learning management systems (LMSs). Descriptions and uses are discussed and a summary table is provided (Table 1.1).

TABLE 1.1   Online Learning Environment Technology Tools and Uses

Category	Technology	Use
Learning Management System	Blackboard www.blackboard.com Canvas www.instructure.com Desire2Learn www.desire2learn.com Docebo www.docebo.com Moodle www.moodle.org Sakai www.sakaiproject.org	Learning management systems offer many different uses for assessment. Some uses include the ability to integrate rubrics, the ability to create and deliver quizzes and exams, and the ability to provide discussion tools that can be used to assess if learning is taking place. Their potential alone, or in conjunction with other technologies, allows instructors to embed assessment directly into the online learning environment. Since courses could be created in a sequential format, where students are required to complete one lesson prior to entering the next, instructors can verify their understanding of content prior to moving to the next.
Rubric Generators	iRubric www.rcampus.com/indexrubric.cfm Isocrates www.isocrates.org/front Roobrix roobrix.com/ RubiStar rubistar.4teachers.org/ Sites4teachers www.rubrics4teachers.com Teach-nology www.teach-nology.com	As a whole, rubric generators can be used to include specific learning objectives for an assignment, activity, etc. They not only provide students with the criteria for that learning activity, they are a quick and easy way for the online instructor to grade. This is especially important in larger classes where the amount of work to be graded can be cumbersome.
Online Authoring Tools	Course Lab www.courselab.com Google's Course Builder code.google.com/p/course-builder/ SoftChalk www.softchalk.com Udemy www.udemy.com Udutu www.uduto.com	Online authoring tools provide instructors with the ability to create packaged course material. They can be used to create a lesson that starts with the learning objectives for the lesson, provide content to teach the material, and then provide learning assignments, activities, quizzes, etc. to assess if the students have learned the material and met the objective of the lesson.

(continued)

TABLE 1.1   Online Learning Environment Technology Tools and Uses (continued)

Category	Technology	Use
Discussion/ Collaboration Tools	Adobe Connect www.adobeconnect.com Google+ plus.google.com Blogger www.blogger.com Course Networking www.coursenetworking.com Wikispaces www.wikispaces.com WordPress www.wordpress.com	Through synchronous and asynchronous discussions instructors can gauge the level of learning that is taking place. Instructors can see if students are correctly using the terminology, concepts, and material of a lesson and then provide feedback to the students. Since many of these discussion tools are not secure sites, their use should be done with caution.
Online Response Systems	Socrative www.socrative.com QuestionPress www.questionpress.com Poll Everywhere www.polleverywhere.com	Online response systems can be used to determine if students have learned material, especially in synchronous online learning environments. As an instructor presents material he or she can then determine through a poll, survey, or quick quiz if the material has been correctly processed.
Student Feedback Tools	Turnitin www.turnitin.com Google Docs docs.google.com	Turnitin, and like tools, can offer student feedback immediately on writing proficiency. If used as a learning tool it can help instructors assess students' understanding of what constitutes original material in a paper. GradeMark provides feedback on spelling, grammar, and writing mechanics. PeerMark can be used to have students evaluate and provide feedback to each other.
Other Tools/ Technology	Quizlet www.quizlet.com Educaplay www.educaplay.com Eclipse Crossword www.eclipsecrossword.com	There are many online tools that allow instructors to create and then embed learning activities into their online learning environments. These can be used to have students assess themselves to determine if learning has taken place. They may also provide instructors with feedback of which concepts may need to be repeated.

Learning Management Systems

The learning management system (LMS) is a software application that instructors can use to meet assessment strategies, specifically by "clarifying and sharing learning intentions and criteria for success" and "providing feedback that moves learners forward" (Leahy et. al., 2005, p. 20). Many learning management systems provide ways to include content, exams, learning assignments, and related materials within the application itself. In Canvas by Instructure, instructors can develop rubrics to assist students in understanding the requirements of assignments and also can create exams. Similar features can be found in most learning management systems. Since Canvas is cloud-based, it offers additional ease in feedback. Piña (2013) explains that "Canvas features a speed-grader system that displays students' written assignments as a graphic image on the left side of the screen with rubrics, grading and feedback tools on the right, allowing for grading and feedback to occur without having to open and save documents onto the instructor's computer" (p. 14). This ease in grading is important for feedback to be provided quickly and effectively to students.

Most learning management systems also offer tools to provide exams or quizzes. Whether used weekly or less frequently, these assessments can provide instructors with a measurement of student learning. Common features of learning management systems "include a test/assessment manager for creating and deploying exams, a generator for creating different types of questions…and question pools or text banks to store questions that can be used for multiple exams" (Piña, 2013, p. 3). These tools make it easier for instructors to be able to use the same assessments in various courses or sections.

Online Authoring/Creation Tools

According to Diwakar, Patwardhan, and Murthy (2012), authoring tools "allow its creators to integrate an array of media to create customized, professional, engaging, and interactive content" (p. 84). SoftChalk is an authoring tool that allows instructors to include content and assessment in one easy format. SoftChalk's required license can provide either a desktop or cloud application. This design tool works with most LMSs and in any learning environment and can be used to include all the elements of a course. The objectives are stated at the beginning of the learning sequence; content and activities are embedded throughout; and quizzes can be linked to a grade book. Instructors can use many of the different activities from SoftChalk for students to self-check their own learning along the way. Using these embedded assessments allows students to be self-regulated learners. According to Banks (2012), SoftChalk lets "students know immediately if they have not mastered the content and can work through the content until they gain mastery" (p. 85). She points out that SoftChalk is easy to use and can be a fun way for students to learn. Different types of activities can be used so students can determine if they properly understand the material. Examples of formative assessment activities in SoftChalk include crossword puzzles that students can use to test themselves on terminology, timeline activities to allow students to self-check their understanding of the history relevant to the course subject, or pairing activities that require students to show they can pair equations with their theoretical foundation. Students having difficulty can contact the instructor, who can clarify the material or provide additional resources. A SoftChalk quiz feature can be tied directly to the lesson. At the completion of the learning sequence, the students take a quiz to demonstrate understanding of the sequence material. The quiz feature includes an option of instant feedback for students to see if they understand the material before moving on.

Another authoring tool that can be embedded in LMSs is EclipseCrossword. This cloud-based tool allows instructors to create crosswords specific to their learning objectives and then load them into an online learning environment. These can be used for student self-check, which helps students determine if they should proceed. Embedding assessments continuously throughout the content gives students the ability to determine if they understand the material well enough to move on or if they should contact the instructor to get additional clarification. Enabling students to take ownership of their learning further helps address concerns about reliability and validity that are especially acute where online learning is concerned.

Many other technologies can provide similar activities for students. Many publishers involved in expanding online learning environments also provide faculty with learning activities that students can connect to through companion sites. There are also many free sites that students can access to explore their readiness for summative assessment of material.

Rubrics

The technologies discussed thus far concentrate on "providing feedback that moves learners forward" and "activating students as owners of their own learning"; additional technologies can be used "clarifying and sharing learning intentions and criteria for success" (Leahy et al., 2005, p. 20). Online rubric development tools are especially helpful in this area and are readily available on the Internet. Due to its compatibility with many learning management systems in its paid, premium version, iRubric is discussed here, but many others, such as RubiStar, Rubrics4teachers, and Roobrix, are also available. Rubrics are essential for embedded formative assessment, since they provide specific criteria when given prior to or with an activity or assignment. Embedding rubrics within an online learning environment enables students to understand the objectives and grading criteria ahead of time. iRubric allows for the rubrics to be included within the assignment itself and can save instructors time with grading by locating all the necessary material in one place. It is becoming more common for learning management systems to include integrated rubrics in their design, since formative assessment is critical for student success in online learning. Systems such as Blackboard have an interactive rubric feature, and open-source learning management software such as Moodle and Canvas also include rubric features.

Discussion/Collaboration Tools

To meet the need for effective discussion and questions in assessment (Leahy et. al., 2005), online instructors can include synchronous or asynchronous discussions with students. Not only do students need to provide clear and concise responses to an initial prompt, but they also need to cultivate critical thinking skills as they respond to other students within the online learning environment. Responding and reflecting on other students' answers enhances student evaluation skills, affords a broader range of feedback, and decreases the workload of the instructor (Anderson, 2004; Bostock, 2000). New technologies being created better allow for seamless discussions in online classes. One such technology is Course Networking (CN), a discussion tool that brings social media features that students might be familiar with into a structure that is tailored to educational needs. Instructors can create course discussions where students become followers and members; the similarity to Facebook or Twitter can help students feel comfortable in holding discussions in the format. These discussions, in turn, can be reviewed by the instructor to determine if students are able to speak to the objectives of the learning sequence. Course Networking employs an online reward system of "seeds" that students can earn through increased activity; rewarding students encourages motivation and ownership of learning. Online discussion also allows students to be resources to each other, since many can provide additional details. Course Networking can be linked from various learning management systems, giving students greater ease of access by allowing them to work through their own institution's site.

Technologies including collaboration, blogs, and wikis offer other ways to assess students through discussion. Several students can work simultaneously in these tools, collaborating and editing in real time. Collaboration tools such as Blackboard Collaborate, Adobe Connect, or Google Drive (formerly Google Docs) include group project features that show history and sharing features for student–teacher interaction. They also allow instructors to post an online rubric to assess group participation and project effectiveness. Through the group project feature, students are placed into groups by the instructor; the instructor has an option to send each group a virtual "handout," such as a project rubric that students can work with. The instructor can set a timer for students to work together online or to meet during another class session. Arranging for students to work in groups during class time allows the instructor to go into each group project and assess each individual student as well as the group process. When a project is due, students can "present" their work to the whole class. The instructor can fill out the rubric and post the graded rubric and feedback soon after students' presentations have been given. A private group reflection can be submitted later if the instructor so chooses. Group reflections help limit nonparticipation, improve overall involvement, increase communication, and enhance group skills (Crockett & Peter, 2002). In a study by Chu and Kennedy (2011), undergraduate students reported using MediaWiki and Google Docs in a group project as a positive experience, with Google Docs being particularly user-friendly. Both platforms supported collaboration in an online learning environment and both have a history function for ease of monitoring activities. Instructors reported that drafts of papers were no longer needed and that in comparison with traditional learning environments, more immediate, detailed feedback could be given regardless of which platform was used, MediaWiki or Google Docs.

Incorporating collaborative learning and reflection as part of the learning process once again allows students to take ownership of their education, increasing the value of thorough self-awareness. Most so-called digital natives are comfortable working in collaborative learning atmospheres, which allows for better cognitive retention regardless of the subject. A study by Wang (2011) supports the value of collaboration with other students in an online class, finding that it enhanced student learning outcomes. Students who worked collaboratively with peers in an online environment found that they had "the opportunity to learn from other resources than just the textbook and the instructor" (p. 87), which provided students with an opportunity for self-reflection of their own work. Technology tools can facilitate that. For example, almost every course has some type of reading requirement. Creating small-group Wikis, where students can post one key element that they thought was important and then reflect upon how it relates to them, promotes critical thinking and increases students' engagement with and thus learning from the material. Assessing the Wiki then becomes an important aspect of evaluating students' content knowledge as well as assessing students' sense of community. It is equally important for the instructor to participate in each group and provide personal reflections, which facilitates becoming a part of the community and enables the instructor to continuously offer embedded assessment.

Student Feedback Tools

Other students can be part of the formative assessment connection when they review and offer feedback on each other's work. Turnitin.com has a feature called PeerMark that allows instructors to make students responsible for reading and providing anonymous initial feedback on papers and assignments. In addition, Google Sites, a website and wiki authoring service, could be used, although this tool does not provide anonymous feedback. This collaborative learning approach not only provides many different levels of feedback to students, it also allows the student reviewer to become a better writer. A study by Travares, Chu, and Weng (2011) of peer monitoring found that students' ability to leave feedback and comments for their peers enabled another level of learning to occur. Additional advantages were noted by a student: "If we use Google Sites as the collaborative platform, we read the writings from other classes and comment on our classmates' work in order to exchange views. If we write it on paper, we can just read a few pieces of writings" (p. 3). By providing embedded formative assessment a student reviewer learns through teaching others. Mosert and Snowball (2012) found that being able to assume the role of educator or assessor is important to students. They develop a higher level of critical thinking by evaluating others' work than they do by just receiving feedback from peers.

This type of assessment works regardless of the number of participants, but is particularly useful in larger environments where the instructor might not be able to give each student substantive feedback. Using peers to initially review student work allows for more expedient feedback. Students also find peer assessment helpful to their overall learning. In a study of undergraduates using formative peer assessment, Vickerman (2009) reports that "many students [indicate] that it brought increased confidence, understanding of the requirements of the task, enhanced subject knowledge and appreciation of the intricacies of assessing their own and others' work" (p. 229).

Turnitin.com can also provide preliminary writing feedback to students with its GradeMark tool. The instructor can set the application to automatically display feedback to students, or the instructor can add additional feedback to improve the writing of students' papers. Research also supports positive reactions from students regarding formative embedded assessment (Chang et al., 2012).

Online Response Systems

Online response systems grew out of the classroom response systems that have been used in face-to-face classes. According to Beatty and Gerace

(2009) "a classroom response system (CSR) is technology that helps an instructor pose questions and polls students' answers during class" (p. 146). It requires students to have a device, such as a clicker, to input answers and requires students and instructor to be in the same location; it is therefore not readily adaptable to online learning environments. The creation of online response systems brings this same approach into the online environment. With these systems, students can respond from their own phones, tablets, or personal computers. Cloud-based response systems such as polleverywhere. com allow online instructors the same benefits of the classroom response systems. They can ask questions of their class to determine if learning has taken place. It might be just a quick poll or survey to determine if students understand the material, or may be more formal to determine if students have completely grasped a concept under review.

Beatty and Gerace (2009) suggest that using questions in learning is beneficial. They suggest that asking questions can help in many ways, "including learning about the students' knowledge and thinking; helping students become more aware of their own and each [other's] knowledge and thinking; preparing a fertile context for subsequent instruction; catalyzing small-group discussion and peer learning; provoking, motivating, grounding, and shaping whole-class discussion of a topic; and precipitating student insights and realizations" (p. 158). Questions can be posed during a synchronous online session to help students through difficult topics, or they can be used in an asynchronous session, which will help determine if the students are ready to move onto new material.

An Example

There are many different technologies used for embedded formative assessment. To give an example specifically for an undergraduate online course, an instructor could start by adding content with a tool such as SoftChalk. The first page of the online learning sequence lists the objectives. Continuous embedded assessments such as quick quiz poppers, embedded self-assessment questions, might be added with a couple of questions for students to check for comprehension. As students move through additional content, another activity, such as a crossword, could be included. Once students have worked through all the content and embedded formative assessments, an assignment could be the next part of the learning sequence. A rubric clearly outlining the criteria used by the instructor could be included. The assignment could easily be graded based on the rubric criteria and would provide quick feedback for students to check comprehension. To promote collaboration, allowing students to clarify things with others, a discussion could take place around concepts that students do not understand; the discussion could be asynchronous or synchronous, depending on the online learning environment and the instructor's preference. This would allow students to bring additional questions about content that could be answered by either the instructor or fellow students. Once students have worked through all the content and feel comfortable, the instructor could use a summative assessment.

CONCLUSION

This chapter does not explain all the different technologies and their uses; however, it does provide an introduction to online instructors looking to improve the performance of their students. Embedding formative assessments offer instructors solid indications regarding achievement, both application and knowledge based, and whether learning objectives were met. Viewing embedded formative assessment as a process in online or blended learning environments is essential. This understanding mitigates threats to reliability and validity and ensures that course objectives are met and student learning is achieved. The success of quality online learning environments depends on the usage of prompt and well-delivered assessment; therefore, it is important to consider assessment as an integral part of the course that when used properly has immediate effects on student learning. It cannot be seen as an add-on, but instead must be designed right alongside content. Embedded assessment and content are an integral part of each other in any course design, particularly so in online learning environments.

REFERENCES

Anderson, T. (2004). Teaching in an online learning context. In T. Anderson & F. Elloumi (Eds.), *Theory and practice of online learning* (pp. 273–294). Athabasca, Alberta, Canada: Athabasca University. Retrieved from http://cde.athabascau.ca/online_book.

Angelo, T. A., & Cross, K. P. (1993). *Classroom assessment techniques: A handbook for college teachers* (2nd ed.). San Francisco, CA: Jossey-Bass.

Bajzek, D., Brooks, J., Jerome, W., Lovett, M., Rinderle, J., Rule, G., & Thille, C. (2008). Assessment and instruction: Two sides of the same coin. In C. Bonk et al. (Eds.), *Proceedings of World Conference on E-Learning in Corporate, Government, Healthcare, and Higher Education 2008* (pp. 560–565). Chesapeake, VA: AACE. Retrieved from http://www.editlib.org/p/29661.

Bakerson, M., & Rodriguez-Campos, L. (2006). The evaluation of Internet usage within the graduate-level classroom. *International Journal of Learning, 13*, 15–72.

Banks, K. (2012). Use of SoftChalk software to create interactive content. In R. K. Morgan & K. T. Olivares (Eds.), *Quick hits for teaching with technology: Successful strategies by award-winning teachers* (pp. 84–85). Bloomington, IN: Indiana University Press.

Beatty, I. D., & Gerace, W. J. (2009). Technology-enhanced formative assessment: A research-based pedagogy for teaching science with classroom response technology. *Journal of Science Education and Technology, 18*(2), 146–162.

Betts, L. R., Bostock, S. J., Elder, T. J., & Trueman, M. (2012). Encouraging good writing practice in first-year psychology students: An intervention using Turnitin. *Psychology Teaching Review, 18*(2), 74–81.

Bloom, B. S. (1956). *Taxonomy of Educational Objectives, Handbook 1: Cognitive Domain.* New York, NY: Addison Wesley.

Bostock, S. (2000). Student peer assessment. Retrieved from http://www.reading.ac.uk/web /FILES/engageinassessment/Student_peer_assessment_-_Stephen_Bostock.pdf.

Bond, L., Herman, J., & Arter, J. (1994). Supporting educational improvement with alternative assessment. *In Improving science and mathematics education: A toolkit for professional developers: Alternative assessment* (pp. 1–26). Portland, OR: Northwest Regional Educational Laboratory. Retrieved from http://eric.ed.gov/?id=ED381360

Butler, E., Tatner, M., & Tierney, A. (2010, July). *Online reflective diaries: Using technology to strengthen the learning experience.* Paper presented at Improving University Teaching, 35th International Conference, Washington DC. Retrieved from http://eprints.gla.ac.uk/ 54590/1/54590.pdf.

Chang, N., Watson, B., Bakerson, M., Williams, E., McGoron, F., & Spitzer, B. (2012). Electronic feedback or handwritten feedback: What do undergraduate students prefer and why? *Journal of Teaching and Learning with Technology, 1*(1), 1–23. Retrieved from http://jotlt.indiana.edu/article/view/2043/1996.

Christen, B. (2003). Designing online courses to discourage dishonesty. *Educause Quarterly, 26*(4), 54–58.

Chu, S., & Kennedy, D. (2011). Using online collaborative tools for groups to co-construct knowledge. *Online Information Review, 35*(4), 581–597.

Crockett, G., & Peter, V. (2002, February). Peer assessment and team work as a professional skill in a second year economics unit. TL Forum: Focusing on the Student. Proceedings of the 11th Annual Teaching Learning Forum. Perth, Australia: Edith Cowan University. Retrieved from: http://otl.curtin.edu.au/professional_development/conferences /tlf/tlf2002/crockett.html.

Dewald, N., Scholz-Crane, N., Booth, A., & Levine, C. (2000). Information literacy at a distance: Instructional design issues. *Journal of Academic Librarianship 26*(1), 33–45.

Diwakar, A., Patwardhan, M., & Murthy, S. (2012). Pedagogical analysis of content authoring tools for engineering curriculum. *Proceedings of the 2012 IEEE Fourth International Conference on Technology for Education,* 83–89.

Fink, L. D. (2003). *Creating significant learning experiences: An integrated approach to designing college courses.* San Francisco, CA: Jossey-Bass.

Goldstein, J., & Behuniak, P. (2012). Can assessment drive instruction?: Understanding the impact of one State's alternate assessment. *Research and Practice for Persons with Severe Disabilities, 37*(3), 199–209.

Krathwohl, D. R. (2002). A revision of Bloom's taxonomy: An overview. *Theory into Practice, 41*(4), 212–218.

Leahy, S., Lyon, C., Thompson, M., & Wiliam, D. (2005). Classroom assessment: Minute by minute, day by day. *Educational Leadership, 63*(3), 18–24.

Lowe, T., & Hasson, R. (2010, September). Assessment for learning: Using Moodle quizzes in mathematics. In D. Green (Ed.), *Continuing Excellence in the Teaching and Learning of Maths, Stats and OR (CETL-MSOR) Conference* (pp. 39–41). Birmingham, UK. Retrieved from http://mathstore.ac.uk/headocs/ Proceedings2010.pdf#page=39.

McMillan, D., & Chavis, D. (1986). Sense of community: A definition and theory. *Journal of Community Psychology, 14*, 6–23. Retrieved from: http://communities. autodesk.com/india/sites/default/files/secure/docs/McMillanChavis—psychological-Sense-of-community.pdf.

Mosert, M., & Snowball, J. D. (2012). Where angels fear to tread: online peer-assessment in a large first-year class. *Assessment and Evaluation in Higher Education,* pp. 1–13.

Piña, A. A. (2013). Learning management systems: A look at the big picture. In Y. Kats (Ed.), *Learning management systems and instructional design: Best practices in online education* (pp. 1–19). Hershey, PA: Information Science Reference.

Popham, J. W. (2011, February), *Formative assessment: A process, not a test. Education Week,* 30(21). Retrieved from http://www.edweek.org/ew/ articles/2011/02/23/21popham .h30.html?tkn=RSXFOfuqzOb7hKGCLEhY nPUpaIePTsq2KR0Z&print=1.

Richardson, R., & North, M. (2013). Strengthening the trust in online courses: A common sense approach. Journal of Computing Sciences in Colleges, 28(5), 266–272.

Scriven, M. (1967). The methodology of evaluation. In R. W. Tyler, R. M. Gagne, & M. Scriven (Eds.), *Perspectives of curriculum evaluation* (Vol. 1, pp. 39–83). Chicago, IL: Rand McNally.

Sewell, J., Frith, K., & Colvin, M. (2010, March). Online assessment strategies: A primer. *MERLOT Journal of Online Learning and Teaching, 6*(1), 297–305.

Stiggins, R. (2005). From formative assessment to assessment FOR learning: A path to success in standards-based schools. *Phi Delta Kappan, 87*(4), 324–328.

Tinto, V. (2009, February). *Taking student retention seriously: Rethinking the first year of university.* Keynote address presented at FYE Curriculum Design Symposium, Brisbane, Australia. Retrieved from: http://www.fyecd2009.qut.edu.au/resources/ SPE_VincentTinto_5Feb09.pdf.

Travares, N., Chu, S., & Weng, M. (2011). *Experimenting with English collaborative writing on Google Sites.* Paper presented at CITE Research Symposium, University of Hong Kong, Hong Kong.

Vickerman, P. (2009). Student perspectives on formative peer assessment: An attempt to deepen learning? *Assessment and Evaluation in Higher Education, 34*(2), 221–230.

Vonderwell, S. (2004). Assessing online learning and teaching: Adapting the minute paper. *TechTrends, 48*(4), 29–31.

Vonderwell, S., Liang, X., & Alderman, K. (2007). Asynchronous discussions and assessment in online learning. *Journal of Research on Technology in Education, 39*(3), 309–328.

Wang, S. (2011). Promoting student's online engagement with communication tools. *Journal of Educational Technology Development and Exchange, 4*(1), 81–90.

Wiliam, D. (2011). *Embedded formative assessment.* Bloomington, IN: Solution Tree Press.

CHAPTER 2

EMPOWERING LEARNERS TO ENGAGE IN AUTHENTIC ONLINE ASSESSMENT

Jennifer V. Lock
University of Calgary

Petrea Redmond
University of Southern Queensland

INTRODUCTION

Nationally and internationally there has been a rapid expansion of online and blended learning. Allen and Seaman (2011a) reported in the United States that 6.7 million higher education students are enrolled in at least one online course. They noted that "[t]he proportion of all students taking at least one online course is at an all-time high of 32.0 percent" (p. 4). With the increased demand for online and blended learning, attention should be given to the assessment practices used within these learning environments.

The purpose of this chapter is to share an authentic assessment practice that was used for an online and blended course that utilized an online task as both a learning activity and an assessment item. The assessment required students to identify their best contributions in the activity and submit those

Assessment in Online and Blended Learning Environments, pages 21–38

items for assessment. This shift in practice required students to reflect on their learning, to identify what they believed counted as evidence of their learning, as well as provided an opportunity for them to further develop their metacognition skills.

BLENDED AND ONLINE LEARNING

There are diverse definitions used for the terms *blended learning* and *online learning*. Allen and Seaman (2006, 2010, 2011b) have defined blended learning as a course with 80% of the content being delivered online, with a blended course being one where 30–79% of the content is delivered online alongside face-to-face sessions. Masie (2002) defined blended learning as "the use of two or more distinct methods of training" (p. 59). The terms *blended learning, flexible, mixed mode,* or *hybrid delivery* are often used interchangeably. Graham, Allen, and Ure (2003) reviewed many definitions of blended learning and came up with three common themes: combining instructional modalities or media, combining instructional methods, and combining online and face-to-face instruction. Graham (2005) then created the definition: "Blended learning systems combine face-to-face instruction with computer-mediated instruction" (p. 5).

The terms *online learning* and *e-learning* are often used interchangeably. According to Garrison (2011), e-learning represents a "paradigm shift from the ideal of autonomy and the industrial production of prepackaged study materials characteristic of mainstream distance education. It represents a distinct educational branch with its roots in computer conferencing and collaborative constructivist approaches to learning" (p. 2). Furthermore, Garrison has argued, "[o]nline learning integrates independence (asynchronous online communication) with interaction (connectivity) that overcomes time and space constraints in a way that emulates the values of higher education" (p. 3).

The challenge is that many instructors do not have the skills to design or redesign their face-to-face courses to take advantage of the opportunity provided in an online space for learners to gain a deep conceptual understanding of the content through interaction, engagement, collaboration, and critical thinking. Learners need multiple cognitive opportunities to connect theory and practice by "engaging in attention, enactment, reflection, critique, adaptation, [and] articulation" (Laurillard, 2000, p. 136). Blended and online learning approaches provide multiple opportunities to facilitate engagement and interaction, to present information, and to represent theoretical concepts in different forms to assist learners in their processes of knowledge connection, deconstruction, and reconstruction.

Dialogue for Learning

Dialogue is a result of collaborative knowledge generation (Misanchuk & Anderson, 2001). Romney (2003) has suggested that "[d]ialogue is focused conversation, engaged in intentionally with the goal of increasing understanding, addressing problems, and questioning thoughts or actions. It engages the heart as well as the mind" (p. 2). Dialogue provides an important contribution to learning in higher education. The Organization for Economic Co-operation and Development (OECD) guide *Higher Education Institutions* stated that "[s]tudent engagement is most powerful as a driver of quality teaching when it involves *dialogue*, and not only information on the student's experience" (Henard & Roseveare, 2012, p. 21). This idea is supported by a number of researchers (Aminifar & Bahiraey, 2010; Bereiter, 1992; Hoskins & Van Hooff, 2005; Schallert, Reed, & the D-Team, 2003) who have suggested that dialogue, collaboration, interaction, and engagement are key to learning and teaching that promotes deep learning and higher-order thinking.

Online and blended learning environments provide opportunities for both synchronous and asynchronous communication. Dialogue can provide a visible demonstration of students' learning or understandings (Bernstein, 2009). When speaking or writing their ideas and making them available to others during the learning process, it is easier for the instructor to diagnose and respond to misconceptions both at the group and individual levels because the group meaning is then interpreted by individuals (Stahl, 2004). In many situations, students' misunderstandings are only available at the point of assessment. At this point, it is often too late to improve their learning and course results and many students take limited opportunities to learn from feedback provided at the end of the semester. It is more effective to support students' learning during the learning process rather than at the completion of the semester.

Asynchronous online communication provides an extension of time for dialogue. It also allows students to review the information provided, reflect on the ideas presented by others, and research additional information before responding to others. Furthermore, using asynchronous dialogue in an online space offers a number of other advantages, for example: it is not time nor place dependent, there is more time to respond, the participants can respond by sharing different media types, the air time can be shared by all, and participants can decide how, when, and how often they participate because they do not need to wait for others to contribute (Henri, 1992; Stacey & Gerbic, 2007). Access to the conversations, using asynchronous communication, means that students can go back to them as often as they like as they deconstruct, reconstruct, and co-construct knowledge.

The technology affords students the opportunity to communicate with numerous people beyond the traditional teacher–student interaction.

Communication with others provides a variety of information sources; multiple perspectives; a diversity of explanations and understandings; a range of prior experiences and knowledge to draw from; and opportunities for disagreement, debate, and the testing-out of ideas. Schallert et al. (2003) have found that "online conversations are far more complex and students' experiences are much less predictable than we had expected" (p. 105) and require high cognitive processes. "By externalising thinking processes, students make statements and counter statements, defend and challenge each other's assumptions, all of which are processes leading to higher-order thinking" (McLoughlin & Luca, 2000, p. 7). If the contributions lead to substantive conversations that are extended and focused, these conversations would include "indicators of higher order thinking such as making distinctions, applying ideas, forming generalizations, raising questions, and not just reporting experiences, facts, definitions, or procedures" (Newmann & Wehlage, 1993, p. 10).

When researching blended learning, Stacey and Gerbic (2007) established that "online discussions helped all the students to learn, reading the online posting prompted engagement, writing the postings aided deeper understanding, [and] the need to communicate to peers clearly and persuasively also aided their understanding" (p. 5). Dynamic student engagement and focused dialogue requires a cycle of posting and responding to others to keep the discussion going rather than individuals posting disconnected or integrated monologues. This requires thoughtful design to support dialogue as well as purposeful facilitation.

The role of the online facilitator is a crucial and complex one including tasks such as creating ground rules, generating activities or questions that promote high-level dialogue, and ensuring effective time management to keep the discussion productive (Spector & de la Teja, 2001). It has been suggested by Muilenburg and Berg (2000) that "asking the right questions is almost always more important than giving the right answers" (p. 10). Lipman (2003) believed that "if the question is a meaningful one and the questioner does not know the answer, the classroom discussion that follows will likely demand that each participant think more and more judiciously" (p. 117). Larreamendy-Joerns and Leinhardt (2006) have elucidated that "successfully orchestrating a dialogue demands fairly sophisticated skills.... The outcome of this complex appraisal is a sense of the amount and quality of the guidance that specific contributions and the conversation as a whole require to support learning" (p. 591).

Authentic Assessment

If something in education is thought of as being authentic it is often thought of as being or mirroring "real-world" activities or being useful or relevant beyond the classroom. The term *authentic assessment* has a range of different meanings and is implemented in a variety of ways: "[T]here is not always agreement as to the important elements that make an assessment authentic" (Frey, Schmitt, & Allen, 2012, p. 1).

From a review of the literature (Herrington, 2006; Herrington & Herrington, 1998; Herrington, Reeves, & Oliver, 2010; Newmann & Wehlage, 1993; Schmidt et al., 2009), the following are some common themes or characteristics of authentic assessment:

- The activity or context of the activity is realistic or connected to the real world.
- The task is performance based, cognitively complex, and ill structured, allowing for multiple responses.
- The students collaborate with others to complete the task and justify or defend their solution or product.
- The criteria or indicators for mastery of learning or task completion are valid, reliable, and known to the students.

According to Reeves (2011), authentic assessments require students to "deal with realistic situations or problems—that is, situations or problems that occur outside classrooms and schools. The more closely a performance assessment matches a task that people do in 'the real world,' the more authentic it is said to be" (p. 110). Reeves goes on to say that in the world outside of school, people "usually have time to think about problems, consult with others, and review the product they create" (p. 110). This is in contrast to a traditional form of assessment where there is only one chance to demonstrate what a person has learned.

Gulikers, Bastiaens, and Kirschner (2004) suggested that authentic learning will result in increased transfer of knowledge and authentic instruction and authentic assessment. They also revealed that the "dimensions can vary in their level of authenticity" (p. 70) and we should consider authenticity as being on a continuum rather than being authentic or not (Newmann & Wehlage, 1993). Gulikers et al. developed the five-dimensional conceptual framework for authentic assessment, which shows how authentic instruction and authentic assessment can be aligned. Their five-dimensional framework provides a lens to be used to unpack the authentic assessment and authentic instruction of our project, which is based on professional practice. Table 2.1 provides a description for the dimensions, along with a guiding question for each dimension. Gulikers et al.'s five-dimensional framework is used to present the learning activity and assessment discussed previously. The next sections examine and discuss the experience in terms of the alignment of authentic instruction and authentic assessment.

TABLE 2.1 Summation of the Five-Dimensional Conceptual Framework for Authentic Assessment

Dimension	Question	Description
Assessment Task	What do you have to do?	Needs to be relevant and valued to both the student and others; it should be complex and requires authentic content or prior knowledge and the integration of knowledge from multiple areas.
Physical or Virtual context	Where do you have to do it?	Needs to be relevant and include scaffolding and relevant information and resources and takes consideration of time.
Social Context	With whom do you have to do it?	Should be similar to a context that takes place outside of school and include both collaborative and individual aspects.
Assessment Result or Form	What is the result of your efforts?	Should include a product or performance that demonstrates relevant competencies across an array of tasks and the work should be presented to others.
Assessment Criteria	How will what you have done be judged?	The criteria/standards should be explicitly provided prior to beginning the task.

Source: Adapted from Gulikers et al. (2004).

THE PROJECT

Learning Context and Project Design

Preservice teachers (students), teachers (experts), and academics were engaged in a 6-week cross-institutional online collaborative activity as part of a Middle Years curriculum and pedagogy course. The students took the course in their second year of a 4-year teacher education program or the first semester of a 1-year graduate diploma at a regional university in Australia. The course could be taken in either online or blended modes. The online task described in this chapter was designed using a constructivist framework to provide the students with an opportunity to live the experience of being online collaborators inquiring into real-world teaching and learning issues in a digital global classroom. Although asynchronous discussions played a critical role in the activity, synchronous communication was also used.

The students participated in a three-phrase initiative that required them to engage in online discussion with their peers and with experts in various discipline areas. The first phase involved students to introduce themselves to their peers and to read a novel related to one of the key themes (ESL and cultural diversity, bullying, Indigenous perspectives, and special needs). The novels were used to stimulate thinking and discussion related to the key themes. An example of one of the stimulus novels is Hadden's book *The Curious Incident of the Dog in the Night-Time* (2002), which related to the special needs theme. The students then worked in teams to provide an overview of the book relating it to curriculum and writing inquiry questions focused on pedagogical implications. Phase two involved students responding to inquiry questions related to the pedagogical implications they provided in phase one. Also in phase two, students interacted synchronously and asynchronously online with teacher experts from Australia and Canada in the key theme areas. The third phase required students to respond to an authentic scenario and to reflect on the learning they gained through the activity and the learning processes they had engaged in during the activity. For each phase, multiple forums were available related to each of the themes.

The students' inquiry, engagement, and assessment formed part of the general learning activity within the online learning environment, meaning they were assessed directly on their contributions to the learning activity and not as a separate assessment task. The students' participation in the activity formed 40% of the overall assessment for the course. At the completion of the three-phase activity, students self-selected their best online discussion posts to be submitted for assessment. The evaluation of their work was not based on a quantitative perspective (e.g., how many times they posted) but on the quality of their online contribution to the dialogue. The criteria for this assessment reflected the learners': timeliness of posts, constructive and supportive responses to others, ability to participate in sustained professional dialogue, ability to promote deep discussion with clear efforts to make personal and group meaning, integration of ideas from a variety of sources, and reflective synthesis of key content and pedagogical issues from one of the themes and their personal learning.

In preparing students for the online discussion component, they were provided with deidentified online posts from previous semesters for the purpose of analysis. As they analyzed the posts, they provided such feedback in terms of readability, likelihood of reading it, and structure and made recommendations for ways to improve the posts. The goal of this task was for students to identify qualities of good online discussion posts and then for them to mirror those qualities in their own work; it also made them familiar with the criteria for their assessment.

There have been several iterations of this authentic learning and assessment activity project. The focus of this chapter is based on the design and implementation used for one semester in 2012 where 65 students participated. This chapter provides a narrative analysis of the student reflections and the instructor experiences during this one semester. The five-dimensional framework for authentic assessment (Gulikers et al., 2004) provides a lens to report on the lived experience of both students and instructors, with the focus on students.

Authentic Nature of the Work

From the analysis, the following five key themes emerged related to authentic learning and authentic assessment that aligned with Gulikers et al.'s (2004) five-dimensional framework for authentic assessment. These themes were authentic task and authentic content, virtual context, social context, assessment result or form, and assessment criteria.

Authentic Task and Authentic Content

From the activity and assessment, there were three factors that influenced the authenticity in terms of the content. First, the key themes of the activity and assessment—ESL and cultural diversity, bullying, indigenous perspectives, and special needs—mirror those issues that teachers deal with everyday in their classrooms. Through the stimulus novels, students were confronted by issues that are real and relevant in their professional practice. The issues under inquiry were complex and the student responses required them to integrate information and experience from multiple sources.

Second, "the use of stimulus novels laid the foundation for a shared experience designed to trigger online dialogue and provide an anchor for preservice teachers when new ideas were introduced or challenged" (Lock & Redmond, 2011, p. 21). The plot and characters were realistic and mirror real-life incidences; as such they could be used in the discussion but also this was the place where students began to make connections to their own experiences and brought in information and resources related to the topic or issue. Furthermore, they asked additional questions that extended and deepened the discussion. One student commented, it "made me more informed and aware of the issues that occur in almost every school." This highlights that the students were able to identify the relevance of the content to their professional lives.

From the start of the work, the students were asked to identify and share online their own inquiry questions. A selection of these questions was used to prompt further facilitated online discussion. The student questions were the focus of the online discussions and further inquiry rather than questions provided by the teacher. As they advanced through the phases of the activity, students were able to choose which discussion forums they wanted to engage in, as well as what topics they wanted to explore and to what depth. The students drove the nature and the direction of the learning based on their perceived gaps in knowledge. As noted by one student, "Being able to interact with many other students exposed me to some great information that I may never have learnt otherwise." A second student commented, "This project has been a very interesting experience. Being able to express my own opinions and read the opinions of other students has opened my eyes to many ideas and concepts I had not previously considered."

Having students consider the pedagogical implications and questions resulting from their experience, reading, and discussion and then respond to a real-life scenario mirrors the work completed by teachers. Part of each synchronous session involved the examination of a real-life scenario. Each scenario was based on the theme from one of the stimulus novels but contained elements of what teachers encounter in classrooms. With the presentation of each scenario:

> Preservice teachers and experts engaged in discussion to come up with strategies for addressing the situation. Out of this experience, preservice teachers identified areas they needed to learn more about and were encouraged to develop professional growth plans identifying elements of pedagogical practice and classroom application. (Lock & Redmond, 2011, p. 22)

As one student commented, "This assessment has generated many key points that are of great importance not only to middle year's learners, but a school as a whole." The synchronous learning event enabled the participants to explore a range of responses to the scenario with a practicing teacher who could comment on the proposed resolutions from their extensive practical in-school experience.

Teachers are reflective practitioners and reflection on learning is a daily activity. As such, the students in this initiative were required to reflect on the learning outcomes and processes of the activity integrating their learning from the content and tasks. The tasks were authentic to their professional practice and also to their learning processes.

Virtual Context

Teachers, as practitioners, often use online forums or online communities to discuss professional issues and pedagogical quandaries relevant to their day-to-day work. For the student work, the authentic learning and assessment tasks were held within an online space where information was provided and dialogue was afforded at a time and place selected by the students. The challenge when working in an online space is to provide the necessary structure and scaffolding that is needed to foster dialogue, not monologue. A key factor noted by Muilenburg and Berge (2000) is "asking the right questions" (p. 10) that will engage people to explore the topic beyond a surface level. Lipman (2003) goes on to say that if it is a meaningful question that is taken up through discussion it will require students to think deeply and in more thoughtful ways. It is through careful facilitation and creation of the expectation of dialogue that will result in meaningful learning.

During this learning and assessment activity, students engaged in authentic discussion with topics and processes imitating teacher professional conversations and including teacher professionals in the conversations. The authentic discussion in this work is recognized in three ways.

First, students drove the nature of the conversation through asking questions and exploring issues that were relevant to their personal learning and were student-centred.

Second, the online discussions based on the thematic areas were taken from the inquiry questions students posted in phase one. The student questions launched the discussion of the topics and the exploration of the issues that they wanted to examine as part of the work. In phase three when they had the opportunity to dialogue with experts, again the questions came from the students relating to real-world teaching and learning issues. One of the students made the following remark, "The discussions have prompted me to look further into issues that I otherwise could have passed over." Another comment was that "The discussions have also allowed me to view the gaps in my knowledge." Second, students engaged in conversation with experts in the field, real teachers who encounter such issues in their day-to-day practice that students were investigating: "The opportunity to interact with students and staff around the globe has been interesting and is a way in which this project has clearly utilised a strength of ICT integration."

Third, these were real discussions driven by interest in the topic rather than by assessment. Students shared their experiences and resources as they engaged in conversation around the topics and considered personal responses to the scenarios. The students were learning with and from others through the online discussion, which resulted in the co-construction of meaning. As noted by one student, "Without the input of the forum members, and being required to work through their findings, I would have been unaware of many of these insights, issues, and resources." Another student noted,

> I enjoyed participating in the forums and looked forward to checking back to read other people's responses. I found that much of what we were discussing related to other subjects I have been studying concurrently (it is all interlinked!). I found my classmates and the experts to be very supportive and I felt comfortable to express my opinion for academic discussion.

Social Context

In real life, teachers often work both with others in groups and individually. They regularly contact other teachers to gain knowledge and tips regarding issues within their classrooms. The book overview task required the students to work in a collaborative team; however, all other items were individual, relying on the cooperation from others to keep the dialogue going.

Students engaged and interacted with multiple others who are situated in different social contexts because the students and the teachers were based all over the world, have different educational experiences themselves as learners, and had different professional placement experiences to draw from. One student reported that she enjoyed the collaborative and pluralistic nature of the project: "I enjoyed seeing the different ways in which different students developed such diverse options regarding and responses to the same material, which definitely gave me a good deal of food for thought in more than one instance."

Another benefit that emerged from this experience was that of a learning community. The idea of learning with and from each other was an empowering learning experience for some students. As noted by one student, "Our group continues on as a study group, supporting each other's learning and helping overcome frustrations or lack of understanding." Another student commented, "This experience has illustrated to me the benefits of providing an online community in both a learning and teaching capacity."

Within this social context, students were able to vicariously test ideas or share their thoughts on how they may deal with some of the issues under discussion. This ongoing feedback from people with different experiences should broaden the students' overall learning and enhance their practice.

Assessment Result or Form

"It is clear that students must perceive participation in e-learning discussions as a major component of the program of studies. Thus, assessment activities must be integrated within the e-learning activities" (Garrison & Anderson, 2003, p. 95). Within this work, the assessment was embedded in the day-to-day online discussion. The form of this assessment was for them to self-select their best participation in the learning activity over the 7-week period. There were guidelines and minimum requirements but students had the opportunity to show their best work. One student reported: "I also like the idea of an ongoing assessment, to allow students the opportunity to not leave the entire piece to the end of the period."

As in real life, students participating in the online discussion received ongoing feedback on their ideas and questions both from peers and from experts. The work was set up as a form of continuous assessment, assessment *for* learning rather than *of* learning. In describing assessment as part of the learning journey, one student spoke of the "ongoing nature reinforced learning." Another student noted that through this process they received

...immediate and ongoing feedback on ideas. The ability to gain instant feedback on an idea is very important, yet much of the assessment we are often required to do unfortunately fails in this regard. As such, I see this project's encouragement for the ongoing germination of a single idea or focus to be a recognizable strength.

From the student reflections, it is clear that there is authentic longevity of their learning. The activity was designed to be a professional learning experience where students could explore in-depth real-world educational topics and issues that were relevant to their own learning needs. Students valued the direct linkages between the activity and assessment and their future professional lives. As one student commented, "The information I have gained from this project will drastically influence my pedagogy" and another revealed, "This has been an interesting assessment piece and has been a great experience that can be applied to my future teaching career."

At the completion of the activity, students were to identify their own next steps for what they needed to learn and how they would learn this so to prepare them for their future classrooms. "This project has given me some great ideas for starting this, but more than that it has shown me the areas where I need to be more vigilant in monitoring and preparation of the use of technology as a tool," commented a student. Another student said, "I am grateful that the staff has taken on this difficult assessment task when they could have easily sat back and assigned a single report question."

One student remarked, "Having to constructively build information and use it, instead of simply pool it to a 'bucket' that may or may not get used." This statement is interesting, in that the nature of the learning required students to use information as a means of knowledge construction. What they were doing in this work required them to use and apply their new understandings. It was not a matter of memorizing information that may or may not be used in their work. As in the real world, a person needs to be able to use new information to make meaning and apply in it new situations.

Assessment Criteria

The criteria and standards for the assessment were provided to the students at the beginning of the semester. In addition, students were provided with the opportunity to unpack the criteria and align practice posts to the criteria, enhancing their understanding of the expectations and standards. From this work, they would have developed a clearer understanding of the level of performance expected to guide their ongoing participation. The students suggested that having the criteria, however, did impact on the nature of their participation. One student suggested that "[h]aving the posting style publicized as a marking criteria has resulted in some interesting and irritating posting conventions."

"The primary difficulty in making any assessment of an asynchronous discussion forum is the huge volume of data that are available to be assessed"

(Andresen, 2009). To overcome this issue, the course instructor asked students to self-select a number of strong examples of their online posting to be used for assessment that aligns with the published criteria. Garrison and Anderson (2003) "argue that it is possible to have students present their own evidence of meaningful participation in e-learning activities" (p. 98). This self-selection required the students to carefully consider what they valued in terms of quality postings. As a result, all students had to take ownership of the selection of the work that showed what they have learned, how they have learned, and why it was important for their learning.

By providing clear criteria for quality participation and prior posts for student participants to analyze, they were able to reflect on their contributions to the online discussions and make improvements to their contributions through the length of the activity. Furthermore, students were required to reflect on the quantity and quality of their contributions, the process of the learning activity, and the knowledge outcomes of their participation.

Having students self-select their best posts supported the development of metacognition in two ways. First, it required them to develop a greater self-awareness of their own knowledge. Second, they needed to have awareness of the quality of that knowledge. As noted by Sawyer (2006), "[a]rticulating and learning go hand in hand. . . . In many cases, learners don't actually learn something until they start to articulate it—in other words, while thinking out loud, they learn more rapidly and deeply than studying quietly" (p. 12).

SIGNIFICANCE TO TEACHING AND LEARNING

The authentic learning activity was used as an authentic assessment task for the course that involved the student asynchronous discussions and other artifacts and reflective items to be graded. One of the techniques that has proven to be successful with this activity has been to have the students self-select their best contributions in the asynchronous discussions to be assessed. This is a major shift away from the former assessment practices of asynchronous communication where an instructor provided a grade based on counting the posts or a grade was provided based on the degree of participation in the online discussion. Or, another way of assessment was to provide a grade based on all their contributions, which have been unmanageable to track over several weeks.

By shifting the practice to allow the students to self-select their best contributions in the online discussion, this empowered students to self-assess their online discussions. Through viewing their contributions to the various discussions forums, they were able to make thoughtful decisions about what counts as evidence of learning and to what degree they had engaged in the nature of the discussion. Furthermore, by examining their own inquiry, they were able to identify and reflect on their depth of understanding of the topic.

At the same time, by using this practice, it showed the students what was important in terms of learning and how they should approach learning. This provides an opportunity for the students to engage in self-regulatory cognition. Through this work, they become active learners of their own learning and further develop their ability to reflect on their learning and own knowledge. According to Sawyer (2006), "articulation is so helpful to learning that it makes possible reflection or *metacognition*—thinking about the process of learning and thinking about knowledge. Learning scientists have repeatedly demonstrated the importance of reflection in learning for deeper understanding" (p. 12).

IMPLICATIONS

Three implications emerged from the work. First, in higher education, how do we better assist instructors to create assessment practices within online environments that support assessment *of* learning and assessment *for* learning? A shift needs to move from summative assessment practices and/or testing at the end of the work. Rather, when developing authentic learning tasks, it requires appropriate assessment practices that not only evaluates the performance but provides ongoing feedback to inform the work.

Second, how can authentic assessment practices be used in online learning environments? Support needs to be in place to help instructors to design online courses to create meaningful authentic learning tasks and to ensure appropriate assessment practices are in place. Conceptual frameworks such as that provided by Gulikers et al. (2004), Newman and Wehlage (1993), or Herrington et al. (2010) must be shared with educators wishing to plan and implement authentic learning and assessment.

Third, structures need to be in place to support learners in understanding what they are learning through self-regulatory cognition. Sawyer (2006) noted that a "central topic in the learning sciences research is how to support students in educationally beneficial reflection" (p. 12). They need to be supported in how to develop their metacognitive abilities but also to have the necessary scaffolding in place to support meaningful reflection.

RECOMMENDATIONS FOR RESEARCH AND PRACTICE

Gulikers et al.'s (2004) five-dimensional framework provided a lens to deconstruct the authenticity of the assessment that learners were involved in as part of the project. As noted by Gulikers et al.'s framework for authentic assessment, there needs to be an alignment with authentic instruction and authentic assessment. The authenticity of the activity was validated by the teachers, as experts, and also by the student participants rather than only by the course instructor. "Authenticity is subjective, which makes student perceptions important for authentic assessment to influence learning" (Gulikers et al., 2004, p. 69). The learning activity and assessment described in this chapter provides an example of constructive alignment between content, pedagogy, and assessment (Biggs, 1996) and resulted in leaning within an authentic context and the use of authentic assessment.

The online or blended environment affords users various opportunities that allow them to engage in learning in new and innovative ways. Yet, care must be taken in the design of the authentic learning task and to ensure the necessary scaffolding is in place to support students as they learn through the online dialogue, but also learn about their learning through using an authentic assessment practice that allows for further development of their metacognitive abilities.

From the study, three key recommendations are to be considered. First, structures need to in place to guide students when selecting examples of their contributions that provide strong evidence of learning. They need to be aware of criterion that helps them to determine what makes a valued online contribution. Then they need to be given the opportunity to use such criteria to assess their work and to select contributions that they feel best reflects quality. Their articulation of why such contributions are quality provides insight into their learning.

Second, instructors need to clearly articulate criteria that will be used to assess student asynchronous discussion contributions. These criteria will need to be used to help students in making decisions with regard to their selected contributions. Such criteria can be research informed, as well as co-created by the students. However, they need to be developed and shared at the start of the work so that students have guidelines to help them in their ongoing online discussions but also for what posts they will select to be assessed.

Third, research needs to be conducted to examine the impact this assessment practice has on student metacognition in online learning environments. Careful selection of appropriate methodology and methods needs to be conducted so as to evaluate what the impact is and the degree of impact it has on a student's metacognitive ability.

CONCLUSION

With the shift to online learning, greater attention needs to be given to assessment. The evidence from this authentic task demonstrates how the students were empowered to participate in authentic assessment by selecting their contributions to be assessed by their instructor. They have taken on an active role in their assessment but have also used this opportunity to learn about their own learning. As such, the challenge is for online instructors to find meaningful ways to create authentic learning opportunities supported through the use of authentic assessment practices.

REFERENCES

Allen, I. E., & Seaman, J. (2006). *Making the grade: Online education in the United States.* Retrieved from http://sloanconsortium.org/publications/survey/pdf/making_the_grade.pdf.

Allen, I. E., & Seaman, J. (2010). *Learning on demand: Online education in the United States.* Needham, MA: Sloan Consortium.

Allen, I. E., & Seaman, J. (2011a). *Going the distance: Online education in the United States.* Retrieved from http://www.onlinelearningsurvey.com/reports/goingthedistance.pdf

Allen, I. E., & Seaman, J. (2011b). *Going the distance: Online education in the United States.* Newburyport, MA: Sloan Consortium.

Aminifar, E., & Bahiraey, D. (2010). *Online learning and teaching at higher education.* Paper presented at the World Conference on Educational Multimedia, Hypermedia and Telecommunications, Toronto, Ontario, Canada.

Andresen, M. A. (2009). Asynchronous discussion forums: success factors, outcomes, assessments, and limitations. *Educational Technology and Society, 12*(1), 249–257.

Bereiter, C. (1992). Referent-centred and problem-centred knowledge: Elements of an educational epistemology. *Interchange, 23*(4), 337–361.

Bernstein, J. L. (2009). Introduction: Making learning visible to whom? *Scholarship of Teaching and Learning at EMU, 2*(1), 2.

Biggs, J. (1996). Enhancing teaching through constructive alignment. *Higher Education, 32,* 347–364.

Frey, B. B., Schmitt, V. L., & Allen, J. P. (2012). Defining authentic classroom assessment. *Practical Assessment, Research and Evaluation, 17*(2), 2.

Garrison, D. R. (2011). *E-learning in the 21st century: A framework for research and practice* New York, NY: Routledge.

Garrison, D. R., & Anderson, T. (2003). *E-learning in the 21st century: A framework for research and practice.* New York, NY: Routledge.

Graham, C. R. (2005). Blended learning systems: Definition, current trends, and future directions. In C. J. Bonk & C. Graham (Eds.), *The handbook of blended learning: Global perspectives, local designs* (pp. 3–21). San Francisco, CA: Pfeiffer.

Graham, C. R., Allen, S., & Ure, D. (2003). *Blended learning environments: A review of the research literature.* Unpublished manuscript, Provo, UT.

Gulikers, J. T. M., Bastiaens, T. J., & Kirschner, P. A. (2004). A five-dimensional framework for authentic assessment. *Educational Technology Research and Development, 52*(3), 67–86.

Hadden, M. (2002). *The curious incident of the dog in the night-time.* Toronto, Ontario, Canada: Doubleday Canada.

Henard, F., & Roseveare, D. (2012). *Fostering quality teaching in higher education: Policies and practices.* Retrieved from http://www.oecd.org/edu/imhe/QT%20 policies%20and%20practices.pdf.

Henri, F. (1992). Computer conferencing and content analysis. In A. R. Kaye (Ed.), *Collaborative Learning through computer conferencing: The Najaden papers* (pp. 117–136). Berlin, Germany: Springer Verlag.

Herrington, J. (2006). Authentic e-learning in higher education: Design principles for authentic learning environments and tasks. *Proceedings of World Conference on E-learning in Corporate, Government, Healthcare, and Higher Education,* pp. 3164–3173.

Herrington, J., & Herrington, A. (1998). Authentic assessment and multimedia: How university students respond to a model of authentic assessment. *Higher Education Research and Development, 17*(3), 305–322.

Herrington, J., Reeves, T. C., & Oliver, R. (2010). *A guide to authentic e-learning.* New York, NY: Taylor & Francis.

Hoskins, S., & Van Hooff, J. (2005). Motivation and ability: Which students use online learning and what influence does it have on their achievement? *British Journal of Educational Technology, 36*(2), 177–192.

Larreamendy-Joerns, J., & Leinhardt, G. (2006). Going the distance with online education. *Review of Educational Research, 76*(4), 567–605.

Laurillard, D. (2000). The impact of communications and information technology on higher education. In P. Scott (Ed.), *Higher education reformed* (pp. 133–153). London, UK: Falmer Press.

Lipman, M. (2003). *Thinking in education* (2nd ed.). Cambridge, UK: Cambridge University Press.

Lock, J. V., & Redmond, P. (2011). International online collaboration: giving voice to the study of diversity. *One World in Dialogue, 1*(1), 19–25.

Masie, E. (2002). Blended learning: The magic is in the mix *The ASTD e-learning handbook* (pp. 58–63). New York, NY: McGraw-Hill.

McLoughlin, C., & Luca, J. (2000). Cognitive engagement and higher order thinking through computer conferencing: We know why but do we know how? *Teaching and Learning Forum 2000.* Retrieved from http://lsn.curtin.edu.au/ tlf/tlf2000/mcloughlin.html.

Misanchuk, M., & Anderson, T. (2001). Building community in an online learning environment: Communication, cooperation and collaboration. *Middle Tennessee State University Teaching Learning and Technology Conference.* Retrieved from http://frank.mtsu.edu/~itconf/proceed01/19.html.

Muilenburg, L., & Berge, Z. (2000). *A framework for designing questions for online learning.* Retrieved from http://www.iddl.vt.edu/fdi/old/2000/frame.html.

Newmann, F., & Wehlage, G. G. (1993). Five standards of authentic instruction. *Educational Leadership, 50*(7), 8–12.

Reeves, A. (2011). *Where great teaching begins: Planning for student thinking and learning.* Alexandria, VA: ASCD.

Romney, P. (2003). *The art of dialogue.* Retrieved from http://romneyassociates. com/pdf/Consulting_Diversity.pdf.

Sawyer, R. K. (2006). The new science of learning. In R. K. Sawyer (Ed.), *The Cambridge handbook of the learning sciences* (pp. 1–16). Cambridge, UK: Cambridge University Press.

Schallert, D. L., Reed, J. H., & the D-Team. (2003). Intellectual, motivational, textual, and cultural considerations in teaching and learning with computer-mediated discussion. *Journal of Research on Technology in Education, 36*(2), 103–118.

Schmidt, D., Baran, E., Thompson, A., Koehler, M., Punya, M., & Shin, T. (2009). Examining preservice teachers' development of technological pedagogical content knowledge in an introductory instructional technology course. In I. Gibson et al. (Eds.), *Proceedings of Society for Information Technology & Teacher Education International Conference 2009* (pp. 4145–4151). Chesapeake, VA: Association for the Advancement of Computing in Education (AACE).

Spector, J. M., & de la Teja, I. (2001). Competencies for online teaching. *ERIC Digest EDO-IR-2001-09.* Retrieved from http://searcheric.org/scripts/seget2.asp?db=ericft&want=http://searcheric.org/ericdc/ED456841.htm.

Stacey, E., & Gerbic, P. (2007). Teaching for blended learning—Research perspectives from on-campus and distance students. *Education and information technologies, 12*(3), 165–174.

Stahl, G. (2004). Building collaborative knowing: Elements of a social theory of CSCL. In J. Strijbos, P. Kirschner & R. Martens (Eds.), *What we know about CSCL: And implementing it in higher education* (pp. 53–86). Berlin, Germany: Springer Verlag.

CHAPTER 3

ASSESSING TECHNOLOGY-ENHANCED LEARNING

A Process-Oriented Approach

Philip Bonanno
University of Malta

ASSESSMENT OF AND ASSESSMENT FOR LEARNING

Digital technologies are transforming education by radically changing the way we acquire, create, and share knowledge. The exponential growth of online Open Educational Resources is facilitating new ways of learning "characterised by personalisation, engagement, use of digital media, collaboration, bottom-up practices and where the learner or teacher is a creator of learning content" (European Commission, 2012b, p. 9).

The boundaries between formal and informal modes of learning are increasingly getting blurred. Through technology, learners shift from one mode to the other without any form of time, geographical, or institutional barriers. Through mobile and locative media, "the surrounding physical environment and the digital environment can be dynamically merged into augmented, ad-hoc Personal Learning Environments" (Buchem & Perez-Sanagustin, 2013, p. 1). As a result, individualized and collaborative

Assessment in Online and Blended Learning Environments, pages 39–53
Copyright © 2015 by Information Age Publishing
All rights of reproduction in any form reserved.

modes of learning are becoming integrated into continuous, coherent technology-mediated learning experiences. Actions, resources, situations, and relationships are distributed between physical and online networked contexts transforming e-lifelong-learning into a sociotechnical system in which knowledge and learning are both the form and the content as for their social and relational meaning (Pettenati & Cigognini, 2007). Blended and online learning are emerging as highly natural practices embedded in and integrating all dimensions of our lives: learning, socializing, personal healthcare, finance, leisure, and entertainment. It is deeply rooted in our daily behavior and in our social interactions enhancing our communication and learning practices, together with knowledge creation and transmission. Assessment has thus to be considered within the context of this internet of ideas, learning objects, processes, and relationships.

The merging of formal with informal learning by technology-enhanced or technology-mediated learning systems necessitates the rethinking of underlying pedagogical frameworks. Didactical approaches, characterized by acquisition learning, are being complemented, and in many situations superseded, by participatory and contributory modes of learning inspired by constructivists, constructionists, and connectivist epistemologies. The Australian framework, *Digital Education—Making the Change Happen* (MCEETYA, 2008), proposes a three-stage pedagogical framework according to the level of school development: the developing, the accomplished, and the leading school. On the same vein, UNESCO's (2011) ICT Competency Framework for Teachers proposes a pedagogical developmental process moving from the integration of technology in the curriculum (within the technology-literacy approach) to the use of digital tools to solve complex problems (in the knowledge-deepening approach) and ultimately to an approach focused on developing self-management competences (knowledge-creation approach).

The pedagogical practice within the "technology-literacy" approach involves the integration of various technologies and digital content as part of whole-class, group, and individual student activities to support didactic instruction. Assessment of this pedagogical approach includes improving basic linguistic and numeracy skills through technology and adding the development of ICT skills in other subjects through a range of relevant ICT resources and productivity tools. The "knowledge-deepening" approach highlights complex problem-solving and requires changes in the curriculum that underscores depth of understanding over coverage of content, and assessments that emphasize the application of understanding to real-world problems and social priorities. Assessment changes focus onto complex problem-solving and embeds assessments into the ongoing activities of the class. The "knowledge-creation" pedagogical approach focuses on knowledge society skills such as problem solving, communication, collaboration, critical thinking, and autonomous learning. Self-management is an important skill to be developed so that students work in a learning community in which they are continuously encouraged to determine their own learning goals and plans, engaged in creating knowledge products and building upon their own and each other's knowledge and skills. Assessment is itself a part of this process, involving self and peer evaluation. In line with this, the policy of the European Union is to develop key competences in formal education together with relevant assessment modes that ultimately shape the learning process. The key challenge for education systems in many member states is the assessment of these competences.

> Assessment is one of the most powerful influences on teaching and learning but it tends to put too much emphasis on subject knowledge, and less on skills and attitudes, and to neglect altogether the increasingly important cross-curricular competences such as learning to learn or entrepreneurship. Progress has to be made on assessment approaches to take into account all competences needed for the 21st century. (European Commission, 2012a, p. 3)

To achieve this, assessment methodologies have to be renovated considering both the "product" and the "process." Moving beyond the ubiquitous subject-oriented modes of assessment, new more process-oriented conceptualizations have to be considered in which competencies (comprising knowledge, skill, and attitude) are defined in terms of learning outcomes that in turn guide both formative and summative modes of assessment. "In this context, the potential of new technologies to help find ways of assessing key competences needs to be fully explored" (European Commission, 2012a, p. 3).

ASSESSING LEARNING
IN TECHNOLOGY-INTENSIVE ENVIRONMENTS

The assessment dilemma takes another dimension when one considers the assessment of key competences or assessment of knowledge, skills, and attitudes through ICT. Technology-mediated methods of assessment that measure different types and modes of learning are still at a rudimentary stage. "ICT-based assessment is often recommended but it is rarely indicated how it should be applied. For personalised and flexible learning, the use of technologies should be embedded in educational practice" (European Commission, 2012b, p. 9).

Consequently, there has been a constant need to measure, evaluate, and acknowledge individual or collective learning endeavors. Assessment methodologies need to adapt to the evolving educational scenario, taking into consideration the different learning processes arising from the various pedagogical orientations characterizing technology-intensive learning environments. The "assessment OF" and "assessment FOR" technology-intensive learning environments is becoming integrated into process-oriented pedagogies that promote 21st-century competences as an extrapolation of subject-content knowledge (Dede, 2010). For example, The Partnership for 21st Century Skills (2009) proposes the development of 21st-century competences using subject-oriented curricular contexts. The proposed three major categories of 21st-century skills are learning and innovation skills (critical thinking; oral, written, and digital communication; collaboration, team, and networking skills; and creativity and innovation); information, media, and technology skills; and life and career skills (flexibility and adaptability, initiative and self-direction, social and cross-cultural skills, productivity and accountability, and leadership and responsibility). Comprehensive assessment models that consider such diversity of competences should be developed and explored.

Traditional models of assessment based on content and task analysis are inadequate in measuring the development and elaboration of such competences. In assessing technology-enhanced learning, both content and processes have to be considered as structured and mediated by digital tools and environments. This demands a more integrative approach considering both "assessment OF learning" and "assessment FOR learning" for different pedagogical approaches such as learning through instruction, exploration, designing, through collaboration and sharing, and through reflection. Teachers and learning designers are challenged to move beyond the traditional assessment approach based on content and task analysis, and adopt a process-oriented assessment methodology based on dimensions and levels of interactions according to the pedagogical orientation of the learning activity. Competences are thus defined and assessed according to the type and frequency of interactions characterizing the learning activity. The actual challenge is to assess the learning process considering the manifested interactions as the learning outcomes. This demands the revisiting of didactical, constructivist, and constructionist pedagogies from a connectivist (Siemens, 2004) perspective considering learning and knowledge building as the establishment of increasingly elaborate networks and modes of interactions with the domain in question, with the community of practice of that particular domain, and with the mediating technology (Bereiter, 2002). Learning is transformed from a process of progressive "knowledge accumulation" to a process of establishing and preserving connections with a particular domain, its "community of practice," and the mediating technologies.

A PROCESS-ORIENTED MODEL FOR ASSESSING TECHNOLOGY-ENHANCED LEARNING

Against this epistemological backdrop, a process-oriented model is proposed for assessing learning in blended and online environments. This

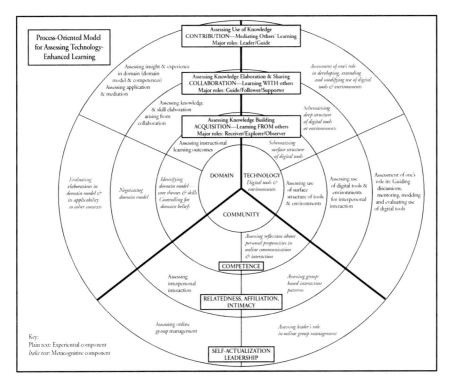

Figure 3.1 Process-oriented model for assessing technology-enhanced learning.

can be summarized as "Valued Technology-Mediated Learning Experiences = F [Pedagogy; Content; Community; Technology; Metacognition]." Figure 3.1 represents a model that organizes interactions according to these fundamental elements of learning and thus proposing an assessment framework for TEL. Interactions are organized along three dimensions and three pedagogical levels. The dimensions are the domain, the technology, and the community. Each dimension comprises two categories of interactions: those at the experiential level and those at a metacognitive level. The former include all interactions with the external environment, mediated through specific digital tools that comprise task-oriented and person-oriented activities. Interactions at the metacognitive level include all those intraindividual or collective reflections about the activities at the experiential level. But these experiential and metacognitive interactions are determined by the pedagogical orientation of the (technology-mediated) organizing context. Depending on learners' competence level, activities evolve from an acquisition, through participatory up to contributory modes of learning. Hence the model also organizes interactions across three pedagogical levels that cut across the three dimensions: the acquisition level comprising interactions of novice learners; a participatory/collaborative level dealing with interactions of more experienced learners; and a contributory level describing interactions characterizing highly experienced or expert learners.

Based on this theoretical framework a systemic process is proposed for assessing the different learning processes along the identified dimensions. This is summarized in Table 3.1.

Activities in the different pedagogical levels will be assessed considering the type, frequency, and directionality of interactions. Interactions along the domain dimension will be categorised according to content or task analysis characterizing the associative design approach (Beetham & Sharpe, 2007) considering the hierarchy of learning outcomes (facts, concepts, rules, procedures, and problem solving; psychomotor skills and cognitive strategies; and attitudes). Along the technology dimension, interactions with the "surface" and "deep" structure of the digital tool or environment will be considered in relation to the acquisition of domain knowledge and skills and to one's participation and collaboration in knowledge building and sharing. The surface structure deals with the physical features of the tool, mainly interface layout, menu options, navigation, and other action tools. The deep structure considers the interactions mediated by the tool or environment with the internet of objects, people, and locations.

TABLE 3.1   Assessing Learning Processes and Dimensions of Interactions

Pedagogical Level	Dimensions of Interactions		
	Domain	Technology	Community
Acquisition (Learning by instruction and exploration; typically assessed by a more experienced learner or tutor)	Assessment of acquired knowledge and skills	Assessment of knowledge and skills in the use of tools	Assessment of interactional skills
Participation (Learning by collaboration and sharing; typically assessed through peer evaluation)	Assessment of interactions in dedicated online spaces and CoPs in relation to domain knowledge and skills	Assessment of collaborative use of tools for communication, group management, and sharing	Assessment of different roles in contiguous and virtual communities
Contribution (Learning by designing and reflection; typically assessed through personalized knowledge- and competence-sharing tools like ePortfolios)	Assessment for designing, developing, and evaluating learning activities related to domain knowledge and skills	Assessment of tools or environments developed for mediating others' learning and for knowledge building and sharing	Assessment of activities involving managing, leading, facilitating, and evaluating in contiguous and virtual communities

Assessment along the community dimension can take different forms. Adopting an interactions approach based on learner analytics, the *type, frequency*, and *directionality* of interactions will be considered for assessing a learner's evolving role and identity. Interaction patterns can be developed to determine one's evolving role within the learning group starting from the basic receiver role that moves on to a supporting, guiding, and ultimately a leading role. Type, frequency, and directionality of interactions can also be quantified using learning networks such as those linked to ePortfolios or netfolios. ePortfolios may also be employed to assess collaborative online learning through peer assessment.

This model can serve as a template to assess learning in a blended or online environment organized within a virtual learning environment, an ePortfolio, a social (learning) network, or in personal learning spaces on the "cloud." It has the potential to be used in adaptive assessment systems involving pedagogical agents capable of tracing and recording interactions, comparing these to stored data, and then creating interactions profiles for a particular person or activity. Besides serving as formative or summative assessment tools, these interaction profiles can be used by the adaptive systems to propose lines of action for the learner.

Assessing Acquisition Learning

The acquisition of knowledge and skills in a particular domain can be assessed through computer-based or online tools specifically designed for developing tests or quizzes. Some provide the possibility to structure the test in a game format, which may be more attractive with younger learners. This traditional assessment approach can be used for the summative and formative assessment of instructional activities based on content and task analysis. Test items are developed to target specific learning outcomes at the knowledge, skill, or attitude level. At the knowledge level, assessment targets mental constructions including verbal information, concepts, and rules. Problem solving, cognitive strategies, and psychomotor skills are assessable domain-related skills. At a metacognitive level, mental organization of domain-related information and knowledge to core themes and skills can be assessed through concept maps in connection with an ePortfolio. If concept maps at different stages of conceptual development are recorded in an ePortfolio, the various levels of elaboration of a particular concept or network of concepts can be quantified and evaluated. In this way both content and process can be assessed. One can also assess the meta-affective level of learning using personal reflections entered in relevant sections of the personal ePortfolio. Acquired domain or technology-related attitudes can be analyzed considering the three components of an attitude: cognitive [thinking that involves perceived control and use], affective [feelings when using a particular tool], and conative [behaviors manifesting user choices].

In approaches where domain competence is acquired through the use of various digital tools, digital fluency becomes a key competence that should be monitored and nurtured through assessment. There are two aspects that should be considered. By "assessment OF digital competency," one attempts to quantify the knowledge and skills gained through the use of the tools mediating domain content and procedures. This involves determining the level of efficiency in using the different functions of the application or environment mediating domain content and procedures. For example, this may include assessing competence in using the different functions of a modeling tool in mathematics or science, the use of online tools for searching and sharing information, or other tools used in inquiry-based learning such as WebQuests. On the other hand, "assessing FOR digital competence" focuses on the metacognitive activity that is triggered by the use of the tool. This includes both tool-related organizational strategies that are employed by learners for schematizing surface structure of a tool and corresponding affective evaluation of the experience. If a learner manages to develop an integrative conceptualization of the different functions of a tool that gives him or her a sense of mastery, then a positive affective evaluation of the experience will be done. If a learner fails to identify an effective organizational scheme to the different affordances of the tool, the probability is that a negative evaluation is done driven by lack of perceived control.

Considering gender-related tendencies in the use of digital tools, assessment should be sensitive to the neurocognitive propensities of male and female learners. This implies controlling for female "rehearsing" versus male "manipulating" memory processing, female "linguistic" versus male "visuospatial" information representation and re-presentation strategies, and male "task-oriented" versus female "person-oriented" learning strategies (Bonanno, 2005, 2008). "Assessing FOR digital competence" can be done through reflection in dedicated sections of a student's or class ePortfolio. These sections will be monitored or managed by the tutor through provocative dialogue about one's thoughts and feelings while using specific tools. Collective reflection provides a comparative context for this technology-related introspection.

Considering the social context of online communication and knowledge-sharing tools, learners can follow a learning path to develop the interactional skills needed for effective functioning in groups. At the competence level one can consider assessing interactional skills focussing on type, frequency, and directionality of interaction. In gaining group competence learners may be involved in task-oriented interactions, such as asking for help in understanding some concept or in using some tool function. They may get engaged in more person-oriented interactions asking for another's opinion about their progress and their feelings about the domain and the mediating technology. Using a learner analytics approach, assessment of these interactional skills can be carried out through "interactions profiles," detailing the type, the frequency, and the learners involved. Each learner may be initiating or receiving interactions so that the interactions profile quantifies the divergent versus convergent activity of each participant.

Quantitative and qualitative analysis of task- and person-oriented interactions related to assessment can also be done through analysis of content in knowledge-sharing tools such as blogs, fora, or ePortfolios. Individual contributions are analyzed for content- or task-related information or for personal communication. Through this analysis an interactions profile based on type, number, and directionality of interaction can be used to assess a learner's performance within a group.

Assessing Participation and Collaboration

Collaborative technology-mediated learning necessitates the assessment of interactions along the domain, technology, and community dimensions. The most promising approach is to use embedded systems that gather interactional data on student engagement in these environments and provide formative and summative feedback. Using type, frequency, and directionality of interactions, learner behavioral tracking coupled with intelligent tutors can provide personalized and collective feedback about collaborative activity.

Along the domain dimension, assessment of collaborative activity considers the elaborations of domain-related knowledge and skills that arise from group-based negotiation of meaning and argumentation. Concept and skill elaborations can be assessed through relevant concepts and skill-mapping tools. Following learning engagements within a group, a learner develops a concept map of the domain content/skill in question. This is compared with other maps developed earlier through individual reflection. Any resulting elaborations arising from interactions within the group can be quantified in terms of added or modified nodes and links within the map.

An alternative method is to track these elaborations while students are collaborating on a task through a wiki. Comparing entry-level conceptualizations or skill levels with those manifested at different stages of the collaborative session in the wiki provides an empirical measure for knowledge and skill development. Using the same methods, one can assess metacognitive activity by quantifying the elaborations about the domain-related model or skill repertoire resulting from interaction with the learning group.

Along the technology dimension, assessment should consider competences in technology-mediated communication and knowledge building and sharing. Assessment may focus on knowledge of such tools (naming tools in relation to tasks) that can be assessed through a survey or quiz. Skill assessment, involving use of different functions of a particular tool while executing communication and knowledge building or sharing tasks, can be done through analysis of screencasts recorded during collaborative activity. One can also assess the attitude developed as a result of using these collaborative tools. Attitude to collaboration tools can be measured through analysis of individual or group reflections captured in knowledge-sharing tools such as ePortfolios, blogs, or wikis.

Analysis, discussion, and reflection on screencasts can be used to assess the metacognitive level of the use of tools for collaboration. This involves assessing the insight gained into the structure and use of the tool or digital environment inquiring about the schematization of its deep structure and identifying tool-related interaction patterns. Learners should show the ability to list the different interactions the tool can mediate with the domain (i.e., modes of interacting with subject matter); the possibilities offered to connect to other learning, communication, and collaboration tools; and interactions with communities of practice, online communities, and social/learner networks. Analysis of screencasts can also reveal and thus enable assessment of interaction patterns that can be quantified by identifying the type, frequency, and directionality of interactions within learners' networks.

Along the community dimension, two approaches may be used to assess group involvement, cohesion, and needs satisfaction. One's relationship with the group can be assessed through affective typifications using audio- and video-based online conferencing tools that capture and record the type of body language, voice tonality, and facial expression. This capitalizes on the intraindividual social monitoring process of mentalizing through which individual impressions are formed about the group process and the evolving collective learning experience. The availability of these auditory and image-based communication tools makes the learning process much closer to real face-to-face communication, considered as the highest form of human interaction. Socioemotional profiling categorizing the various degrees of positive or negative facial and body expressions can be used.

In technology-mediated learning environments the level of communication and sharing can also be quantified through the type, frequency, and directionality of person-oriented interactions (Bonanno, 2008). Even the socioemotional climate of an online community can be quantified through the degree of interaction with the various communication and knowledge-sharing tools. A fully engaged participant will definitely show a higher variety and frequency of interaction in an online environment than a detached, disengaged, or uncommitted member. Their interactions profile would definitely contrast. Constructing individual and group interaction profiles based on task- and person-oriented interactions is a very effective mode for assessing group dynamics and progress (Bonanno, 2011).

Some tools already provide this mode of assessment based on learner analytics. For example, the online social learning environment *Edmodo* (*www. edmodo.com*) already provides such a group-monitoring and assessment tool. It includes an interactions-monitoring tool, the Insights option, that lets the teacher view interaction trends and totals based on how students are reacting to posts, assignments, quizzes, and other categories of interactions. The degree of interaction is represented metaphorically by face icons linking size to frequency of interactions. The large faces to the left side of the interface show the overall mood of the classrooms based on individual reactions. The small faces represent the most popular reactions that are occurring in the groups. There is also a Trends tool that functions in conjunction with the large faces showing the overall mood of the group/class. The small arrows next to the large faces indicate whether more recent reactions are trending positively or negatively.

Assessing Knowledge Creation and Mediation

The third pedagogical level of the proposed model focuses on how learners can use digital tools and environments to generate knowledge and mediate it to others. Through their refined portfolio of skills in their area of expertise and in line with the technology, pedagogy, and content knowledge framework (Mishra & Koehler, 2006), highly competent learners are able to foster a range of technology-mediated interdisciplinary and transdisciplinary skills. This "wisdom" level thus describes the ability of highly competent members of a particular "community of practice" to use knowledge for motivating and helping less competent members to understand and develop situated, domain-related competences and become proficient in using digital tools for learning, communicating and knowledge building and sharing. They also have a role in helping other members to develop technology-mediated social skills and interactional competences such as networking skills, group monitoring, management, and evaluating skills.

Experts or highly experienced members of the learning community provide more than knowledge and skills to less competent learners, they embody knowledge and skills and are capable of providing situated knowledge by modeling expert behavior in authentic contexts. Their insight into technology, pedagogy, and content knowledge comprising pedagogical content knowledge (PCK), technological content knowledge (TCK), and technological pedagogical knowledge (TPK), and their ability to apply this in authentic learning situations enables them to operate in learning contexts characterized by the higher levels of Bloom's (1956) cognitive domain, that is, the level of synthesis, design, and evaluation. Koehler, Mishra, Akcaoglu, and Rosenberg (2013) propose the learning technology by design (LT/D) framework as an effective instructional technique to develop deeper understanding of technological pedagogical content knowledge. This constructionist approach is convergent with UNESCO's "knowledge creation approach" (UNESCO, 2011) through which technology-intensive solutions to real-life problem situations are developed.

One important phenomenon that emerges in collaborative online environments is "distributed expertise." These contexts can be better described as "symbiotic associations" of different types of expertise. While some members provide insight into domain knowledge and pedagogical content knowledge, other members provide insight into the use and application of technological tools and environments in that particular domain. Their level of expertise in technological content knowledge and technological pedagogical knowledge can supersede that of the other group members who are more domain competent. Thus in technology-mediated collaborative learning contexts it is more appropriate to think of "distributed mediation of learning" and "complementary roles" in the co-construction of the learning experience. Learning in such contexts is a multilayered constructionist experience. Learners construct their understanding of a subject or field by participating in learning communities who are continually co-constructing their experience. Learning by designing is the common thread, co-designing the evolving learning experience is the practical collective application of this principle.

The ePortfolio approach is the most effective mode for assessing both the "product" and the "process" of this mediational constructionist approach along the three dimensions of technology-enhanced learning. Along the domain dimension, assessment should focus on the design, development, and evaluation of learning activities targeting the promotion of knowledge and skills in less competent learners. The ePortfolio should organize these and make them available for peer evaluation considering one's insight into the domain model and manifested domain-related competences including mediational skills. These include the tools or environments used or developed for mediating different modes of learning for less competent learners. The criteria to assess this mediational activity includes one's awareness about the degree of transformation of domain knowledge and skills by the technological tools used; modeling use of the tool; mentoring use of the tool; criticizing use of the tool for learning, communication, and knowledge building and sharing; use of tools for monitoring and managing community processes.

The community dimension is assessed considering those activities involving managing, leading, facilitating, and evaluating contiguous or online learning communities. From a process-oriented perspective experienced learners have to be assessed on their abilities to manage and evaluate technology-mediated task and person-oriented interactions. Their insight into the domain models and mediating technological tools puts them in a position to anticipate interaction patterns by individual members or the whole group.

They are able to evaluate quickly group activity and propose relevant guiding or corrective measures. On an individual level they may challenge negative impressions and beliefs about collaborative technology-mediated learning. They model the use of tools for enhancing collaboration; provide guidance and support; and encourage members lacking in confidence to take more active roles. On a collective level their role is to nurture group affinity by addressing task- and tool-related interactions and by managing the socioemotional climate of the group. By analyzing group goals and prevalent interaction patterns, they will be able to guide group strategy, challenge inefficient approaches, and suggest alternative group structure through changing the group-based roles shown by different members of the group.

One of the most important metacognitive activities that experienced learners may be assessed for is their role in promoting reflection within the learning group about a participant's evolving role and corresponding identity. Mature identities motivate participants to identify a strategy for upgrading various competences in an attempt to bridge the gap between current and more evolved identities in contiguous and virtual groups. The role of experienced participants is to mediate this process by continually challenging less competent participants, or those showing low levels of interactions, to adopt more assertive and active group roles. This shifts their comportment from a passive to a more leading and contributing one. At the group level they should encourage rotation of roles and control in-group formations arising from exclusive patterns of interaction. At the same time competent participants should encourage a more inclusive approach by interacting with all group members and habitually addressing the whole group.

From a process-oriented perspective these different aspects of contribution outline how technology-intensive environments for collaborative learning could be used to "mediate others' learning" by providing a context and a set of tools so that a teacher or a more experienced learner can help others become active contributory nodes in the social interactional network. These environments provide the context in which all interactions occur that can be easily captured through session recording facilities, which can be utilized for monitoring and managing group activity. They also provide an online environment that can be discussed, evaluated, and adapted according to the evolving interactional needs of the group. Yet this online environment provides these experienced users with the tools to help them mediate the further growth of learners in domain-related knowledge and competences, and in the proficient use of technology for learning, communicating, and interacting with other learners and experts. A connectivist perspective to growth within a domain assumes the elaboration of networks through which one interacts with different levels and roles within a learning group in an effort to achieve the projected "mature identity." These are all assessment criteria that could be utilized to valuate this dynamic and evolving contributory experience.

CONCLUSION

Assessing technology-enhanced learning, whether in blended or totally on-line contexts, is a very complex task as it involves so many dimensions and levels of interaction. One cannot assess learning along the domain dimension without considering learning along the other two dimensions. At the same time, assessment should be competence-sensitive—adapting to learners' levels of experience in any of the three dimensions of interactions. This demands careful design of assessment considering the use of different instruments and modes of assessment targeting different competences. Instead of focussing on the traditional mode of assessing domain content, one should determine the underlying learning and interactional processes in a specific technology-enhanced context, and then devise the most appropriate assessment mode. For this purpose, assessment design should be data-driven. Using the information obtained through observation, from interactions profiles or interactivity indicators, specific assessment procedures can be developed for different individuals or groups. The analysis of the results obtained from these modes of assessment should serve to identify the degree of influence the online environment had on the individual learners and on groups. Assessment should help learners reflect about the sense of mastery the online environment is developing in them regarding the acquisition of knowledge and skills in the curricular subject and about online collaboration. The improvement of one's sense of competence develops more positive attitudes about the online learning experience.

The proposed process-oriented model attempts to link different modes of assessment to the range of domain-, technology-, and community-related competences that underlie technology-enhanced learning. It shifts focus from the sole assessment of domain competences to include interdisciplinary and trans-disciplinary competences—critical analysis, creativity, technological-pedagogical skills, and collaborative and team management skills. It explores how comprehensive assessment can be achieved by integrating the assessment of the "product" with the assessment of the "process," that is, "assessment OF technology-enhanced learning" with "assessment FOR technology-enhanced learning." This is the highly evolving field of "assessment design for technology-enhanced learning."

REFERENCES

Beetham, H., & Sharpe, R. (2007). *Rethinking pedagogy for a digital age: Designing and delivering e-learning.* London, UK: Routledge.

Bereiter, C. (2002). *Education and mind in the knowledge age.* Mahwah, NJ: Erlbaum.

Bloom, B. S. (1956). *Taxonomy of Educational Objectives, Handbook 1: Cognitive Domain.* New York, NY: Addison Wesley.

Bonanno, P. (2005). Categorising and investigating gender-based neurocognitive propensities influencing gameplay: An interactions-oriented approach. In M. Burmester, D. Gerhard, & F. Thissen (Eds.), *Digital game based learning: Proceedings of the 4th International Symposium for Information Design* (pp. 59–82). Karlsruhe, Germany: Karlsruhe University.

Bonanno, P. (2008). *Learning through collaborative gaming: A process-oriented pedagogy.* Joensuu, Finland: University of Joensuu.

Bonanno, P. (2011). A process-oriented pedagogy for ubiquitous learning. In T. Kidd, & I. Chen (Eds.), *Ubiquitous learning: Strategies for pedagogy, course design, and technology* (pp. 17–35). Charlotte, NC: Information Age.

Buchem, I., & Perez-Sanagustin, M. (2013). Personal learning environments in smart cities: Current approaches and future scenarios. *eLearning Papers, 35.* Retrieved from http://openeducationeuropa.eu/en/article/Personal-Learning-Environments-in-Smart-Cities%3A—Current-Approaches-and-Future-Scenarios?paper=133343.

Dede, C. (2010). Technological supports for acquiring 21st century skills. In E. Baker, B. McGaw, & P. Peterson (Eds.), *International encyclopedia of education* (3rd ed., pp. 158–166). Oxford, UK: Elsevier.

European Commission. (2012a). Assessment of key competences in initial education and training: Policy guidance. In *Accompanying the communication from the Commission on Rethinking Education: Investing in skills for better socio-economic outcomes.* Strasbourg, France: Author.

European Commission. (2012b). *Rethinking education: Investing in skills for better socio-economic outcomes.* Retrieved from http://www.cedefop.europa.eu/EN/Files/com669_en.pdf.

Koehler, M. J., Mishra, P., Akcaoglu, M., & Rosenberg, J. M. (2013). Technological pedagogical content knowledge for teachers and teacher educators. In N. Bharati & S. Mishra (Eds.), *ICT integrated teacher education models* (pp. 1–8). New Delhi, India: Commonwealth Educational Media Center for Asia.

MCEETYA. (2008). *Digital education—Making the change happen.* Retrieved from http://www.det.wa.edu.au/detcms/cms-service/download/asset?asset_id=13814129.

Mishra, P., & Koehler, M. J. (2006). Technological pedagogical content knowledge: A new framework for teacher knowledge. *Teachers College Record, 108*(6), 1017–1054.

Partnership for 21st Century Skills. (2009). *P21 framework definitions.* Retrieved from http://www.p21.org/storage/documents/P21_Framework_Definitions.pdf.

Pettenati, M. C., & Cigognini, M. E. (2007): Social networking theories and tools to support connectivist learning activities. *International Journal of Web-Based Learning and Teaching Technologies, 2*(3), 39–57.

Siemens, G. (2004). Connectivism: A learning theory for a digital age. *Elearnspace.* Retrieved from http://www.elearnspace.org/Articles/connectivism.htm.

UNESCO. (2011). ICT competency framework for teachers. Retrieved from http://unesdoc.unesco.org/images/0021/002134/213475E.pdf.

CHAPTER 4

STUDENTS AS "ASSESSORS" AND "ASSESSEES" IN AN ERA OF SOCIAL MEDIA

Gail Casey
Deakin University, Australia

INTRODUCTION

The discussion in this chapter is part of a larger study that used the action research process to build a social learning framework investigating three foci (students, learning, and the teacher). The larger study included 13 classes involving information technology and mathematics curriculum over an 18-month time frame. It was found that social and participatory media could offer an interactive and positive learning experience for students and links to social constructivist teaching as well as chaos and complexity theories, which are discussed in Casey and Evans (2011). The study explores the unique qualities that social and participatory media brought to the classroom; it required the teacher to redesign her curriculum delivery, discussed further in Casey (2011). A more in-depth examination of the social tools within this simple, yet complex hybrid (blended) environment is discussed in Casey (2013b). A short teacher-focused article on social media in mathematics can be found in Casey (2012) and an in-depth discussion of

Assessment in Online and Blended Learning Environments, pages 55–75
Copyright © 2015 by Information Age Publishing
All rights of reproduction in any form reserved.

the new literacies and multimodal methods within student online activities is discussed further in Casey (2013a).

This chapter focuses on how the research was implemented in one classroom. The action research extended the walls of the classroom as it examined ways to support students in becoming active and valued participants in the learning process. It explored the unique qualities of online social media and Web 2.0 tools within the face-to-face teaching program in an Australian public secondary school. The teacher redeveloped curriculum programs in order to take advantage of the interactive learning environment where formal and informal learning opportunities were encouraged as students created online interest groups to integrate their knowledge and experiences into the social media site. Designing such a learning framework required a rethink in approach to teaching and learning and, hence, to assessment. This chapter describes how one teacher, within one of her 13 secondary school classes, incorporated a multidimensional student-centered approach to assessment. The author was both the teacher and doctoral researcher and she used the action research spiral to build a learning framework while investigating three research foci:

1. *Students:* What are the complexities in developing such a framework and what scaffolding is needed to help students learn within such complexity?
2. *Learning:* How can this framework help meet the learning and curriculum needs for schooling?
3. *Teachers:* What new demands could this type of framework bring to teachers and what professional development is needed to support such change?

This chapter provides an extensive project example from one class to help explain how the teacher used a student-centered approach to create a triangulation of assessment data, one that included peer assessment, self-assessment, and teacher observations. This provided rich evidence for the school reporting process.

Within this study, Nuthall's (2007) "lens on learning," where sensitivity, adaption, and adjustment to the "here-and-now," provided important elements for the teaching and learning framework. Nuthall's lens focuses on peer-to-peer learning and supports teacher intuition when making decisions as a lesson or activity progresses. These were fundamental for this study as the teacher used the action research spiral to build one social network, called Ning (*http://uk.ning.com*), to share with all of her students in a given semester. The teacher posted many of her class projects on the social networking site and students used the different social spaces and tools, within the site, to interact. This included posting content for projects as well as using and creating online groups, chat, blogs, and discussion forums. Using such social and interactive spaces provided an environment where students had multiple methods of receiving peer support and feedback.

Valuing such knowledge can be a difficult task within a secondary school curriculum program, but within the social networking site students were encouraged to create online groups based on their interests, allowing them to bring their life experiences and out-of-school knowledge into the classroom. This allowed both formal and informal learning to occur within the social media site and it supports many concepts of extending learning experience beyond the set classroom (Alsop, 2008; Bean & Dunkerly, 2012; Beetham & Sharpe, 2007; Bonk, 2008; Boyd & Ellison, 2007; Coleman, 2011; Jewitt, Clark, & Hadjithoma-Garstka, 2011; Lankshear & Knobel, 2006; Mason, 2008; Palfrey, 2008; Pullen & Cole, 2010). The online nature of both the formal and informal learning, within this study, provided many opportunities for a more visible teaching and learning approach to exist.

> When students become their own teachers, they exhibit the self-regulatory attributes that seem most desirable for learners (self-monitoring, self-evaluation, self-assessment, self-teaching). Thus, it is visible teaching and learning by teachers and students that makes the difference. (Hattie, 2012, p. 14)

As explained by Hattie (2012), levels of achievement are important, but there is also the question of how to move each student forward from wherever they start through the progression of learning.

SITUATING THE RESEARCH

Assessment not only measures learning, but it also contributes to learning (Hricko & Howell, 2006). However, traditional-based assessment, as discussed by Hricko and Howell (2006), does not always meet the needs of the online environment. Peer assessment is an educational arrangement where students judge a peer's performance quantitatively and/or qualitatively and that stimulates students to reflect, discuss, and collaborate (Strijbos & Sluijsmans, 2010). In the past two decades a conceptual shift has occurred in the practice of assessment, from teacher directed to one that involves students, as discussed by Strijbos and Sluijsmans (2010), and although they argue that the effectiveness of any assessment depends on the quality of assessment and how it is incorporated by students in subsequent performance, Lan, Liu, and Zhou (2012) offer a different perspective on peer assessment within technology-assisted environments.

In their study, Lan et al. (2012) examine how students, playing the roles of assessors and assessees in technology-assisted peer assessment, contributed to students' performance. They discuss the assessees' ability to critically judge and act upon peer feedback, and their findings suggest that the quality of feedback, provided by students in reviewing the work of their peers, correlated positively with the quality of their own work. Their findings are relevant to this study because they contradict the common belief that receiving higher-quality feedback leads to better student performance. In other words, their findings focus on the benefit of the students from performing the assessor's role rather than the assessee's role. Lan et al. suggest that one possible explanation of their perplexing picture is that students may not respond to peer feedback in the same way that they respond to instructor feedback. They go on to clarify that such findings strongly support a theoretical explanation of the value of active engagement as well as critical thinking in peer assessment. In their study, students who benefited more from the peer assessment process not only tended to be more engaged in finding the weaknesses and strengths of their peers' work but also show superior ability to discriminate good versus misleading comments from their peers. Lan et al.'s findings are noted in this research study because their discussion on the value of active engagements as well as critical thinking in peer assessment relates well with the interactive nature of Casey's classroom social media site, which provided opportunities for such engagement and assessment.

Although discussing peer feedback in an undergraduate setting, and within the context of gaining feedback for writing, Cho and MacArthur (2010) discuss peer feedback as an important alternative to instructor evaluation and feedback. The aim of their research was to increase understanding of peer reviewing in order to inform improved practice. They investigated how students revise drafts based on feedback from peers and whether their revisions improve writing quality. Their research also compares peer review to expert and instructor review. Cho and MacArthur found that multiple peer reviews led to greater quality improvement. In discussing their findings, they suggest that multiple peer reviews are easier to understand than an expert review and easier to use in revision. Their findings are consistent with their previous research. Cho and MacArthur's discussion of the research of others supports the concept of peer reviews as reasonably valid and reliable. They also argue that, at least under some conditions, students are able to provide useful feedback to their peers without training, although they also point to research that has found that such training is important. Cho and MacArthur's research is particularly helpful in looking at the peer feedback and assessment processes in this study because of the general lack of depth of the peer feedback. They argue that peer reviews also help authors improve their audience awareness by providing responses from the perspectives of multiple readers, and the ability to read one's own writing, from a reader's perspective, is important to effective communication.

In this study, the research site comes under the umbrella of the Department of Education and Early Childhood Development (DEECD), in Victoria, Australia, and the learning objectives for all classes at the school were required to meet the DEECD Victorian Essential Learning Standards (VELS); these have similar standards to their newly updated version of AusVELS (*http://ausvels.vcaa.vic.edu.au*). All schools at the time within the DEECD jurisdiction were expected to adhere to the following assessment advice:

> Assessment is the ongoing process of gathering, analysing and reflection on evidence to make informed and consistent judgements to improve future student learning. Assessment for improved student learning and deep understanding requires a range of assessment practices to be used with three overarching purposes:
>
> - Assessment FOR learning—occurs when teachers use inferences about student progress to inform their teaching,
> - Assessment AS learning—occurs when students reflect on and monitor their progress to inform their future learning goals,
> - Assessment OF learning—occurs when teachers use evidence of student learning to make judgements on student achievement against goals and standards
>
> …Assessment is most effective when it reflects the fact that learning is a complex process that is multi-dimensional, integrated and revealed in student performance over time. (DEECD, 2009, p. 1)

THE RESEARCH FRAMEWORK

This qualitative study used Armstrong and Moore's (2004) action research framework. Some aspects of the research framework are discussed in the following pages, although the focus of this chapter is to provide a practice-oriented approach rather than include a full description of the research process. The full research study took place in an Australian public secondary school with students between ages 13 and 16 over an 18-month period. The author was both the teacher and the doctoral researcher and data was collected from July 2010 through December 2011 from within the author's 13 (Year 7–10) mathematics and information technology classes that she taught during that time.

The school's student population was approximately 900 with a midrange socioeconomic profile and the proportion of students with English as a second language was classified as low-middle. The average class size was 25 and most classes were timetabled for five periods per week except for

Year 7 classes, which were only two periods per week and were part of an integrated curriculum program; one period was approximately 50 minutes in duration.

The research data were organized around the three research foci: students, learning, and teachers. Each theme was broken up into categories and the collected data were tagged and stored within these categories; one piece of data could be associated with more than one category. A large quantity of the data included screenshots of student online interactions and user-generated content; an overview of the range of data collected within the student and learning foci is shown in Figure 4.1.

The data collected from the teacher focus included:

- Planning documents
- Field notes
- End-of-week reflections
- Midterm and end-of-term reflections
- Critical friend and teacher feedback

Each semester, the teacher created one social networking site, using Ning, to share with all of the teacher's classes during that semester. Figure 4.2 shows a screen clip of the main page of the Ning social network. The main navigational menu used is shown near the top left-hand side of

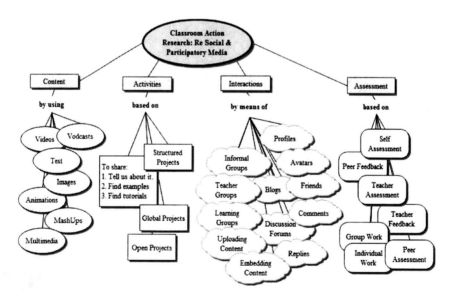

Figure 4.1 The range of activities and data collected throughout the action research study.

MS CASEY'S CLASSES

Learning by sharing

Main | My Page | Members | Photos | Videos | Blogs | Groups |

Welcome to
Ms Casey's Classes
Sign Up
or Sign In

All classes working together to support each other - some content from this site may be used for educational research.

/// MEMBERS

/// CONDITIONS OF MEMBERSHIP

Enjoy communicating and learning together while being respectful of each other.
NOTE:
1. Please do NOT post any identifyable information of yourself or others
2. Please do NOT post pictures of yourself or anyone else
3. Please use your fake name at all times
4. You must make your own Avatar - use one of these sites to make your avatar then take a screen clip then upload it to your 'My Page' under settings.

   M&M avatar - http://www.mms.com/us/becomeanmm/
   Lego avatar - http://www.reasonablyclever.com/mini/kidsafe.htm
   Wild avatar - http://www.buildyourwildself.com/

At times we hope to connect globally with other schools through Skype, email, chat and blogs. To keep track of our visitors we shall use the cluster map below

523 Visitors
25 Feb 2011 - 1 Nov 2012

/// GROUPS

Google Earth in Maths
9 members
0 ▪ 0

Maths & the Real World
15 members
0 ▪ 3

May - Student Help Video...
18 members
45 ▪ 3

Maths Help - Tips and Tr...
1 members
0 ▪ 6

Figure 4.2 An example of a Ning social network used in this research study.

Figure 4.1 and this menu appears on all pages within the site. For quick access, the teacher-directed groups are situated down the left-hand side of the main page.

All students, for privacy reasons, used pseudonyms and avatars to represent themselves online. Many Web 2.0 tools were embedded or linked to the site. Within the Ning site, each student had their own "My Page," which provided quick access links to all of their content, such as blogs, groups, discussion forums, pictures, and video. This page also listed their latest activity on the site and listed their online "friends" and "likes." The "My Page" also allowed students to develop their own profile and to publish their own page theme. Students could leave comments on a peer's "My Page." This area was also seen by the teacher as a type of informal ePortfolio.

During the initial stage of this research study, the teacher identified that the time taken to develop and moderate the social media site, within the face-to-face classroom setting, required more time than available. As a consequence the teacher began a process of finding how "best" to use classroom and organizational time. Through the action research spiral, the issue of reducing teacher time continued to be at the forefront of many changes. As the teacher redesigned the assessment processes she took particular note of the words from Weedon, Winter, and Broadfoot (2001), who assert that marking takes up many hours of a teacher's week, but much of this time is spent checking that work has been completed, rather than being more focused on identifying learning problems and helping pupils to identify and to resolve problems for themselves.

An Example of One Classroom Project Using a "Bucket" Blog

The following provides an extensive example of one class project and describes the associated, designed assessment processes. This particular project uses a concept called a "bucket" of information, developed from Hendron (2010), who used this as part of his "info-seeking gluency" framework. The concept, in this study, of a "bucket" blog involved students creating "buckets" of information that were accessible and shared by other students. This, Hendron argues, embraces, rather than ignores, the digital nature of information today and takes advantage of three major sources of online media:

- Networked and social resources such as discussion forums and online interaction

- Read/write/remix resources such as blogs, video-sharing websites, and Web 2.0 tools
- Traditional "trusted" resources such as databases and encyclopedias

Within this study, the concept of a "bucket" of information was used in a number of projects in different subjects and with students of different ages. The specific example discussed in the following pages involved students age 15–16 years from an information technology elective subject. Assessment for the project included peer assessment (where the student worked with three peers), self-assessment (which included a detailed account of the work completed and a reflection of their effort), and teacher observations (mainly focusing on the student's ability to provide constructive and critical feedback to their peers). It should also be noted that this project was one of many that occurred during the data collection period and it was chosen, for this chapter, because it highlights the ease and value of interacting and sharing resources. However, this particular example does not highlight the wide variety of user-generated content that was also possible online. This aspect was highlighted during the final semester of data collection where many Web 2.0 tools were used and linked from the "Get Creative" page provided by the teacher on the social site at http://webtowhere.ning.com/group/getcreative

---

TASK 1: FAVORITE FOOD

Target skills: find, save, and upload resources onto the social site as well as identifying sources

This was an introductory task to establish some understanding of the range of tools available on the social site. Students used the Internet to find pictures of their favorite foods then saved their picture to their computers and uploaded them to the social site where they then left a description of their favorite food and links to websites that identified their sources. These details enabled their peers to check the information provided and obtain further information if needed. Students were asked to leave comments and feedback for at least three peers.

Assessment:

- Assessment FOR learning: An informal formative assessment by the teacher carried out through observation.
- Assessment AS learning: An informal assessment by the student carried out through an examination of the uploaded content and comments posted by their peers and compared with their own.

TASK 2: TAGS AND RATINGS

Target skills: concepts of online tags, ratings, and photo albums

Students were required to include additional information and organization of their food pictures from Task 1. This included adding tags to their food pictures, which ensured that these were searchable within the social site. It also included the creation of photo albums, which helped to organize the pictures. Students were asked to provide constructive comments and to rate the food photos, in relation to their own likes and dislikes. The rating was done by clicking on the "star rating" system displayed under each picture, five stars being the highest rating. The options to add ratings to content provided students with additional methods of communication, feedback, and assessment within the social site.

Assessment:

- Assessment FOR learning: An informal formative assessment by the teacher carried out through observation.
- Assessment AS learning: An informal assessment by the student carried out through an examination of the ratings and comments posted.

TASK 3: CREATING AND SHARING A "BUCKET" BLOG

Target skills: finding and sourcing information as well as examining the reliability of information

Students were asked to choose their own research topic, within the area of new technologies or new software types. Students then created a blog to store their information, which was the start of a working space for this project. On their blog, students were asked to explain their topic and list five things they hoped to find out or explore in regard to their topic. All students could read each other's blogs and leave comments, if they so desired. Students were also asked to list words or sentences that could be used when searching for information on their topic. This became the student's "bucket" of information. Initially, the students were asked to simply copy and paste slabs of information from the Internet into their buckets (encouraging students of all learning abilities to get started and to not be discouraged by the language or detail of the information). Students were also asked to rate and tag their different slabs of information, hence to make decisions on the reliability of the information and sources.

Note:

- This task created a type of modelling process where peers could see how the Buckets of others were developed.
- Slabs of information were cut and pasted into the buckets before students, in a later task, carved away the unnecessary information

to get closer to the essence of the content, as discussed by Hendron (2010), and to answer their research questions.

Assessment:

- Assessment FOR learning: Informal formative assessment focused on the students' ability to identify and examine the validity and usefulness of their sources.
- Assessment AS learning: An informal assessment by the student carried out through an examination of the posted ratings and comments.

TASK 4: STUDENT-DESIGNED ASSESSMENT CRITERIA

Target skills: reflection and critical thinking, focusing on past assessment practices and different learning styles

In this task, students were required to reflect on their own learning style as well as their past experiences as an "assessee." The assessors of a bucket blog were to be three peers and the assessment criteria that would be used by the assessors were to be determined by the student owner of the bucket blog.

Assessment:

- Assessment AS learning: Informal formative assessment focused on students reflecting and analyzing their learning style and their previous assessment experiences.

TASK 5: KNOWLEDGE-BUILDING, SHARING BUCKETS

Target skills: identifying and analyzing buckets that have similar or connected research topics

Students used the main "Blog" menu to access a complete list of blogs published on the site. From this list they were to find at least three peer buckets that contained research topics that related to their own. Students were to read the slabs of information pasted on each of these buckets then visit the website sources listed on the bucket to find resources for their own research. When a student found a peer's bucket useful, they were expected to leave supportive comments and to thank the peer for sharing their research. Each student was also expected to invite their peers to visit their own bucket by leaving a website link to their bucket.

Assessment:

- Assessment FOR learning: Informal formative assessment, focused on the quality of the peer feedback.
- Assessment AS learning: Identifying and analyzing peer buckets.

Comment by Tam on November 19, 2010 at 10:30
http://www.fi.edu/fellows/fellow5/may99/History/history.html
Is a great link from Warney
http://ghs2010.ning.com/profiles/blogs/warneys-animation-bucket

Comment by Tam on November 19, 2010 at 10:23
I love the website
http://hhs.hilmar.k12.ca.us/Departments/FineArts/Animation/Types%20...
from Ninja
Check out their bucket here: http://ghs2010.ning.com/profiles/blogs/ninja-amimation-bucket

Comment by Tam on November 19, 2010 at 10:19
Some great infomation from sandwich here:
http://ghs2010.ning.com/profiles/blogs/sandwichs-animations-bucket
I like the http://en.wikipedia.org/wiki/Educational_animation

Figure 4.3 Comments from one student with pseudonym "Tam" as they share different "buckets" of information.

Figure 4.3 displays three comments left by a student whose pseudonym was "Tam." In these comments, Tam has acknowledged the value of peer blogs from "Warney," "Ninja," and "Sandwich," hence attempting to display her own ability to critically analyze the content of peer blogs. These comments from Tam also provided a model to her peers, displaying one appropriate way of carrying out Task 5. (Note that all students were asked to use pseudonyms to ensure they could not be identified online.)

These comments are an average representation of the standard of comments for this task. Although the comments were constructive, the teacher believed that more work needed to be done to scaffold support for students to help them add depth of information into their comments.

TASK 6: PRODUCE

Target skills: summarizing and synthesizing information

In this task, students needed to carve away the unnecessary information from their buckets to get closer to the essence of their research content. They were to summarize and synthesize their information and determine the way in which they would publish their research within the social site. The teacher offered a number of options for online publishing, including a selection of Web 2.0 software tools, listed below. All of these were used by students at some point during the project work.

http://www.voki.com
http://www.tagxedo.com
http://animoto.com
http://www.wallwisher.com
http://blabberize.com

http://goanimate.com
http://www.xtranormal.com
http://taggalaxy.de
http://zoom.it/arOi

Assessment:

- Assessment FOR learning and Assessment AS learning: Informal formative assessment focused on the student's ability to summarize and synthesize.

The teacher also offered more traditional methods for organizing students' research. Students were given the option to make a poster, use a Word document, make a movie using Photo Story/Movie Maker, create a PowerPoint, or use Publisher. These could be uploaded to the social site as a means to publish their research. The teacher noted that the Web 2.0 tools most successful were:

1. *Voki*, which created an animated podcast that was very quick and easy for students to use. Students enjoyed using a Voki because they had options to either type in their text (a computer-generated voice would read their text) or record their voice using a microphone. There was also a wide variety of animations that could be used as a talking avatar. Peers were also keen to watch and listen to these animated podcasts and, hence, were often learning from them without realizing.

2. *Animoto*, which allowed students to make very quick 30-second videos that could include the "free" use of music tracks. Students were limited to 30 seconds (for a free Animoto account) and this had the advantage of forcing them to be very selective in what they were creating. The content was fully online and could be embedded into the class social network. This also had the advantage of eliminating many issues involving file formats (viewing could be done online anywhere and anytime) and did not take up any storage space within the class social network.

TASK 7: PUBLISHING ONLINE

Target skills: *publishing on a blog*

The teacher did not attempt to influence how students published their research. It was interesting to note that most students chose to present their work in a traditional form using a Word document, uploaded to their bucket blogs. The teacher's reflection data indicated that this may have been due to the time restraint for the project and/or the lack of "play" time needed to explore the Web 2.0 alternatives. Perhaps, when considering peer modeling, if the first students published using Web 2.0, others may have followed in their path. Perhaps the concept of research was seen by students as a more textual form of information provision.

Assessment:

- Assessment FOR learning: Informal formative assessment focused on the teacher identifying different modes of presentation that would be suitable for the range of student abilities.
- Assessment AS learning: Informal formative assessment focused on organizational skills.

TASK 8: PEER AND SELF-ASSESSMENT

Target skills: critical review and reflection

For each student, two out of three peer assessors where chosen at random. As students published their blog it appeared in a list on the main "Blogs" page. From this list, students would find their own blog. They would then identify the blog belonging to the student above them on the list and the one below them on the list. These two blogs were ones the student was required to assess and they should also assess one more blog, being any other of their choosing.

Assessment:

- Assessment FOR learning: Informal formative assessment focused on the teacher supporting the self-assessment and peer-assessment processes.
- Assessment OF learning: Summative assessment focused on students through the self-assessment and peer-assessment processes.

Figure 4.4 shows the average standard of student critical feedback. In this example, the student with the pseudonym JMSBANMDTMATM has provided his assessment criteria in the bottom of the three posts. The two posts above show the peer feedback and assessment from two peers with the pseudonyms "KANGAS" and "Bigcat." "M" indicates a medium standard and "H" indicates a high standard of work. The simple instructions to the "assessors" indicating what constitutes high, medium, or low are shown in the screen clip in Figure 4.5.

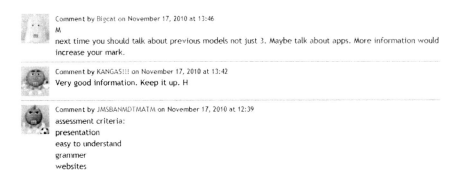

Comment by Bigcat on November 17, 2010 at 13:46
M
next time you should talk about previous models not just 3. Maybe talk about apps. More information would increase your mark.

Comment by KANGAS!!! on November 17, 2010 at 13:42
Very good information. Keep it up. H

Comment by JMSBANMDTMATM on November 17, 2010 at 12:39
assessment criteria:
presentation
easy to understand
grammer
websites

Figure 4.4 The student with pseudonym "JMBNDMTMATM" posted his assessment criteria and two students "Bigcat" and "KANGAS" provided peer feedback and assessment.

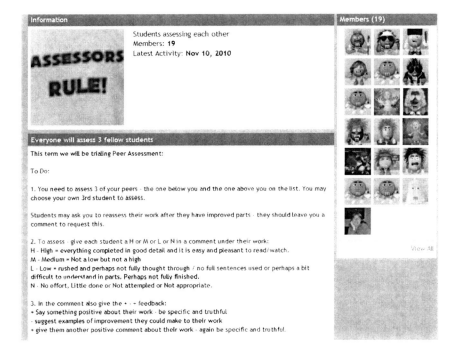

Figure 4.5 Scaffolding used to guide student peer-assessment.

IMPLICATIONS OF THE PROJECT

Initially, the teacher was mindful of the negative perceptions that many educators had with social media environments and students were to adhere to strict rules of appropriate behavior that would not disappoint the school principal. When breaches of the rules were identified, the student would lose access to the site until a discussion between the student and the teacher occurred. Initially, this could be for the slightest misdemeanor, such as using a cartoon avatar rather than creating their own (as instructed) or using slang that the teacher did not understand. One female student had her access removed for adding love hearts to a comment left for another female. As the research progressed over the 18-month period, the teacher became more flexible, knowledgeable, understanding of the way in which students liked to interact online. The following pages discuss the implications of this flexibility within the curriculum design and approach to assessment.

Students

Although peer feedback often appeared to offer little constructive support for improvement, it was interesting to note that students valued their peer feedback, and in the face-to-face classroom, and they sought out this feedback if their "assessors" were slow to provide it online. Initially, students were shocked and intrigued to hear that they were to choose their own assessment criteria, but once they gained a picture of their past years of experience with assessment they began to discuss it with interest. This was an area of assessment that needed much more investigation. Students made connections to "cheating" when discussing the open nature and social design of the learning environment, such as having access to all student buckets of information. As the project progressed, the students became aware that the task became individualized and the ability to think, critically analyze, and research were the important elements and concerns about cheating did not arise after initial conversations.

Teacher

The teacher began to move her focus away from being the dominant authority figure and into a more supportive role with a focus on helping students to learn good online behavior. An example of this change includes allowing students to use cartoon characters for their avatars as long as the teacher considered them "G"-rated. The teacher's approach to student comments also became more lenient and when a student posted the comment "Geelong Cats Suck," the teacher responded with an online comment pointing out the inappropriateness of the comment and asked that they please delete the comment and choose their words more carefully. The teacher also encouraged all students to post comments similar to this type if they were not comfortable with a comment or other uploaded content.

As the research progressed, it became rare for a student to lose their access to the site for inappropriate behavior. The action research spiral helped the social site to evolve into an active shared learning space where students and the teacher began to work together with less teacher–student traditional hierarchy and more within a concept of a shared learning environment.

The research data indicates that improving student constructive and critical feedback continued to be a challenge for the teacher. However, the teacher continued to note in her reflection data, that students appeared to gain a deeper understanding of the requirements of the project through carrying out peer assessment, even though their peer feedback may have lacked detail or critical analysis. This, the teacher pointed out, was partially due to forcing the students to view the work of their peers; the teacher provided an example where one student who, after being directed by the teacher to provide peer feedback, responded, "Is that all I have to do?"

Project

In the face-to-face classroom the teacher clarified the general school rules and made clear other rules more specific to her classroom. On the social media site, the rules focused on students being respectful to each other as well as remaining anonymous; these were published on the site and can be seen on the screen clip in Figure 4.2, listed under "Conditions of Membership." It was also made clear to students that, when online, school rules still applied.

Within the self-assessment process for this project, students were asked to discuss problems they had in each of the eight tasks. They were also asked to indicate how much of each task was completed. The teacher found that it was important to encourage students to document any issue or complaint that may have been due to hardware, software, personal, health/absenteeism, project support, etc. This appeared to help students maintain a positive view of the assessment process by providing them with empathy and an understanding that these issues would be considered at the end of the assessment process and could add weight to their self-assessment.

The Assessment Process

Teacher reflection data noted that some students changed their assessment criteria toward the end of the project. This was an interesting issue and one that requires more analysis to determine its significance. In the teacher reflection data, it was occasionally noted that a student complained that feedback was not appropriate or was offensive. When this issue arose, the teacher asked the student to very politely reply to the feedback online to indicate that they were offended and to please delete the feedback and provide something more appropriate. It was rare for such a problem to become an issue, but, when it did, the teacher discussed school rules with the student and this resolved the issue.

The teacher observation assessment data focused on the students' ability to provide constructive and critical feedback to their peers. Students were aware of this throughout the project and were often approached by the teacher on a one-to-one basis with advice on how to improve their peer feedback.

The social networking site used provided a list of the "Latest Activity" on the main site page. This also appeared on each of the student "My Pages" and helped to reduce the time taken for the teacher to moderate student activity. In minimizing issues of lost work or students not knowing what to do, the teacher endeavored to post all instructions and/or handout sheets on the site. It should also be noted that all interaction and activity on the site was automatically date-stamped and the site had search facilities.

RECOMMENDATIONS FOR FURTHER RESEARCH AND PRACTICE

During parent–teacher interviews, parents were particularly pleased with the 24/7 access to class resources and the facilities for their child to post queries online if they had difficulty with a task. The teacher also presented the research at local and international conferences where she received positive and constructive feedback. This included a first place award from the International Society for Technology in Education in June 2012, in recognition of the innovative learning opportunities the social site offered (*www. iste.org/docs/pdfs/iste_awards_archives.pdf?sfvrsn=6*). More specific analytical data from parents and critical friends identifying strengths and weaknesses of such a framework would be very valuable.

During the final semester of data collection the teacher, while designing an online project with classes from Russia and Romania, thought it useful to develop a type of training area on the social site. This was developed by creating an online group called "Getting Started" (*http://webtowhere.ning. com/group/gettingstarted*). This provided some step-by-step instructions as well as links that were aimed to help new members become familiar with a range of activities and tools within the site. Some examples include instructions on how to sign up and to be cyber smart. This support structure needs further exploration and development to identify the scaffolding needed to work globally with other schools.

Although the example given in this chapter was based on researching new technologies in an Information Technology class, the underlying concept was also used in the teacher's Mathematics classes and in a Year 7 integrated subject and the action research process continued to help modify the approach to each different circumstance. Other projects within this research included students making video help tutorials to support the learning of peers in both mathematics and information technology. These, again, saw the role of the teacher move away from being the dominant knowledge provider. As student projects became more flexible in content, the research data showed that students were more able to extend their own abilities and interests. This further developed the concept of the teacher as a learner in the classroom and confirmed the importance of peer and self-assessment. In discussion with critical friends it was noted that the teacher's ability to become more flexible is dependent on a number of factors such as their confidence and familiarity with the online environment. Further research is needed to identify the support structures needed for teachers with a range of abilities.

Peer feedback, self-assessment, and teacher observations were three important elements within the assessment process. Peer assessment and self-assessment required students to reflect, to critically analyze, and to justify their thinking in regard to each individual task within the larger project. This provided the teacher with invaluable detail regarding "what" the student did, "when" they did it, "how" they did it, and "why" they did what they did. The teacher noted that the self-assessment was, usually, a true and accurate record of the students' work and aligned with teacher observations. The peer assessment, although this often varied from peer to peer, provided additional data to draw comparisons and often strengthened the self-assessment data. A rich triangulation of assessment data was strongly evidenced through each student's "My Page." Students and parents appeared to be pleased with this triangulation of assessment data and there were no issues raised in regard to final marks.

Each student should have multiple peers for whom they were expected to provide feedback during individual tasks, as well as to perform the role of assessor at the end of the project. Self-assessment should also include a detailed analysis by each student of what, when, why, and how they completed each task, as well as the details of any issues encountered. Students were usually honest when completing the self-assessment process and each student's "My Page" provided them with many links to their own work as well as their online activity, which they could refer to as a reminder of their past work. Teacher observations focused on each student's ability to be the assessor and to provide constructive and critical peer feedback.

In regard to assessment of student outcomes within the school mathematics program, there was no evidence or concern that student performance suffered in any way. The next step would be to conduct a more analytical study to investigate possible evidence of an increase in student learning outcomes.

CONCLUSION

The project example discussed in this chapter was one of many class projects within the study. As the teacher integrated social and participatory media within the face-to-face classroom, the action research process was used to support the redesign of class projects and assessment practices while incorporating the use of social tools as well as the interactive nature of the social site. Actively involving students in assessment provided them with opportunities to be valued by their peers and to become more involved in their own learning, as well as the learning of their peers.

By developing simple guidelines for assessment (involving high, medium, and low as standards of measurement) and without any complex assessment criteria, the teacher developed a multidimensional approach to include peer assessment, self-assessment, and teacher observations. This helped to create a student-centered approach to assessment involving students as "assessors" and "assessees" and it was found that consequently, teacher "time" issues reduced significantly due to the reduction in emphasis on teacher assessment. It was found that as students analyzed the work of their peers, as assessors, they more fully understood the task at hand and, hence, gained insight into how to improve their own work. This experience also provided them with insight as they worked through the self-assessment process.

REFERENCES

Alsop, R. (2008). *The trophy kids grow up: How the millennial generation is shaking up the workplace.* San Francisco, CA: Jossey-Bass.

Armstrong, F., & Moore, M. (2004). Action research: Developing inclusive practice and transforming cultures. In F. Armstrong & M. Moore (Eds.), *Action research for inclusive education: Changing places, changing practice, changing minds* (pp. 1–16). London, UK: RoutledgeFalmer.

Bean, T., & Dunkerly, J. (2012). Adolescent literacy: Looking back and moving forward in the global flow. *Journal of Adolescent and Adult Literacy, 55*(8), 669–670.

Beetham, H., & Sharpe, R. (2007). An introduction to rethinking pedagogy for a digital age. In H. Beetham & R. Sharpe (Eds.), *Rethinking pedagogy for a digital age* (pp. 1–10). New York, NY: Routledge.

Bonk, C. J. (2008). *Empowering online learning: 100+ activities for reading, reflecting, displaying, and doing.* San Francisco, CA: Jossey-Bass.

Boyd, D. M, & Ellison, N. B. (2007). Social network sites: definition, history, and scholarship. *Journal of Computer-Mediated Communication, 13*(1), 210–230.

Casey, G. (2011). Knowledge-building: Designing for learning using social and participatory media. *eLearning Papers, 27,* 1–7.

Casey, G. (2012). Social media in the math classroom. *Learning & Leading with Technology, 40,* 36–37.

Casey, G. (2013a). Interdisciplinary literacy through social media in the mathematics classroom: an action research study. *Journal of Adolescent and Adult Literacy, 57*(1), 58–69.

Casey, G. (2013b). Social media in the classroom: a simple yet complex hybrid environment for students. *Journal of Educational Multimedia and Hypermedia, 22*(1), 5–24.

Casey, G., & Evans, T. (2011). Designing for learning: Online social networks as a classroom environment. *The International Review of Research in Open and Distance Learning, 12*(7), 1–26.

Cho, K., & MacArthur, C. (2010). Student revision with peer and expert reviewing. *Learning and Instruction, 20*, 328–338.

Coleman, B. (2011). *Hello, Avatar: Rise of the networked generation.* Boston, MA: MIT Press.

DEECD. (2009). *Prep to year 10 assessment–Assessment advice.* Retrieved from www.education.vic.gov.au/studentlearning/assessment/preptoyear10/assessadvice/default.htm.

Hattie, J. (2012). *Visible learning for teachers: Maximising impact on learning.* London, UK: Routledge.

Hendron, J. (2010). Developing info-seeking fluency. *Learning and Leading with Technology, 38*(2), 31–32.

Hricko, M., & Howell, S. (Eds.). (2006). *Online assessment and measurement.* Hershey, PA: Information Science Publishing.

Jewitt, C., Clark, W., & Hadjithoma-Garstka, C. (2011). The use of learning platforms to organise learning in English primary and secondary schools. *Learning Media and Technology, 36*(4), 335–348.

Lan, L., Liu, X., & Zhou, Y. (2012). Give and take: A re-analysis of assessor and assessee's roles in technology-facilited peer assessment. *British Journal of Educational Technology, 43*(3), 376–384.

Lankshear, C., & Knobel, M. (2006). *New literacies: Everyday practices and classroom learning* (2nd ed.). Maidenhead, Berks, UK: Open University Press/McGraw-Hill.

Mason, R. (2008). *E-learning and social networking handbook: Resources for higher education.* New York, NY: Routledge.

Nuthall, G. (2007). *The hidden lives of learners.* Wellington, New Zealand: New Zealand Council for Educational Research.

Palfrey, J. (2008). *Born digital: Understanding the first generation of digital natives.* New York, NY: Basic Books.

Pullen, D. L., & Cole, D. R. (2010). *Multiliteracies and technology enhanced education: Social practice and the global classroom.* Hershey, PA: IGI Global.

Strijbos, J., & Sluijsmans, D. (2010). Guest Editorial, Unravelling peer assessment: Methodological, functional, and conceptual developments. *Learning and Instruction, 20*, 265–269.

Weedon, P., Winter, J., & Broadfoot, P. (2001). *Assessment: What's in it for schools?* London: RoutledgeFalmer.

CHAPTER 5

ASSESSMENT METHODS IN ONLINE GRADUATE COURSES

Shijuan Liu
Indiana University of Pennsylvania

INTRODUCTION

Online education has made inroads into higher education in recent decades (Moore & Anderson, 2003). Allen and Seaman (2013) reported in their survey results that "there were 572,000 more online students in fall 2011 than in fall 2010 for a new total of 6.7 million students taking at least one online course" (p. 17). Online graduate courses and programs are especially attractive to adult learners since they can advance their education while staying with their families and maintaining their full-time jobs (Martinez, Liu, Watson, & Bichelmeyer, 2006). As the number of online courses and programs expands, concerns arise regarding their quality. One critical element for course and program quality assurance is the assessment used in individual courses for student learning (Anderson, 1998). What assessment methods instructors use usually indicates what they think is important for students to learn in the courses. Assessment also affects the depth of student learning, the learning strategies students take, and how they manage

Assessment in Online and Blended Learning Environments, pages 77–101
Copyright © 2015 by Information Age Publishing
All rights of reproduction in any form reserved.

their study time (Brown, Bull, & Pendlebury, 1997). Boud (1995) points out that students can escape bad teaching (e.g., finding an excuse for being absent from a class), while they cannot escape bad assessment. Not surprisingly, therefore, assessment is acknowledged as a fundamental element in course design (Christen, 2003).

While much has been written on assessing students in traditional environments, there is a paucity of research studies on assessment of students in online environments (Reeves, 2000, 2002). Among the limited empirical studies, extremely few of them were conducted in the context of graduate education. This chapter reports on a recent study that examined assessment methods used in online graduate courses. The study addressed the following research questions: What were the major characteristics of assessment methods used in online graduate courses, and what considerations did the instructors have for the assessment methods they used?

LITERATURE REVIEW

As Robles and Braathen (2002) suggest, "looking to suggested traditional teaching practices can help us to shape the assessments for online courses" (p. 41). Simonson, Smaldino, Albright, and Zvacek (2002) put the assessment methods into two categories: traditional assessment tools and alternative assessment. Traditional assessment refers to exams, including multiple-choice, true or false, fill-in-the-blank, and essay. The alternative assessment includes self-assessment, peer assessment, portfolios, projects, and others. The literature shows that traditional assessment has been challenged recently, and alternative assessment is gaining favor in higher education.

Online environments are argued to have special characteristics not found in traditional environments (Dewald, Scholz-Crane, Booth, & Levine, 2000; Robles & Braathen, 2002). These special characteristics are believed to bring advantages and disadvantages for assessing students in online environments. Comeaux (2005) summarized 10 benefits in assessing students online. These included the ability to track, monitor, and document students' activities automatically; unlimited and self-paced access to course materials; and an increased emphasis on student thoughts and reflections. In the meantime, researchers find some disadvantages associated with the online assessment. For example, the disadvantages that Kibby (2003) listed include students may need specific instruction in online assessment; and instructors may have limited ability to control the time and have no control over the resources that students can access when they take online exams at a distance.

Much of the literature on online assessment (e.g., Oosterhof, Conrad, & Ely, 2007; Rovai, 2000) is anecdotal or opinion-based. Among the limited available empirical studies, many of them only examined the use of assessment in one course (e.g., Macdonald & Twining, 2002). While some studies investigated online assessment across courses, many of them focused on individual specific assessment tasks such as online discussions and participation (e. g., Liu, 2007). Extremely few empirical studies are available that provide a comprehensive view of online instructors' current practices in using assessment tasks across courses. In addition, there is a paucity of research on why instructors choose certain assessment tasks in their courses, especially in the context of online graduate courses. This study is an attempt to respond to this need.

METHODOLOGY

An exploratory, qualitative approach was adopted for this study. There is scant empirical research found on assessment methods used in online environments. If a topic needs to be explored but minimal research has been done on it, then it merits a qualitative approach (Creswell, 1998, 2003). Compared to quantitative methods, qualitative methods have the advantage in helping investigate a topic in depth (Patton, 1990).

Participants

Participants were chosen from five different master's programs offered by a large, public Midwestern research university. These five master's programs were (a) Language Education, (b) Instructional Design and Technology (IDT), (c) Adult Education, (d) Nursing, and (e) Business Administration (MBA).[1] The purpose of selecting participants from different programs was to explore assessment tasks used in a variety of disciplines. Choosing programs offered by one university was based on the consideration that the examined courses were offered in a similar context, and hence they could be reasonably compared and contrasted with each other.

Twenty instructors were purposely sampled from the five programs mainly based on the courses they taught and their willingness to participate in this study. Nine of the participants were male and 11 were female. The 20 instructors taught 22 courses (two of them taught two courses), which were core courses or major courses of the five programs.

It is worth mentioning that similar to the methodology employed by Delandshere and Jones (1999), the focus of this study was not on the individual instructors, but on their reflections on the rationales and considerations underlying their practices. In other words, these instructors were not considered as separate cases, but rather constituted a collective case for helping understand the assessment tasks in online environments comprehensively.

Data Collection and Analysis

Document Analysis

Information was first collected from the university websites concerning programs that offered online graduate courses. After analysis of the curriculum design of the programs, the syllabi of the courses available online were examined. According to Ford (2002), a syllabus is like a contract between the students and the instructor. It usually includes the description of the assessment tasks that the instructor uses to assess students. The syllabi of the 22 courses taught by the 20 instructors were all analyzed. In addition to the syllabi, other relevant documents were also obtained from the instructors, such as the detailed descriptions of the assessment methods they used and some grading templates that were not included in their syllabi.

Fraenkel and Wallen (2003) suggest two ways to analyze the documents collected. One is to determine the categories before any analysis begins. The other is to become extremely familiar with the descriptive information collected and allow the patterns, themes, or categories to emerge as the analysis continues. Because of the exploratory purpose of this study, the latter analysis approach was employed. The assessment methods described in the syllabi and related documents of the 22 courses were read and analyzed numerous times and at different stages (e.g., before and after the interviews with the participants, during analysis of the interview data, and in the write-up process).

Interviews

The 20 instructors were interviewed on a one-on-one basis. The interviews were semi-structured. Prior to each interview, the syllabus and other available documents of the course(s) that the instructor taught were examined. Their courses were also observed if the researcher had access to them. Analyzing the syllabi and course materials, as well as observing the courses in advance, helped the researcher to focus the interviews on collecting data that could not be obtained from document analysis, and hence make the best use of the interview time. Similar to the document analyses, the interview data were also analyzed in an inductive manner. Inductive analysis, as Patton (1990) defines it, means that the patterns, themes, and categories emerge out of the data rather than being imposed on them prior to data collection and analysis. The researcher referred to the guidelines that Carspecken (1996) provided in the analysis process. Codes were added to the individual interview transcripts during the process of listening to the recorded digital files and reading the transcripts. In the meantime, the researcher created a separate file to summarize the codes generated from each interview. This file was used as a main document in which the codes were further grouped and analyzed.

FINDINGS

The assessment methods that the 20 interviewed instructors used in 22 online courses were grouped into 21 large categories, which include:

1. Participation in asynchronous discussions (used by 16 instructors in 17 courses)
2. Critiques (10 instructors)
3. Projects (nine instructors)
4. Essays (used by eight instructors in nine courses)
5. Field reports (seven instructors)
6. Reflections (seven instructors)
7. Quizzes and exams (by five instructors in six courses)
8. Creating questions or design activities (by four instructors in five courses)
9. Case analysis (three instructors)
10. Questions–answers (three instructors)
11. Collecting information and resources (three instructors)
12. Inventory (three instructors)
13. Reading and summarizing (used by two instructors in three courses)
14. Concept-mapping (two instructors)
15. Learning contracts (two instructors)
16. Portfolios (two instructors)
17. Participations other than asynchronous discussions (two instructors)
18. PowerPoint presentations (one instructor)
19. Critique logs (one instructor)
20. Peer editing (one instructor)
21. Other

Details of the 21 categories, subcategories, and operational definitions are available in the Appendix.

The researcher also identified some trends and characteristics of the assessment methods used by the instructors, which were detailed below.

The Use of Asynchronous Discussions

Eighty percent of the instructors required students to participate in asynchronous discussion and counted this toward their final grade. The percentage of this task in the final grade varied among the courses examined, ranging from 10% to 40%, while 20% was the most frequently used weight for students' final grades.

Asynchronous discussions were organized in a variety of ways in the courses examined. Many courses, especially those offered by the Language Education program, asked students to participate in the online discussion weekly. By contrast, some courses required students to participate in the discussion only in some weeks. For example, Dr. Sandy from the Nursing program only required students in her course to participate in the discussion in the first unit (first 2 weeks). Additionally, some courses divided students into groups and designed a variety of activities for the discussion. For instance, in two Adult Education courses, students were required to discuss the tasks within their team and respond to what other teams posted. Dr. Sharon from the nursing program divided students into four groups and gave the groups different tasks each week in the course she taught. In one week, she put four teams in two groups and asked them to debate on the pros and cons of a topic addressed in the course. In another week, she assigned different topics to each team and asked each student to research the topic assigned to his or her team, then post their individual answers in their team space. The team was asked to post a team answer based on what individual members shared, and served as experts answering questions that other teams might have on this topic.

Two major reasons were identified regarding why instructors included asynchronous discussion in their assessment tasks. One was its necessity. Many instructors believed that it was necessary to require students to participate in asynchronous discussions in online courses. Several of them compared this to student participation in live discussions of a residential class. Dr. Joan, one nursing instructor, said: "I see the participation as they [are] sitting in a classroom in a big circle. And someone is saying something. After that, I am, as a professor, trying to get everybody to at least vocalize a little bit in the class."

A couple of instructors further pointed out that asynchronous discussions created interactions among students, which helped differentiate an online course from other formats of distance courses such as a corresponding course or a video broadcast course.

The other reason why instructors included asynchronous discussion in their assessment tasks concerned the advantages of using asynchronous discussions. One advantage that several instructors mentioned was that asynchronous discussions helped build learning communities and decrease isolation among students. Another advantage mentioned by many instructors was that asynchronous discussions helped make students more reflective and thoughtful. Dr. Sharon from the Nursing program explained:

> In the classroom, people just do things spontaneously. They have got reaction, they have made you react. Whereas you do something online, you know, you think about it, you write it, you review it, before you send it. So, I really think it encourages more thoughtful reflection. They realize that what they said goes to public record. . . . They reported to me that they feel like it helps them to be more, a better thinker.

Among the four instructors who did not include asynchronous discussion in their assessment tasks, one was from the MBA program and three of them were from the IDT program. This was not to say, however, that there was no asynchronous discussion in their courses. For example, according to Dr. Felix from the IDT program, students asked a lot of questions concerning the projects in the discussion board. He and their peers provided suggestions. Therefore, although the discussions were not required and did not count for their final grade, there was a significant amount of asynchronous discussion taking place in his course.

Concerning why they did not require students to participate in asynchronous discussions and/or did not give students credit for doing that, Professor Felix asked rhetorically, "Why should I [do that]?!" According to him, asking students to participate in discussions was not one of his course objectives. The course that he taught was not about talking, but about developing e-learning products. He said:

> I am not grading them on their ability to talk, or to recite back what they read from the book. . . . What I am grading, assessing is *(pause)* do they understand the first principles of instruction? Can they apply them in developing e-learning products? . . . That is what I am evaluating. I am evaluating their performance in those tasks. I am not evaluating what they say in the discussion forums. You know what? They said a lot. So did I. And it was valuable. But it was focusing on tasks they were doing. . . . I did not grade whether they participated or not. In fact, there were a couple of people who did not participate at all, but they got good grades. Because that was not, never part of the grades.

Differently, Dr. Cathy, another IDT instructor, explained that she did not include asynchronous discussion in her assessment tasks because she had mixed feelings. According to her, online discussion could be beneficial but could be very problematic as well. She hoped that asynchronous discussions could be used in a natural way in that students could share, receive, and provide help on whatever and whenever they needed it, instead of being forced to participate in a discussion.

Critical Thinking and Other Higher-Order Thinking Skills

Fifty percent of the instructors included critiques in their assessment. The objects that students were asked to critique upon varied, including articles, books, websites, software, lesson plans, tests, and their peers' work. Dr. Hunter from the Adult Education program mentioned that he included book critiques in his assessment tasks because he believed critical thinking skills were necessary skills for all graduate students. Mr. David from the Language Education program, who used several critique-related assignments, held a similar view and further explained his rationale. According to him, the course he taught was designed for in-service and preservice teachers. Critique (evaluation) of others' work as well as one's previous work was essential for one to improve his or her teaching practices. In addition, Dr. Fred from the Adult Education program asked each student to develop a critical thinking type of question for each module, and then to critique the questions that their peers created. He stated in the course syllabus that 20% of the multiple-choice questions in the final exam would come from the questions developed by the class. He also provided detailed guidelines for creating these questions in the syllabus:

> A critical thinking multiple-choice question should be designed to do more than measure knowledge through recall of specific information. It should assess comprehension and application, including the ability to transfer existing knowledge and skills to new situations such as problem-solving situations.

Dr. Fred further emphasized in the interview that being able to ask critical thinking questions was very important for graduate students. Other higher-order thinking skills such as synthesis and analysis listed in the well-known Bloom's (1956) taxonomy were also stressed in many of the courses studied. For example, at least three Adult Education courses asked students to summarize or make annotations for the articles they read. As Dr. Fred described the requirements of this task in one core course he taught, the annotation should include not only the descriptive information about the article (i.e., its title and author), but also a 300-word critique that included:

1. The main conclusions of the article.
2. What the article meant to you, why it had an impact on you and what insights were discovered.
3. What you could personally apply from the article to help you become a better adult educator. Describe what is relevant to you and how you may practically apply the information.

Similarly, in one assessment task used by Ms. Shea, students were asked not only to list the software and hardware that they found useful to their classrooms, but also to explain why they chose certain software or hardware (e.g., low cost, useful functions). Additionally, at least three instructors used case analysis in their courses. Answering the questions associated with the cases asked for analytical and other related higher-order thinking skills.

Quizzes and exams were typically used to test lower-level thinking skills such as the memorization of facts and comprehension (e.g., Simonson et al., 2002). Only five instructors included quizzes and exams in their assessment tasks. Notably, one of them (Ms. Jessie) used the quiz as a mastery learning tool, allowing students to take the quiz multiple times so as to ensure they all mastered the concepts and knowledge that the quiz covered. On the other hand, as some scholars (e.g., Perry, 2006) argued, if well designed, quizzes and exams could also be used to assess higher-order thinking skills. Professor Joyce from the MBA program mentioned that she spent a lot of time and effort in designing and updating the quizzes and exams. She also stated that she referred to Bloom's (1956) taxonomy in creating her test items, and tried to get one or two items from each major concept that the course addressed.

Real-World Assessment Tasks

The majority of instructors emphasized student real-world application skills in the assessment tasks they used. For example, nine instructors asked students to conduct projects involving real-world applications. The three IDT instructors asked students to develop instructional products (e.g., websites) or create instructional materials that could be applied to the real world. Two MBA instructors (Dr. Justin and Dr. Tyler) asked students to apply the knowledge and skills that they learned from the courses in the company where they worked or a real company that interested them. Two Language Education instructors (Ms. Shea and Mr. David) asked students who were in-service or preservice teachers to create instructional materials that they could use in their classrooms.

Additionally, more than one-third of the instructors included field reports in their assessment tasks. For instance, two Language Education instructors (Mr. Jack and Mr. David) asked students to observe a real classroom and submit an observation report. One nursing instructor (Dr. Sandy) asked students to attend a professional meeting and summarize what they learned from the meeting. Five instructors from the five different programs (Dr. Sandy, Dr. Cathy, Dr. Randy, Dr. Tyler, and Ms. Lili) all asked students to interview people that met the requirements of the assessment task and write a corresponding report based on the interviews.

In addition to the assessment tasks categorized under "projects" and "field reports," assessment tasks under other categories involved real-world applications as well. For instance, Dr. Sandy asked students to write a letter to policymakers. Dr. Cathy asked students to write a letter to decline people. While both of the assessment tasks were grouped under the "Essay" category, obviously both were closely linked to the real-world application.

Assessment and Writing

Each of the interviewed instructors used at least one assessment task in written form. In addition, more than half of the 21 categories of the assessment tasks, such as critiques, field reports, reflections, and case analyses, could be loosely grouped into a larger category with a label such as "written assignments" because the final products of these assessment tasks all were in written form.

Among the categorized 21 types of assessment tasks, there was a specific category named "Essay," which includes two subcategories: Structured and Unstructured. Structured essays referred to those in which instructors provided questions for students to answer and specific requirements for students to follow. For instance, Mr. Jack from the Language Education program asked students to use a metaphor to show their understanding of language teaching and learning issues. Similarly, as mentioned earlier, Dr. Cathy and Dr. Sandy both included a task asking students to write a letter. Unstructured essays referred to those tasks in which students had more flexibility and were given options in choosing specific topics they would like to write about. Those that were categorized under this category included writing a literature review, a research proposal, a research paper, and an editorial review.

Only a few categories of assessment tasks seemed not to stress writing skills, such as quizzes and exams, concept-mapping, and PowerPoint presentations. Instructors who used such assessment tasks indicated that they chose these tasks intentionally because they found that too many assessment tasks used in online courses involved heavy writing. For instance, Ms. Jessie mentioned that one of her purposes for using concept-mapping in her course was to provide an opportunity for visual learners. According to her, most of the other assessment tasks demanded high-level writing skills, which were typically beneficial for verbal learners.

Although written assignments dominated the assessment tasks in the courses examined, the instructors' attitudes toward the demand for writing skills in online environments were not the same. For instance, Dr. Rosy from the Nursing program seemed to think this was a disadvantage and had sympathy for students whose writing skills were poor. She used four types of assessment tasks in her course. Two were concerning quizzes and exams. The other two were about case analyses and asynchronous discussions. She mentioned that asynchronous discussions only counted for a small portion toward students' final grades because she wanted to be fair to those students with poor writing skills. Similarly, she asked students to work in teams for the case analysis assessment partly because she hoped that students who had lower-level writing skills could receive help from their teammates who had higher-level writing skills.

In contrast, Dr. Hunter from the Adult Education program seemed to think it was an advantage for students to take courses online in that it could help them become better writers. When asked to comment on the concern that Dr. Rosy had, he mentioned that because one's writing skills were poor, it did not mean that the person could not improve his or her writing skills. As he said, "If they [students who are sloppy writers] want to improve to another level, they need to put effort in it, improve their skills."

Clear and Detailed Assessment

Assessment tasks in most courses examined were written in a clear and detailed manner. Many instructors not only detailed requirements of the tasks but also provided clear instructions for completing the tasks. Additionally, many instructors included detailed grading criteria. Some instructors further provided samples for students to consider in completion of the tasks. It is worth mentioning that several instructors explained their purposes or intent in using specific assessment tasks. For example, Dr. Sandy wrote in her syllabus "This online PowerPoint presentation will help students to understand the process for developing issues and presenting them to influential policymakers in a concise, powerful, and persuasive manner." Likewise, Ms. Jessie included descriptions of her purposes for each of the assessment tasks in the syllabus. For instance, she stated that the purpose of the Literature Review assignment was "to begin working on two of the course objectives: to understand and appreciate the philosophies that undergird and inform research practice and to develop a personal perspective on what constitutes knowledge." Similarly, she described in the syllabus that her purpose for the first qualitative article review task was "to begin working on the following course objective: to become a critical consumer of all types of research and to explore various research tools and techniques."

While most courses presented their assessment tasks in a nearly perfect manner, some of them could probably be further improved. For example, Dr. Randy and Dr. Hunter described the assessment tasks they used for each module in a very comprehensive and detailed manner. However, students might have to search through the documents for the assessment tasks because the information and instruction they provided seemed too long. In addition, there seemed to be a lack of consideration in visual design in terms of font and format. It might be helpful if the instructors could add a summary table of the assessment tasks as Dr. Sandy and Ms. Jessie did, and even reformat the current document.

Additionally, some instructors probably could consider adding a master schedule that includes the assessment tasks with their due dates, and includes the associated modules/topics, as Mr. Jack and Dr. Justin did. Similarly, although Dr. Joyce described her assessment tasks in enough detail in the syllabus, the percentage that each assessment task counted toward the students' final grades was not very clear. Providing a similar table as many other instructors used might help solve the problem effectively.

In general, the assessment tasks in nearly all the courses examined seemed to be written in a much more detailed manner than those in residential courses. This practice might be because as Mr. Jack pointed out, online instructors need to make their instruction, assessment tasks, and feedback as clear as possible to students, since in online courses, everything relies on typing, which is different from residential courses where students can ask for clarifications easily face to face.

Continuous and Ongoing Assessment

All the 20 instructors used continuous and ongoing assessment tasks in the 22 courses they taught. Nearly half of the courses included a master schedule in the syllabi, listing the topic for each week, corresponding readings, activities, and assignments. The other courses divided the courses in modules, units, or lessons, and listed the assignments based on each module, unit, or lesson. For example, Dr. Sandy from the Nursing program divided her course in five units. Additionally, some instructors used a number of assessment tasks throughout the semester. For instance, Dr. Tyler from the MBA program used four projects in his 12-week-long course, with each project lasting approximately 3 weeks. Similarly, Ms. Jessie from the Adult Education program used 11 assessment tasks in her course, which consisted of eight modules in 16 weeks.

On the other hand, some instructors broke down a large project in a series of smaller tasks. For instance, Dr. Felix from the IDT program asked students to develop an instructional project, which accounted for 80% of their final grade. He divided the project into six smaller deliverables and had them submitted at different times, rather than all at once at the very end of the course. Similarly, Dr. Justin from the MBA program asked students to complete a team project that accounted for 60% of their final grade. He broke down the project into five deliverables and asked students to turn them in one by one every 2 or 3 weeks.

Three reasons were identified from instructors' interviews concerning using the ongoing and continuous assessment tasks. First, according to Dr. Joan from the Nursing program, using small and continuous tasks helped students to learn better and helped the instructor to assess student work easier. She reported, "I find that I can break the materials up in their head easier. I can evaluate whether they are progressing, in a small bit, rather than having them do the two large things." Second, a few instructors mentioned that the use of ongoing assessments helped students to expand on what they learned from the readings as well as to keep them on track. Ms. Lili from the Language Education program explained in her email response:

> Each week, I had a specific theme and topic, with readings to go with it. Each assignment usually goes with the theme and topic. I see the assignment as opportunities to expand their learning and practice what they have learned from their reading. Therefore, I would like to keep them "on task" each week.

Ms. Jessie from the Adult Education program concurred and further pointed out that keeping students on track was especially important for online students since the majority of the students were full-time employees and had many commitments with their work and families.

DISCUSSION

In general, the 20 instructors' assessment task practices were in alignment with the principles of good assessment practice suggested by the literature. For example, one principle for best assessment constantly addressed in the literature was that assessment should be ongoing and monitoring the process of student learning (e.g., Robles & Braathen, 2002; Rovai, 2000). As detailed in the previous section, all of the instructors used continuous and ongoing assessment tasks. They evened out the assessment tasks based on the weekly schedule or the modules throughout the courses. Instructors who included large projects in their assessment tasks further broke down the projects into smaller tasks in order to better monitor the student learning process. To help students to achieve better learning outcomes, some instructors also suggested timelines for students in the completion of the assessment tasks.

Clarity is another principle suggested by the literature (e.g., American Association of Higher Education [AAHE], 1992; Brown, Race, & Brenda, 1996). While there was room for some instructors to improve the clarity in the description of some of the assessment tasks they used, in general, the assessment tasks in the examined courses were clearly written in terms of task requirements and grading criteria. Additionally, the descriptions of the tasks seemed to be more detailed than those used in residential courses. As noted by several participants in this study and suggested by the literature (e.g., Liang & Creasy, 2004), this is because communications in online environments (including giving instructions, clarifications, and feedback) mainly rely on writing due to a lack of face-to-face interaction.

Use of diverse assessments is also suggested by the literature for best assessment practice (e.g., AAHE, 1992). A variety of assessment tasks (21 large categories with many subcategories) were identified from the courses examined. Some instructors mentioned in the interviews that they intentionally made their assessment tasks more diverse by using such assessment tasks as concept-mapping and PowerPoint presentations.

However, as reported in the previous section, the final products of most assessment tasks were required in written form. Writing skills, consequently, were greatly demanded in completion of the tasks in the courses examined. Bonk and Zhang (2006) developed a model titled R2D2 (Read, Reflect, Display, and Do) to "make sense of the diverse array of instructional possibilities currently available in distance education" (p. 249). The assessment tasks used by most of the instructors seem to mainly involve activities concerning reading and reflecting (writing). Only a few instructors used assessment tasks involving displaying (e.g., concept maps) and doing (e.g., simulations).

This tendency may be explained by three reasons. First, the objectives of most of the examined courses fall in the cognitive domain. Writing seems to be the most common and appropriate means to assess such skills as analysis, synthesis, critical thinking, and reflection, which were stressed by instructors in this study. Second, as several participants argued, writing skills are very important in graduate education. The emphasis on writing skills was beneficial for students' professional careers. Third, some instructors mentioned that they mainly relied on assessment tasks in written form because of the constraints of the online delivery format. Several of them indicated they used or anticipated using more variety of assessment tasks in face-to-face environments.

For instructors who decided to use written-form assessment tasks based on the first two reasons, their decisions seem to be reasonably justified. For instructors who made decisions mainly based on the third reason, they may want to explore and learn more how to make the best use of the available technologies in the design of assessment tasks in online environments. For instance, such technological tools as Breeze already have the capacity to support instructors in using similar formats for assessment tasks (e.g., live group discussions and presentations) in online environments as they do in residential environments.

Asynchronous discussions were found as the most frequently used assessment tasks in the courses examined (required in 17 out of 22 courses, or 77.2%). This finding is consistent with what Arend (2006) found from her study on the assessment practices at community colleges. According to Arend, among the 60 online courses she examined, 59 of them included discussions in the assessment tasks. Additionally, Yates (2005) found that the majority (63.7%) of the respondents in her study used this assessment task in the online courses they taught.

Researchers argue that online environments bring opportunities for students to develop and display higher-order thinking skills (Muirhead, 2005; Reeves, 2000). Results of the study indicated that the assessment tasks used in most of the examined courses stressed higher-order thinking skills such as synthesis, analysis, critical thinking, and reflective thinking. It is worth pointing out that critical thinking and other higher-order thinking skills have been advocated not only at the graduate and undergraduate levels, but also at the K–12 level, although some researchers (e.g., Black & Wiliam, 1998; Delandshere & Jones, 1999) find that the inconsistency between the call for development of student higher-order thinking skills and the instructors' assessment practices at the K–12 level is associated with external mandated tests required by school districts and/or states.

Many of the assessment tasks used by the instructors focused on real-world applications. This practice is consistent with another principle suggested by the literature that assessment tasks should be authentic, especially in an online environment (e.g., Morgan & O'Reilly, 1999). As several participants in this study pointed out, use of authentic tasks could help increase students' motivation and commitment in completing the tasks. Additionally, using the authentic assessment tasks successfully meets the needs of online graduate students, who typically work full time, in that they can make direct connections between the assessment tasks and their work. Such findings also concurred with the literature (e.g., Liu, Kim, Bonk, & Magjuka, 2007) that students applying what they learn directly in their jobs was one advantage of teaching and learning online.

IMPLICATION AND RECOMMENDATIONS

This study indicates that many general principles of good assessment practice apply in any learning environment and context, although how to implement these principles may differ. The following principles appear especially important for an online environment:

- Assessment tasks should be ongoing, monitoring the process as well as the product of student learning (Rabinowitz, 1995; Rovai, 2000).

- Assessment tasks should be explicit concerning their objectives, values, requirements, and grading criteria (Brown et al., 1996; Simonson et al., 2002).
- Assessment tasks should be authentic, helping students to apply what they learn in the real world (Hjelm & Baker, 2001).

It would be beneficial for professional development staff to provide instructors teaching online courses with some guidelines and other relevant resources concerning the design and use of assessment. This can help save instructors much time in searching for quality resources in this regard. Since instructors teaching online courses can work at any time and at any place they have access to the Internet, it is important to ensure these resources are available online and can be easily accessed by the instructors.

Regarding recommendation for further research, since limited research has been conducted on assessment in online environments, there are many topics that can be explored. For example, one could do a similar study by interviewing instructors teaching online courses at other graduate programs and/or in other disciplines, and then comparing the findings with this study. Additionally, to obtain a more comprehensive picture of instructors' assessment practices, one could survey instructors teaching in different institutions and different disciplines in the United States, or even other nations, exploring patterns and tendencies as well as similarities and differences across disciplines and institutions in terms of use of assessment tasks they used.

LIMITATIONS

As Fraenkel and Wallen (2003) point out, "generalizing is possible in qualitative research, but is of a different type than that found in quantitative studies. Most likely it will be done by interested practitioners" (p. 445). The generalization of this study is similar to other qualitative studies of this kind. Audiences would need to be aware of these limitations when applying the findings of this study in their own cases.

APPENDIX
Summary of Categorized Assessment Methods

Assessment Methods	Operational Definitions	Subcategories	Instructors Who Used This Method	Number of Instructors (and courses)
1. Participation in asynchronous discussions	Students are required to participate in activities associated with asynchronous discussion forums.	Having discussions on a regular basis (weekly, or each module)	Shea, David, Jack, Xiang, Lili, Fred, Hunter, Jessie, Randy	16 (17 courses)
		Having discussions only on some specific topics	Leo, Sandy, Justin	
		Providing feedback to peers' work only	Rosy, Leo, Joan	
		Having a variety of activities for discussions	Lili, Sharon, Randy	
		Role playing (e.g., in court forum)	Fred, Joyce	
2. Critique	Students are required to analyze and evaluate objects that are physically visible and exist.	Critiquing a book	Hunter, Randy, Sandy	10
		Critiquing an article	Jack, Jessie,	
		Critiquing a lesson plan	Xiang, David	
		Critiquing a scholarly piece	Sharon	
		Critiquing a website/software package	Shea	
		Critiquing a webquest	David	
		Critiquing a language test	David	
		Critiquing peers' work	Brenda	

(continued)

Assessment Methods	Operational Definitions	Subcategories	Instructors Who Used This Method	Number of Instructors (and courses)
3. Projects	Students are encouraged to choose topics in which they are interested. This method stresses assessment of students' application of knowledge and skills in the real world. While the final product may be in the essay format, writing is not the major purpose for this method.	Selecting a company and analyzing its characteristics	Tyler, Justin	9
		Evaluating a program	Randy (one option for the final project), Fred	
		Developing instructional products	Brenda (3 projects), Felix (1 project)	
		Developing instructional materials	Shea, Cathy	
		Creating a portfolio evaluation form and describing how the form is able to communicate specific types of information	David	
4. Essays	The final product is in a narrative format and relatively long. Students will need to construct a response and supply supporting details or arguments. The essay allows the instructor to assess the students' understanding and/or ability to analyze and synthesize information.	*Structured:* Responding to the specific questions that the instructor asks	Joan (e.g., How would concept analysis help you in doing a research project?) // Fred	8 (9 courses)
		Using a certain format or addressing certain content required by the instructor	Jack (using a metaphor to show their understanding of language teaching and learning), Sandy (writing a letter to policymakers) // Cathy, Fred (writing profiles of two persons who had major influences in the field), Cathy (writing an editorial review)	

(continued)

Assessment Methods	Operational Definitions	Subcategories	Instructors Who Used This Method	Number of Instructors (and courses)
		Unstructured:		
		Choosing an issue, position, and supporting conclusions	Jack	
		Identifying an issue, collecting and analyzing related resources, and reflecting on the findings	Sandy	
		Conducting a literature review	Xiang, Jessie	
		Writing a research proposal	Jessie	
		Writing a research paper	Hunter	
		Writing a theory essay	Fred	
		Contrasting and comparing at least three of the adult development theorists	Hunter	
5. Field reports	Students are asked to do some real-world work and report what they have found.	Conducting and reporting on classroom observations	Jack, David	7
		Conducting interviews and reporting on interview results	Sandy, Cathy, Randy, Tyler, Lili	
		Reporting on a professional meeting they attend	Sandy	

(continued)

Assessment Methods	Operational Definitions	Subcategories	Instructors Who Used This Method	Number of Instructors (and courses)
6. Reflections	Students are asked to reflect on their skills, what they have learned, or their learning process. (To distinguish from critiques, this category does not include reflection on books or articles that they read.)	Writing interactive reflections (informal, letting instructors know what went well, and what could have gone better)	David, Shea	7
		K (what I know), W (what I want to learn), L (what I have learned), W (future wanderings)	David	
		At the beginning, writing "how I write," then near the end of the course, reviewing "how I write."	Cathy	
		Revisiting the metaphor they wrote earlier	Jack	
		Reflecting on at least two concepts/assignments	Lili	
		Reflecting on learning activities (e.g., webquest, reading other students' work)	Hunter	
		Evaluating their skills based on the goals they stated	Sharon	
7. Quizzes and exams	There is at least one item in the format of multiple-choice questions.	Being allowed to take the same quiz more than once (mastery)	Jessie	5 (6 courses)
		Being allowed to take the same quiz/exam only once	Rosy, Joan, Fred, Leo	
8. Students create questions or design activities	Students are asked to create questions for discussion or exams, or design activities for the class.	Creating questions for exams	Fred (2 courses)	4 (5 courses)
		Creating questions for discussions	Jack	
		Designing activities for the class	Hunter, Randy	
9. Case analysis	Students are asked to analyze a case/scenario.	(No subcategory)	Rosy, Tyler, Joan	3

(continued)

Assessment Methods	Operational Definitions	Subcategories	Instructors Who Used This Method	Number of Instructors (and courses)
10. Questions–answers	The instructor provides a list of questions for students to answer. Because the questions are so specific, the answers could not be in an essay format.	Being assigned roles in answering the questions given by the instructor	Xiang	3
		Answering general questions given by the instructor	Leo, Joan	
11. Collecting information and resources	Students are asked to report on relevant information or resources they collected.	Summarizing information about three relevant organizations	Sandy (one option for students)	3
		Listing useful software and hardware	Shea	
		Finding an instructional writing sample and posting in forum	Cathy	
12. Inventory	Students are asked to complete relevant commercial or noncommercial inventories to self-test their knowledge and skills in certain domains.	Taking and retaking the Political Astuteness Tool	Sandy	3
		Taking and retaking the Philosophy of the Adult Education Inventory	Fred	
		Taking the Teaching Perspective Inventory	Hunter	
13. Reading and summarizing	Students are asked to read articles and write summaries of the articles.	Doing a annotated bibliography	Fred (2 courses)	2 (3 courses)
		Reading and summarizing three relevant articles	Hunter	
14. Concept mapping	Students are asked to describe their understandings of relevant concepts with concept maps.	(No subcategory)	Jessie, Hunter	2
15. Learning contracts	Students are asked to establish a learning contract with the instructor regarding the goals they want to achieve.	(No subcategory)	Hunter, Randy	2

(continued)

Assessment Methods	Operational Definitions	Subcategories	Instructors Who Used This Method	Number of Instructors (and courses)
16. Portfolio	Students are asked to collect evidence to show their learning and progress.	Putting together evidence (assignments) for one's achievement and learning progress in the course	Lili	2
		Putting together evidence showing one's competency of realization of one's stated professional goals	Sharon	
17. Participations other than asynchronous discussions	Students are asked to participate in activities other than asynchronous discussions.	Providing support to their peers	Brenda	2
		Participating in discussion planning teams	Randy	
18. PowerPoint presentations	Students are asked to use PPTs to present their understanding of certain knowledge.	(No subcategory)	Sandy	1
19. Critique log	Students are asked to record critiques and feedback that they received, and changes that they have or have not made.	(No subcategory)	Brenda	1
20. Peer editing	Students are asked to edit each other's work.	(No subcategory)	Cathy	1
21. Other	Tasks that seem to be course-specific activities and may not be applicable to other courses.	Using PPTs to reorganize information given Competence checklist (Completing basic technical tasks, e.g., converting a Word document to PDF format)	Cathy Felix	2

NOTE

1. The real names of the programs were changed with the purpose of protecting participants' identities.

REFERENCES

American Association of Higher Education (AAHE). (1992). *Nine principles of good practice for assessing student learning.* Retrieved from http://www.learningout-comeassessment.org/PrinciplesofAssessment.html.

Allen E., & Seaman, J. (2013). *Changing course: ten years of tracking online education in the United States.* Retrieved from http://www.onlinelearningsurvey.com/reports/changingcourse.pdf.

Anderson, R. S. (1998). Why talk about different ways to grade?: The shift from traditional assessment to alternative assessment. In R. S. Anderson & B. W. Speck (Eds.), *New directions for teaching and learning: Vol. 74. Changing the way we grade student performance: classroom assessment and the new learning paradigm* (pp. 5–16). San Francisco, CA: Jossey-Bass.

Arend, B. (2006). *Course assessment practices and student learning strategies in online college courses.* Unpublished doctoral dissertation, University of Denver.

Black, P., & Wiliam, D. (1998). Assessment and classroom learning. *Assessment in Education: Principles, Policy and Practice, 5*(1), 7–75.

Bloom, B. S. (1956). *Taxonomy of Educational Objectives, Handbook 1: Cognitive Domain.* New York, NY: Addison Wesley.

Bonk, C., & Zhang, K. (2006). Introducing the R2D2 model: Online learning for the diverse learners of this world. *Distance Education, 27*(2), 249–264.

Boud, D. (1995). *Enhancing learning through self assessment.* London: Kogan Page.

Brown, G., Bull, J., & Pendlebury, M. (1997). *Assessing student learning in higher education.* London: Routledge.

Brown, S., Race, P., & Brenda, S. (1996). *500 tips on assessment.* London: Kogan Page.

Carspecken, P. F. (1996). *Critical ethnography in educational research.* New York, NY: Routledge.

Christen, B. (2003). Designing online courses to discourage dishonesty. *Educause Quarterly, 26*(4), 54–58.

Comeaux, P. (Ed.). (2005). *Assessing online learning.* Boston, MA: Anker Publishing.

Creswell, J. W. (1998). *Qualitative inquiry and research design: Choosing among five traditions.* Thousand Oaks, CA: Sage.

Creswell, J. W. (2003). *Research design: Qualitative, quantitative, and mixed methods approaches* (2nd ed.). Thousand Oaks, CA: Sage.

Delandshere, G., & Jones, J. H. (1999). Elementary teachers' beliefs about assessment in mathematics: A case of assessment paralysis. *Journal of Curriculum and Supervision, 14*(3), 216–240

Dewald, N., Scholz-Crane, N., Booth, A., & Levine, C. (2000). Information literacy at a distance: Instructional design issues. *Journal of Academic Librarianship, 26*(1), 33–45.

Ford, M. L. (2002). Preparing students for assessment in the on-line class. In R. S. Anderson, J. F. Bauer, & B. W. Speck (Eds.), *New directions for teaching and learning: Vol. 91. Assessment strategies for the on-line class: From theory to practice* (pp. 77–82). San Francisco, CA: Jossey-Bass.

Fraenkel, J., & Wallen, N. (2003). *How to design and evaluate research in education* (5th ed.). Boston, MA: McGraw-Hill.

Hjelm, M., & Baker, R. L. (2001). Evaluating individual student learning: Implications from four models of assessment. *Learning Abstracts, 4*(3).

Kibby, M. (2003). *Assessing students online: Student centred learning.* University of New Castle, Australia. Retrieved from http://www.newcastle.edu.au/discipline/sociolanthrop/staff/kibbymarj/online/assess.html.

Liang, X., & Creasy, K. (2004). Classroom assessment in web-based instructional environment: instructors' experience. *Practical Assessment, Research and Evaluation, 9*(7). Retrieved from http://PAREonline.net/getvn.asp?v=9&n=7.

Liu, S. (2007, April). *Assessing online asynchronous discussion in online graduate courses: The good, the bad, and the ugly?* Paper presented at the annual conference of the American Educational Research Association, Chicago, IL.

Liu, S., Kim, K-J., Bonk, C. J., & Magjuka, R. (2007). Benefits, challenges, and suggestions: What do online MBA professors have to say about online teaching? *Online Journal of Distance Learning Administration, 10*(2), Retrieved from http://www.westga.edu/~distance/ojdla/summer102/liu102.htm.

Macdonald, J., & Twining, P. (2002). Assessing activities-based learning for a networked course. *British Journal of Educational Technology, 33*(5), 603–618.

Martinez, R., Liu, S., Watson, W., & Bichelmeyer, B. (2006). Evaluation of a web-based Masters degree program in a Midwestern research university. *Quarterly Review of Distance Education, 7*(3), 267–283.

Moore, M. G., & Anderson, W. G. (Eds.). (2003). *Handbook of distance education.* Mahwah, NJ: Erlbaum.

Morgan, C., & O'Reilly, M. (1999). *Assessing open and distance learners.* London, UK: Kogan Page Limited.

Muirhead, B. (2005). Foreword. In P. Comeaux (Ed.), *Assessing online learning* (pp. xiii–xiv). Boston, MA: Anker Publishing.

Oosterhof, A., Conrad, R., & Ely, D. (2007). *Assessing learners online.* Upper Saddle River, NJ: Prentice Hall.

Patton, M. (1990). *Qualitative evaluation and research methods.* Newbury Park, CA: Sage.

Perry, D. (2006, June 28). *Effective multiple-choice items for online testing.* Presentation given at Teaching & Learning Technology Centers (TLTC), Indiana University, Bloomington.

Reeves, T. C. (2000). Alternative assessment approaches for online learning environments in higher education. *Journal of Educational Computing Research, 23*(1), 101–111.

Reeves, T. C. (2002). Keys to successful E-learning: Outcomes, assessment and evaluation. *Educational Technology, 42*(6), 23–29.

Rabinowitz, S. N. (1995). Beyond testing: A vision for an ideal school-to-work assessment system. *Vocational Education Journal, 70*(3), 27–29.

Robles, M., & Braathen, S. (2002). Online assessment techniques. *Delta Pi Epsilon Journal, 44*(1), 39–49.

Rovai, A. P. (2000). Online and traditional assessments: What is the difference? *Internet and Higher Education, 3*(3), 141–151.

Simonson, M. R., Smaldino, S., Albright, M., & Zvacek, S. (2002). *Teaching and learning at a distance: Foundations of distance education* (2nd ed.). Columbus, OH: Prentice-Hall. Retrieved May 5, 2013, from http://www.nova.edu/~simsmich/pdf/entire.pdf.

Yates, K. (2005). *Perceived effectiveness of assessments used in online courses in western North Carolina community colleges.* Unpublished doctoral dissertation, East Tennessee State University.

CHAPTER 6

ONLINE COURSE DYNAMIC DESIGN INFORMED BY STUDENT RESPONSE AND FORMATIVE ASSESSMENT

Marius Boboc
Cleveland State University

INTRODUCTION

Online courses and programs are becoming considerably more prevalent in higher education. Based on responses from more than 2,500 colleges and universities in the United States, 63% of participating institutions mentioned online learning as a critical component of their strategic planning processes. Over 5.6 million students took at least one online course during the Fall 2009 term (Allen & Seaman, 2010). The investigation of how online courses accommodate emerging computer technologies relies on determining how Web-based classes are different from traditional, face-to-face equivalents. Depending on the pedagogical strategies used, there are some factors that seem to be more prominent in one particular course format

Assessment in Online and Blended Learning Environments, pages 103–124
Copyright © 2015 by Information Age Publishing
103

compared to the other, such as immediacy (Conaway, Easton, & Schmidt, 2005), level of energy, nonverbal cues/clues (Epp, Green, & Rahman, 2010), time to respond, opportunity to reflect, and so on (Meyer, 2003).

The more online education becomes more prevalent on college and university campuses, the more considerations are made about factors influencing course design, pedagogy, and assessment, thus supporting the use of indicators of effectiveness assurance (McKnight, 2004). The characteristics of e-learning courses and programs provide students with learning opportunities (Hayden, McNamara, & Kane, 2009) that are not restricted by any given physical locale, thus capitalizing on "convenience and flexibility" (Lao & Gonzales, 2005, p. 460). At the same time, effective e-learning design and delivery should take into account the various situational, institutional, and dispositional reasons (Reisetter & Boris, 2004) for which students do not perform well in online classes, such as administrative problems, degree of interactivity, prior academic preparedness, technical skills, motivation level, time and support for learning, costs associated with taking the online class, and availability of technical support designed to troubleshoot (Muilenburg & Berge, 2005). Consequently, in order to avoid the potential for developing a sense of isolation online students may experience (McBrien & Jones, 2009), course design should be student-centered and constructivist (Oztok, Zingaro, Brett, & Hewitt, 2013; Summers, Waigandt, & Whittaker, 2005) by avoiding to be "static" or linear (Liu & Johnson, 2004). Instead, it should be dynamic by providing instructors and learners with ample opportunities to negotiate course-specific content, interactions, and assessment practices.

The example described in this chapter demonstrates how an undergraduate-level teaching methods course in a teacher preparation program focuses on student responses and formative assessment data to design content-specific processes and outcomes (Swan, Matthews, Bogle, Boles, & Day, 2012). Relevant connections between instructional strategies designed to ensure student participation and course-specific assessment procedures will illustrate the flexible, student-centered nature of curriculum implementation and ongoing formative assessment used in this online course.

The range of class activities and assignments that engage students in the online class is represented by the following: (a) a preservice teacher concerns questionnaire used in a pre/post manner at the beginning and end of the semester; (b) weekly journal entries; (c) "hook questions" for a combination of assigned and student-selected reading materials; (d) "things to keep in mind" used in a similar fashion to the "hook questions"; (e) weekly synchronous chat sessions; and (f) clinical observations of preservice teachers delivering an entire lesson to a class of students in middle or high school. Items 1–5 are used to inform the selection of instructional materials that involves students and their instructor. For example, the "hook questions" or "things to keep in mind" could generate discussion topics to be used during online chat sessions. Journal entries could be tapped to identify focal points for subsequent online group activities that could be derived from an emerging misconception or, on the flip side, specific interest students seem to have. During weekly chat sessions, students may negotiate relevant instructional resources that they choose to share with the entire class as they connect to various topics being discussed. As another example, journal entries as well as the preservice teacher concerns questionnaire administered early in the semester could be used to generate voice podcasts that elaborate on concepts or principles or examples of effective practice. Finally, several of these class assignments and activities could be employed to design a set of pre- and post-observation meetings with preservice teachers in their clinical field, as a culmination of their coursework.

The content negotiated collaboratively in a highly interactive environment (Choy, Dong, & Wang, 2004) supports the concept of a "dynamic design," expected to lead to "higher learning outcomes and more positive approaches toward learning" (Liu & Johnson, 2004, p. 2951). In this context, online student-centeredness correlates with "negotiated learning" (Warrick, Connors, & Norton, 2004, p. 2737), as it relies on using gradual community-building strategies, prior personal knowledge, and effective communication (Brinkerhoff & Koroghlanian, 2007). Recommended considerations for instructional designers and faculty revolve around the concept of flexible pedagogy that takes into account the audience members, the set of appropriate instructional and technological tools and strategies, course cadence or pace, and creating and maintaining an online learning community, as well as valid and reliable assessment measures (Liu & Maddux, 2003). These items are part of the larger picture of interest areas to instructional designers of online courses (Barron, Schullo, Rendida-Gobioff, Venable, & Carey, 2004).

PROJECT DESCRIPTION AND METHODOLOGY

The project described in this chapter relies on the analysis of particular ways in which student engagement, feedback, and formative assessment in an online undergraduate course for preservice teachers work in tandem to influence the dynamic implementation of the given planned (or written) curriculum (Glatthorn, Boschee, & Whitehead, 2009). As the course instructor is also the researcher conducting the project, the methodology used focuses on self-study within his rich professional context (Samaras & Freese, 2009), by relying on reflection (Kitchen & Stevens, 2008) as a way to use narrative inquiry methods (Clandinin & Connelly, 2000) to inform future practice. Student engagement, both structured/formal and unstructured/informal, follows the course sequence in the online environment detailed in the next paragraphs. Student feedback is shared either in a series of private communications with the instructor or in the various public fora made available on Blackboard, the learning management system used. Both sets of evidence of student engagement and feedback are used to help the researcher-instructor adapt the course curriculum to the varied needs and interests of students, as they emerge from the wide range of online communicative exchanges. The interpretation of these formative curricular changes attempts to identify particular ways in which the course design process becomes ongoing, as opposed to static once the semester-based instructional sequence commences. The findings support recommendations for future iterations of the flexible design procedures used, with a particular focus on the interplay among various considerations to be made when developing online courses effectively, as referenced in the specialized literature.

As far as the data sources for the project are concerned, they relate to an undergraduate course enrolling 15 students, offered in Fall 2012 as part of the professional core in a traditional teacher preparation program at a midsized, urban state university in the Midwest. The focus of this semester-based (16 weeks) class is on general teaching methods for preservice teachers, meaning that English language arts, mathematics, science, social studies, art, and modern languages are represented as subject or content areas. The program of study for these preservice teachers includes practicum and student teaching that build on this general methods course. Due to increasing demand for course offerings in virtual learning environments, the instructor developed the online version of the class by maintaining curriculum integrity, while adapting the pedagogy to the specifics of Web-based teaching and learning. The instructor's research interest in the dynamics of online teaching, learning, and assessment spurred the emphasis of this particular project. Intended as the first professional course in the program that has a field (or clinical) component necessitating school placements for all students, the course outcomes cultivate skills and dispositions associated with knowledge of various educational settings, diverse student populations, learner growth and development, the full spectrum of special needs, theories of motivation, and the design, implementation, and evaluation of instructional resources and strategies, as well as assessment of student learning.

The course curriculum consists of a required textbook—*Teaching in the Middle and Secondary Schools* by Kellough and Carjuzaa (2006)—enhanced by a series of focused reading materials posted on Blackboard following particular weekly themes. There are multiple opportunities for students to negotiate and apply what they learn by means of both fieldwork and coursework. For fieldwork, there is a requirement that students go to an area school (middle or high) where they interact with learners in a scaffolded manner. Initially, these preservice teachers are expected to observe the interactions in the classroom in which they have been placed. Gradually, they engage in class activities as they become more acclimated to the classroom environment later on. Eventually, they are expected to teach a series of at least three entire lessons to a whole class of students, representing the culminating experience in the general methods course. The mentor teacher working in that school engages the preservice teachers in joint instructional planning of lesson and unit plans, in addition to guiding and observing them perform instructional duties. The course instructor acts as the university supervisor, which means that he goes in to observe one of the lessons taught by the preservice teacher.

Students are prompted to complete a range of writing assignments and engage in several online collaborative activities, both synchronous and asynchronous. There is a teacher concerns questionnaire used in a pre-/post-test fashion, based on the instrument developed by Borich (2007) dealing with self-reporting on a variety of factors that could impact teaching effectiveness, such as planning for instruction, curriculum, and standards; support and respect from peers, students, school administration, and parents; student needs based on which to design effective learning opportunities; workload and associated responsibilities; classroom management; assessment of student learning; being supervised; and overall satisfaction, both for students and teachers. The five-point Likert scale ranges from 1 being equated with "not being concerned at all" to 5 representing a serious preoccupation with the given factor. Other written assignments include a series of activities that prompt preservice teachers to focus their observations of classroom interactions, while transitioning into a more active role in their field (clinical) placements, leading to the teaching of a number of entire lessons to their respective groups of students. Additionally, there are several course assignments that students write over the course of the semester by connecting theory with their own emerging practice, culminating with the inclusion of corresponding artifacts into a required e-portfolio system. Students also have to submit 12 reflective journal entries associated with particular reading materials.

The traditional, face-to-face version of the class features the same journal entries as required written assignments. The writing prompt is identical for all 12 journal entries, as follows: (a) What are the main points made by the author(s)? (b) What am I to learn from these points raised by the author(s)? (c) Do I agree or disagree with the author(s)? In either case, what evidence do I have to support my position on a particular concept or topic? (d) What are some of the main implications of this concept or topic on my future professional practice as a classroom teacher? and (e) Where do I go from here? Does this chosen concept or topic lead to further investigation? If so, what specific information would I be searching for?

Since the format of the course included in this research project is entirely Web-based, the last two questions supporting the journal entry template are of particular relevance to the management of the online exchanges between the instructor and his students. Based on the regular review of student responses to journal entry prompts, areas of interest emerge as they relate to misconceptions about various aspects of classroom teaching that need clarification or examples during the compulsory synchronous chat sessions.

Two additional written assignments used as formative assessment tools serve the same purpose of informing the focus of these chat sessions. There are "Hook Questions" designed to prompt students to identify several topics they could generate inquiries around, based on which they could initiate a conversation on given topics presented in the common prerequisite reading materials for the course (Vonderwell & Boboc, 2013). "Things to Keep in Mind" is intended to provide students with an opportunity to summarize different common prerequisite reading materials or the same one students use to generate Hook Questions for. It should be noted that students have complete control over the topics about which to write Hook Questions and Things to Keep in Mind. Both assignments are designed to personalize the learning experiences students have while interacting with the formal, taught curriculum of the class. The Hook Questions could be coupled with the Things to Keep in Mind as a more complex manner in which to diagnose potential misconceptions students may demonstrate (Vonderwell & Boboc, 2013). The two formative assessment tools were used separately, students having the option to choose submitting either of them based on weekly required reading materials.

Following the progression of topics proposed by the course curriculum, the developmental approach to instruction is revealed by the gradual acquisition of pedagogical knowledge related to effective teaching. To that effect, students' reflective journal entries document how they construct meaning based on the coverage of required reading assignments. Over time, especially after they go to their field placement school and have various opportunities to observe their mentor teachers, there is increasing evidence of emerging teaching skills. Both sets of formative assessment tools—Hook Questions as well as Things to Keep in Mind—show a shift from theoretical comments to analyses of their own teaching. Online classes lack nonverbal cues (Epp et al., 2010) that help instructors diagnose comprehension problems, misconceptions, inaccuracies in reasoning, or logical fallacies, thus necessitating the integration of compulsory synchronous chat sessions as a way to address all pertinent issues identified in journal entries, Hook Questions, and Things to Keep in Mind. Analyzed collectively, student responses as well as formative assessment—both in instances of synchronous and asynchronous conversations—pinpoint changes made to the course curriculum, indicative of a dynamic instructional design process (Liu & Johnson, 2004), as elaborated upon in the next section.

STRATEGIES OF DYNAMIC COURSE DESIGN

Student Responses

There is a distinction between student feedback that emphasizes satisfaction with the quality of online class interactions and student responses that depend on engagement with peers during asynchronous and synchronous conversations. The assignments representing strands of asynchronous discussions used in this online class are as follows: 12 weekly journal entries, five Learning to Teach activities, and weekly Hook Questions and Things to Keep in Mind, as described earlier. The instructor, along with a teaching assistant, provided feedback to every single student posting from the aforementioned list. However, students were not required to respond to any of the instructor's feedback within the same discussion forum because of the integration of synchronous chat sessions into the course on a biweekly basis, as detailed below.

This course is the first methods class that has a clinical component requiring students to go to an area public school where they are expected to complete certain instructional requirements. Students usually start their clinical experiences around week 5 into the semester, and they continue going to their respective school until week 15. Within this structure, the compulsory online chats were designed to start in week 3 until week 12, following a 2-week cycle in order to allow students to choose a session (either Wednesday or Thursday) from either week. The class featured a total of 10 chat sessions of which students were required to attend five depending on their availability by the 2-week cycle. Each chat-session script was recorded in Blackboard and retrieved to run a topical analysis after the semester was over. Due to some technical problems, the first chat session was not properly recorded, rendering the script incomplete. Therefore, the topical analysis is based on nine scripts.

Table 6.1 outlines the various sequences of topics discussed during the nine chat sessions included in the analysis. As regular practice across all synchronous communication sessions, preliminary questions are intended to determine ad-hoc if any participating students have concerns that need the instructor's immediate attention. The focus of these questions used as a formative assessment tool is both on the course structure as well as its associated requirements in the online learning environment and on class assignments. A comparative analysis of all chat-session scripts in terms of the topics addressed reveals the fact that the first session took on a much more orientative, introductory tone by providing students with an overview of the various course features. The rest of the chat sessions increasingly accommodates student prompts, responses to instructor inquiries, and student examples pertaining to applications of the various instructional components being discussed.

In chat sessions 2–9, the sequence of topics being discussed revolves increasingly around the emerging skill sets participating preservice teachers

TABLE 6.1   Sequence of Topics Discussed During Chat Sessions 1–9

	Sequence of Topics Discussed
Chat Session 1 (four participants)	• Preliminary questions • Introductions • Prior teaching experience (as a way to introduce the clinical field requirement for the class) • Blackboard structure/organization • Overview of course assignments • Hook Questions (selection from student postings prior to the chat session) • Overview of main points in required readings up to this week • Explanation of the Teacher Concerns Survey • Overview of TaskStream (e-portfolio platform for the college) • Things to Keep in Mind (selection from student postings prior to the chat session)
Chat Session 2 (13 participants)	• Preliminary questions • Hook Questions (selection from student postings prior to the chat session) • Clarifications/examples for this week's required reading materials • Elaborations and probing into examples provided by students from their field experience settings (as they relate to either the Hook Questions or the most recent required reading materials) • Things to Keep in Mind (selection from student postings prior to the chat session) used as a personalized way to connect theory with practice
Chat Session 3 (five participants)	• Preliminary questions • Hook Questions (selection from student postings prior to the chat session) • Student prompt (their field experience started): (1) the use of student helpers in the classroom; (2) the design and use of icebreaker activities at the beginning of class; (3) student ability differences (within the larger concept of student diversity); and (4) motivation strategies (intrinsic and extrinsic) • Things to Keep in Mind (selection from student postings prior to the chat session) used to reinforce the examples provided by students from their respective classroom settings

(continued)

TABLE 6.1   Sequence of Topics Discussed During Chat Sessions 1–9 (continued)

	Sequence of Topics Discussed
Chat Session 4 (10 participants)	• Preliminary questions • Hook Questions (selection from student postings prior to the chat session) • Classroom management (based on recommendations from students) • Things to Keep in Mind (selection from student postings prior to the chat session) used to reinforce the examples provided by students from their respective classroom settings with regard to classroom management strategies
Chat Session 5 (six participants)	• Preliminary questions • Hook Questions (selection from student postings prior to the chat session) • Comments on school placement (derived from some events that had occurred there that these preservice teachers were trying to interpret) • Applications of strategies discussed/read in class up to date • Seating arrangements (prompted by examples shared by students) • Curriculum integration and flexible instructional planning (part of the larger concept of content management) • Transitioning from one instructional activity to the next (part of the larger concept of classroom management) • Questions from students (related to examples from their respective classrooms) • Things to Keep in Mind (selection from student postings prior to the chat session) used to reinforce the examples provided by students from their respective classroom settings with regard to several of the topics analyzed during this chat session
Chat Session 6 (11 participants)	• Preliminary questions • Blackboard updates • Overview of upcoming class assignments and e-Portfolio artifacts • Hook Questions (selection from student postings prior to the chat session) • Managing student differences (as a way to apply educational psychology concepts to their respective diverse classrooms) • Things to Keep in Mind (selection from student postings prior to the chat session) used to connect theory with practice

(continued)

TABLE 6.1   Sequence of Topics Discussed During Chat Sessions 1–9 (continued)

	Sequence of Topics Discussed
Chat Session 7 (six participants)	• Preliminary questions • Blackboard updates • Overview of upcoming class assignments and e-Portfolio artifacts • Hook Questions (selection from student postings prior to the chat session) • Comments on school placement (derived from one event that had occurred at the placement school of one of the preservice teachers) • Managing student differences (as a way to apply educational psychology concepts to their respective diverse classrooms) • Things to Keep in Mind (selection from student postings prior to the chat session) used to connect theory with practice
Chat Session 8 (nine participants)	• Preliminary questions • Administrative clarifications (related to the instructor's upcoming classroom observations) • Hook Questions (selection from student postings prior to the chat session) • Using the three domains for lesson planning: cognitive, affective, and psychomotor • Overview of teacher-centered instructional strategies • Analysis of examples of teacher/student-talk in the various classrooms • The design and use of group work • Things to Keep in Mind (selection from student postings prior to the chat session) used to connect theory with practice
Chat session 9 (seven participants)	- Preliminary questions - Administrative clarifications (related to the instructor's upcoming classroom observations) - Hook Questions (selection from student postings prior to the chat session) - Overview of teacher- and student-centered instructional strategies - Review of transitioning from one instructional activity to the next (part of the larger concept of classroom management, as it applies to various instructional strategies discussed during this chat session) - Examples of differentiated instruction (shared by students based on their emerging classroom experiences) - Things to Keep in Mind (selection from student postings prior to the chat session) used to connect theory with practice

demonstrate as they attempt to connect theory with their own observations and initial interactions with students in real classrooms. As the course relies heavily on formative assessment tools to inform the focus of each chat session, student responses shape the communicative exchanges in terms of the probing questions, elaborations, and examples used by the instructor. Overall, the topics of student differences and classroom management are reiterated, as both represent very complex areas of practice. Consequently, they were reinforced by making changes to the course curriculum to accommodate them based on the needs of the participating preservice teachers, as elaborated on later in this chapter.

Formative Feedback

The range of formative assessment strategies was designed to provide the course instructor with a variety of data sources by which to determine how to modify the curriculum in order to highlight areas of interest to students, as expressed by them during both the asynchronous and synchronous communicative exchanges mentioned previously, such as the preliminary questions opening each chat session. The Hook Questions and Things to Keep in Mind represent weekly student postings intended to provide the instructor with a glimpse into the manner in which every student engages with the course content. As a way to validate this particular kind of student participation in class as well as to increase the meaningfulness of online interactivity, the instructor selects one or two Hook Questions and Things to Keep in Mind posted by students to include in weekly synchronous chat sessions. The Hook Questions used at the beginning of such a session prompt students to elaborate on particular topics of discussion. As a way to encourage reflection and higher-level thinking skills, the instructor used probing questions as an additional formative assessment strategy by asking students to elaborate on their initial responses to the Hook Questions. Along the same lines, every chat session ends with one or two student-generated Things to Keep in Mind designed to summarize the online synchronous conversation, while promoting the potential for future investigations of the topics being analyzed collaboratively.

Of particular interest to the instructor was the Teacher Concerns survey (Borich, 2007) administered in a pre-/post-test fashion. The rationale behind using such an instrument in an online methods course for preservice teachers had to do with an attempt to present students with a variety of factors that could impact teaching effectiveness to determine which of them they are concerned with at varying degrees. As the five-point Likert scale ranges from 1 being equated with "not being concerned at all" to 5 representing a serious preoccupation with the given factor, the results of the

self-reporting instrument administered at the beginning of the semester allowed the instructor to zoom in on particular emerging areas of interest to
participating students. For example, most of them (10 out of 15) expressed
a moderate concern in terms of being rated favorably at the end of an observation session of their classroom teaching, while nine students showed
a similar moderate concern related to having sufficient time to prepare
for instruction. At the "very concerned" level, there were eight students
who focused on being able to address the full range of student needs present in their respective classrooms. At the highest level of concern (labeled
as "totally preoccupied"), seven preservice teachers chose the issue of being able to assist their own students to develop lifelong learning skills. An
equal number of respondents were similarly concerned about whether or
not their students would be able to reach their potential in class. These data
informed several of the synchronous chat sessions, along with some of the
changes to the course curriculum detailed in the next section. The final
administration of the same survey at the end of the semester allowed the
instructor to analyze how student concerns levels changed over the semester as a result of being engaged in coursework as well as field experiences.

As far as the use of formative assessment strategies in synchronous chat
sessions is concerned, in addition to the preliminary questions described
in the previous section, the instructor implemented probing questions
to elicit student elaborations on particular topics being discussed. Additionally, such questions served the purpose of prompting student examples from their field experiences to illustrate applications of various
theoretical concepts, models, and/or principles relevant to their emerging classroom practice. For example, as indicated by the analysis of the
sequence of topics addressed during synchronous chat exchanges listed
in Table 6.1, coupled by the findings from the initial administration of
the Teacher Concerns survey, there were several online chat sessions de-
voted to conversations about managing classroom settings characterized
by a high degree of student diversity. In those instances, asking students
to share examples of instructional strategies observed or tried by them
in their respective classrooms led to the identification of various relevant
teaching tips related to either how to design and use seating arrangements or differentiate lessons or motivate students.

Dynamic Course Design Informed by Student Response and Formative Feedback

Social presence is the attribute of being involved in an online community by means of a variety of learning opportunities. In order to increase
its dimensions—social context, online communication, and interactivity

(Tu & McIsaac, 2002)—the instructor demonstrated teaching presence to mediate the use of various synchronous and asynchronous communication tools designed to enhance student engagement and enrich the learning environment. As the focus of this general methods course for preservice teachers is on developing the skill sets necessary to be successful as future classroom practitioners, the emphasis of the entire curriculum sequence is placed on identifying applications of various theoretical concepts, models, and principles to actual classroom settings. Therefore, there is a certain degree of authenticity that characterizes the course, defined by connections to real-life teaching situations. Based on this perspective, the assessment structure, both formative and summative, has to be authentic (Allen, 2009) in its relevance to students' professional practice.

The effective design of online learning environments relies, in part, on the ways in which synchronous and asynchronous interactions and communications represent an integral part of the course architecture (McNeil, Robin, & Miller, 2000; Reisetter & Boris, 2004). Under these circumstances, the outline below represents the specific instructional design strategies used to sustain high-activity, relevant venues where online students could co-construct the knowledge and skills supported by the course curriculum.

Asynchronous conversations. The data sources taken into account as a way to accommodate student responses and emerging needs by means of formative assessment were as follows: (a) the last two questions in the weekly journal entries, focused on the implications on future practice and potential for future investigations of given topics; (b) the weekly Hook Questions and Things to Keep in Mind from which a selection was shared during each online chat session to promote student-driven discussions; and (c) the Teacher Concerns questionnaire used at the very beginning of the semester to identify particular areas of interest students seemed to have related to the contents of the course.

Synchronous conversations. The data sources underlying the process of adapting the class curriculum to student responses and emerging needs by means of formative assessment were as follows: (a) preliminary questions that were used at the beginning of each chat session to orient the instructor in terms of the sequence of topics to be addressed that time; (b) a selection from the Hook Questions and Things to Keep in Mind posted by students as a way to ground online discussions in particular concepts or models or principles that appealed the most to learners; and (c) probing questions aimed at encouraging students to reflect on their responses and share additional explanations and/or examples as they relate to given topics being discussed.

Example 1 below demonstrates the use of a Hook Question selected from several student postings to initiate a conversation during chat session 3. In this case, students had inquired about how to use an "icebreaker strategy" in the classroom:

Instructor: What "icebreaker strategy" would you use to get to know your students?

Student A: Being an art teacher, I would probably have them do a project of some sort that represents things they like or things that make them up, and have them maybe write a short story to go along with it, and present it to the class.

Instructor: (Student D, let's think how we could adapt those strategies to different students, after Students B and C share their examples.)

Student D: (Sorry, I am writing my notes, I am getting back to you in a minute.)

Instructor: (Sure.)

Student B: Isn't laughter a part of an icebreaker?

Instructor: It could be.

Student B: I guess for me, I would use some laughter, but not the whole time because I want the students to take me seriously, but I want to incorporate jokes and laughter so that students would not be scared of me. . . . I guess, if it makes sense.

Instructor: Is this part of the "icebreaker" early in the semester?

Student B: Umm, maybe, I am not sure.

Student A: Today at my observation, my mentor incorporated a lot of jokes and laughter to his students, he said you just have to learn your classes; [in] other classes he is strictly business. It was good to see him use both aspects with different classes.

Instructor: Good point. Student B, using humor would be good while asking students to introduce themselves . . .

Student B: I just want my students not to feel like they are in a very strict environment, I want them to have fun in class.

Example 2 below shows how a Thing to Keep in Mind was used to ground the various points made by students during chat session 4 with regard to being able to identify and implement "instructional routines" in the classroom:

Instructor: Everything you see your mentor teacher doing in their respective classrooms could be broken down into "routines" (I mean that in a good way). There is something your teachers tend to do at the beginning of the lesson, then they transition into new content, then they have students work on something (individually or in groups), then there is another set of instructional strategies that represents yet another routine, and, finally, ending the lesson is one last routine. You could analyze your own teaching in terms of these routines. Based on how your students react/behave, you could determine which routine of yours is strong and which could be improved, and that could help you work on classroom management over time.

Finally, example 3 below centers on probing into a student's comment related to the seating arrangement in her placement classroom, inviting her to reflect on how it could accommodate her needs as a preservice teacher about to deliver her first lesson to the entire group of students in that classroom:

Instructor: Student A, speaking of seating arrangements, what seems to be the case in your class?

Student A: No arrangement at all.

Instructor: Does that work alright? (…)

Student A: Everyone sits wherever and moves around (…) No seating arrangement because it's a ceramics class, we move around a lot (…)

Instructor: Do you think you could change the structure of the class if the focus would be … on art appreciation, let's say (or evaluation of their own ceramic art)?

Student A: Yes, I would definitely have a seating arrangement and the class would need a lot more structure. I have not been there for the evaluation, but I'll have to ask her [the mentor teacher] and definitely include it in my lesson.

Instructor: Good, that would be useful (…)

Student A: I think constructive criticism and evaluation are very important in art.

Instructor: Agreed. I asked you that question because there is one thing to keep in mind as we look at classroom management (…) One very encouraging finding based on your feedback is that none of you pointed out that classroom management should be about "controlling" student behavior (which would be primarily behavioral in nature, as in behavior control/management). This is where we could tie together the other pieces of the conversation we have been having tonight—no matter where you teach, no matter what you teach, effective classroom management should rely on three major components—content management (implying how we structure/sequence the contents of our lessons), coupled with context management (implying how we are able to modify the physical environment of our classrooms

                to accommodate learning), and then coupled with student
                behavior management...

Student B: Nice summary.

Instructor: Which is what traditional classroom management used to
                mean. Think of this triad whenever something seems not to
                be going according to plan...

Student C: Agree, those are all very important.

Instructor: And then try different strategies that relate to any of the three
                components mentioned earlier. Questions, comments? (By
                the way, I am recording this session to send you the script.)

Student D: I have been in classrooms that lack all three of them, I
                imagine.

As a result of implementing formative assessment strategies to accommodate student responses in order to increase interactivity in the social context of the online class, the following are the examples of changes made to the course curriculum during the semester.

New content folders were posted on Blackboard, intended to extend learning by providing students with access to additional online resources pertinent to various topics discussed either synchronously or asynchronously. These folders contain links to video clips, archived or current articles and associated documents, course templates, PowerPoint presentations, and handouts. Both the instructor and his students contributed to the list of items generated in these folders, which enhanced the level of student participation in class.

Voice podcasts were used to serve a variety of purposes. On the one hand, they were supposed to clarify and/or extend any complex topics initiated either in asynchronous conversations or online chat sessions. On the other hand, this tool was designed to update students on new additions to the virtual space of the class or upcoming assignments, on relevant field experience information, or on any other general online course management data.

Additional chatrooms were identified by the day of the week when they should be accessed, where students could engage in peer-driven conversations without any instructor interference or mediation. These virtual collaborative spaces were intended to encourage student exchanges of ideas without any prior, formal structuring. Since there were 2 days (Wednesday and Thursday, on a 2-week cycle) when students were expected to join compulsory chat sessions on either day, these additional chat sessions labelled "Saturday chatroom" and "Sunday chatroom" were developed as a result of students expressing interest in working together on the weekend. There was one other additional chatroom designed to be more structured, as groups of students would use it to complete collaborative lesson plans based on templates discussed during several of the compulsory chat sessions. At the same time, this particular chatroom could be used for any other joint project students wanted to collaborate on as a result of their online decision-making process. It should be noted that none of the additional chat sessions could be recorded, which is a Blackboard-specific feature.

New discussion fora were created to accommodate ideas derived from chat sessions as a way to focus further additions of relevant materials posted by students themselves. One such new discussion forum was called "Examples of instructional strategies we use or observe in the field," while another one was labelled "Notes from the field." In the latter case, students were encouraged to share with the entire online class any examples of interactions observed in their field classrooms either to seek an explanation or talk more about how they could replicate particular instructional practices when they would be ready to teach their lessons toward the end of the semester. Finally, one additional discussion forum was connected to the collaborative, peer-directed chatroom where students could discuss how to complete joint projects, after which they would post their finished product on the discussion forum for peer evaluation.

RECOMMENDATIONS AND FUTURE RESEARCH

Flexibility in the curricular decisions made by instructors is important in practicing student-centeredness by encouraging students to make and suggest selections of materials and topics to investigate during class (Schrum & Hong, 2002). The purpose of effective online communities is to provide learners with opportunities to engage in enhanced educational experiences. As noted by Garrison, Anderson, and Archer (2000, p. 88), such experiences are supported by a triad of factors—social presence, cognitive presence, and teaching presence—that work in tandem. There are several areas of convergence that connect these components of educational experience, as follows: supporting discourse brings together social presence and cognitive presence, climate setting coordinates the way in which social presence influences teaching presence in a mutual relationship, and content selection determines the balance between teaching presence and cognitive presence. Given the degree of interactivity in online classes, the need for the use of a constructive approach to teaching, learning, and assessment (Oztok et al., 2013; Summers et al., 2005) is crucial in helping students to co-construct knowledge by making meaning (Bures, Abrami, & Barclay, 2010) of their interactions with content, instructors, and peers (Swan, 2002), as well as the interface provided by the learning management system (Davidson-Shivers, 2009; Wanstreet, 2006).

Student responses and formative feedback connect supporting discourse, climate-setting, and content selection (Garrison et al., 2000) in particular ways that are grounded in the context of the class where the research was conducted. In other words, formative assessment was an integral part of structuring student responses, thus creating a positive learning environment where communicative exchanges were student-centered, as they led to the selection of curricular materials pertinent to students' emerging professional practice. Figure 6.1 represents an adaptation of the model for a community of inquiry proposed by Garrison et al. (2000) by adding formative assessment and dynamic course design as required components supporting enhanced educational experiences.

Time was spent to connect asynchronous discussions with student contributions to online chat sessions, thus becoming a major factor in managing this online class. Future iterations should attempt to strike a balance in terms of the range of structures one can use to provide responses. The course architecture should be inclusive of components that accommodate

Figure 6.1 Interplay of enhanced educational experience components in online classes.

formative assessment in a way that allows the instructor to monitor and provide all necessary feedback to students. The time management of online classes has been shown to represent an important source of concern for online instructors (Davidson-Shivers, 2009; Spector, 2005; Worley & Tesdell, 2009). Future online course design could also include chat participation grades based on required student responses to instructors' feedback to asynchronous discussions as a way to increase accountability and enhance student participation. This would accommodate the need for "social bonding, information exchange, and self-disclosure" as leading to the effective creation of online communities (Kleinman, 2005, p. 15), so the addition of more formal structures could impact the course dynamic as previously presented.

Another feature of effective online classes that has been proven to bear importance on the course design and implementation process has to do with learning opportunities that increase interactivity while promoting student autonomy in making choices that are relevant to their field of study, as well as the emerging professional practice (Kleinman, 2005; McBrien & Jones, 2009). The students in the class analyzed in this research project had several assignments where they could choose what to write about, such as the Hook Questions and the Things to Think About. One strategy that could extend these online student postings to include a self-assessment component would be to require learners to make reference in their journal entries to how a particular topic connects to any of the previous concepts, models, or principles negotiated previously either in a synchronous or asynchronous setting. That information would then be used by the instructor to inform the content of chat sessions in a similar fashion to how the selection of Hook Questions and Things to Keep in Mind was used in this class.

Dynamic course design bears great significance on the way the class analyzed in this research project supports the interplay of enhanced educational experience in online classes presented in Figure 6.1. The clear objectives, expectations, and guidelines needed to develop effective online classes (Kupczynski, Ice, Wiesemayer, & McCluskey, 2010) were shared consistently with the students participating in this project. Moreover, the intersection of social, cognitive, and teaching presence promoted learners' ability to interact within "practice fields" (Polin, 2004) that correlated course assignments and activities with the field experiences for this group of preservice teachers. Grounding the use of formative assessment in the wide range of student responses, both formal and informal and structured and less (semi-) structured, was centered on the instructor's ability to maintain a flexible teaching presence that mediated the way curriculum was presented to students in the online learning environment. Future research could look into differences between theory-focused and skill-building courses in how they implement the dynamic, student-centered design process. Additionally, it would be very helpful to investigate how a given range of ongoing curricular modifications correlate with enhanced educational experiences and improved student performance in virtual environments.

REFERENCES

Allen, I. E., & Seaman, J. (2010). *Class differences: Online education in the United States, 2010.* Retrieved from http://sloanconsortium.org/publications/survey/class_differences.

Allen, M. (2009). Authentic assessment and the Internet: Contributions within knowledge networks. In T. Bastiaens et al. (Eds.), *Proceedings of the World Conference on E-Learning in Corporate, Government, Healthcare, and Higher Education 2009* (pp. 1505–1510). Chesapeake, VA: AACE.

Barron, A. E., Schullo, S., Rendida-Gobioff, G., Venable, M., & Carey, L. (2004). Creating online courses: Instructional designers' perspective. In J. Hall & R. Robson (Eds.), *Proceedings of the World Conference on E-Learning in Corporate, Government, Healthcare, and Higher Education 2004* (pp. 1083–1088). Chesapeake, VA: AACE.

Borich, G. D. (2007). *Effective teaching methods: Research-based practice* (6th ed.). Upper Saddle River, NJ: Pearson.

Brinkerhoff, J., & Koroghlanian, C. M. (2007). Online students' expectations: Enhancing the fit between online students and course design. *Journal of Educational Computing Research, 36*(4), 383–393.

Bures, E., Abrami, P., & Barclay, A. (2010). Assessing online dialogue in higher education. In J. Sanchez & K. Zhang (Eds.), *Proceedings of the World Conference on E-Learning in Corporate, Government, Healthcare, and Higher Education 2010* (pp. 438–448). Chesapeake, VA: AACE.

Choy, D., Dong, C., & Wang, L. (2004). Developing a criterion set for an online learning environment: From the perspective of higher education faculty. In R. Ferdig et al. (Eds.), *Proceedings of the Society for Information Technology and Teacher Education International Conference 2004* (pp. 367–370). Chesapeake, VA: AACE.

Clandinin, D. J., & Connelly, F. M. (2000). *Narrative inquiry: Experience and story in qualitative research.* San Francisco, CA: Jossey-Bass.

Conaway, R. N., Easton, S. S., & Schmidt, W. V. (2005). Strategies for enhancing student interaction and immediacy in online courses. *Business Communication Quarterly, 68*(1), 23–35.

Davidson-Shivers, G. V. (2009). Frequency and types of instructor interactions in online instruction. *Journal of Interactive Online Learning, 8*(1), 23–40.

Epp, E. M., Green, K. F., & Rahman, A. M. (2010). Analysis of student-instructor interaction patterns in real-time, scientific online discourse. *Journal of Science Education and Technology, 19,* 49–57.

Garrison, D. R., Anderson, T., & Archer, W. (2000). Critical inquiry in a text-based environment: Computer conferencing in higher education. *Internet and Higher Education, 2*(2–3), 87–105.

Glatthorn, A. A., Boschee, F., & Whitehead, B. M. (2009). *Curriculum leadership: Strategies for development and implementation* (2nd ed.). Thousand Oaks, CA: Sage.

Hayden, K. L., McNamara, K., & Kane, D. (2009). Assessing effective strategies and design in online learning. In T. Bastiaens et al. (Eds.), *Proceedings of the World Conference on E-Learning in Corporate, Government, Healthcare, and Higher Education 2009* (pp. 2660–2667). Chesapeake, VA: AACE.

Kellough, R. D., & Carjuzaa, J. (2006). *Teaching in the middle and secondary schools* (8th ed.). Upper Saddle River, NJ: Pearson.

Kitchen, J., & Stevens, D. (2008). Action research in teacher education: Two teacher educators practice action research as they introduce action research to pre-service teachers. *Action Research, 6*(1), 7–28.

Kleinman, S. (2005). Strategies for encouraging active learning, interaction, and academic integrity in online courses. *Communication Teacher, 19*(1), 13–18.

Kupczynski, L., Ice, P., Wiesemayer, R., & McCluskey, F. (2010). Student perceptions of the relationship between indicators of teaching presence and success in online courses. *Journal of Interactive Online Learning, 9*(1), 23–43.

Lao, M., & Gonzales, C. (2005). Understanding online learning through a qualitative description of professors and students' experiences. *Journal of Technology and Teacher Education, 13*(3), 459–474.

Liu, L., & Johnson, L. (2004). Static and dynamic design in online course development. In R. Ferdig et al. (Eds.), *Proceedings of the Society for Information Technology and Teacher Education International Conference 2004* (pp. 2946–2951). Chesapeake, VA: AACE.

Liu, L., & Maddux, C. (2003). Online course design and research. In A. Rossett (Ed.), *Proceedings of the World Conference on E-Learning in Corporate, Government, Healthcare, and Higher Education 2003* (pp. 1078–1081). Chesapeake, VA: AACE.

McBrien, J. L., & Jones, P. (2009). Virtual spaces: Employing a synchronous online classroom to facilitate student engagement in online learning. *International Review of Research in Open and Distance Learning, 10*(3), 1–17.

McKnight, R. (2004, January–March). Virtual necessities: Assessing online course design. *International Journal on E-learning*, pp. 5–10.

McNeil, S. G., Robin, B. R., & Miller, R. M. (2000). Facilitating interaction, communication and collaboration in online courses. *Computers and Geosciences, 26*, 699–708.

Meyer, K. A. (2003). Face-to-face versus threaded discussions: The role of time and higher-order thinking. *Journal of Asynchronous Learning Networks, 7*(3), 55–65.

Muilenburg, L. Y., & Berge, Z. L. (2005). Student barriers to online learning: A factor analytic study. *Distance Education, 26*(1), 29–48.

Oztok, M., Zingaro, D., Brett, C., & Hewitt, J. (2013). Exploring asynchronous and synchronous tool use in online courses. *Computers & Education, 60*, 87–94.

Polin, L. (2004). Learning in dialogue with a practicing community. In T. M. Duffy & J. R. Kirkley (Eds.), *Learner-centered theory and practice in distance education: Cases from higher education* (pp. 17–47). Mahwah, NJ: Erlbaum.

Reisetter, M., & Boris, G. (2004). What works: Perceptions of effective elements in online learning. *Quarterly Review of Distance Education, 5*(4), 277–291.

Samaras, A. P., & Freese, A. R. (2009). Looking back and looking forward: An historical overview of the self-study school. In C. A. Lassonde, S. Galman, & C. Kosnik (Eds.), *Self-study research methodologies for teacher educators* (pp. 3–19). Rotterdam, The Netherlands: Sense Publishers.

Schrum, L., & Hong, S. (2002). Dimensions and strategies for online success: Voices form experienced educators. *Journal of Asynchronous Learning Networks, 6*(1), 57–67.

Spector, J. M. (2005). Time demands in online instruction. *Distance Education, 26*(1), 5–27.

Summers, J. J., Waigandt, A., & Whittaker, T. A. (2005). A comparison of student achievement and satisfaction in an online versus a traditional face-to-face statistics class. *Innovative Higher Education, 29*(3), 233–250.

Swan, K. (2002). Building learning communities in online courses: The importance of interaction. *Education, Communication and Information, 2*(1), 23–49.

Swan, K, Matthews, D., Bogle, L., Boles, E., & Day, S. (2012). Linking online course design and implementation to learning outcomes: A design experiment. *Internet and Higher Education, 15*, 81–88.

Tu, C. H., & McIsaac, M. (2002). The relationship of social presence and interaction in online classes. *American Journal of Distance Education, 16*(3), 131–150.

Vonderwell, S., & Boboc, M. (2013). Promoting formative assessment in online teaching and learning. *TechTrends, 57*(4), 22–27.

Wanstreet, C. E. (2006). Interaction in online learning environments: A review of the literature. *Quarterly Review of Distance Education, 7*(4), 399–411.

Warrick, W., Connors, S., & Norton, P. (2004). E-mail, discussion boards, and synchronous chat: Comparing three modes of online collaboration. In R. Ferdig et al. (Eds.), *Proceedings of the Society for Information Technology and Teacher Education International Conference 2004* (pp. 2732–2738). Chesapeake, VA: AACE.

Worley, W. L., & Tesdell, L. S. (2009). Instructor time and effort in online and face-to-face teaching: Lessons learned. *IEEE Transactions on Professional Communication, 52*(2), 138–151.

CHAPTER 7

USING EMBEDDED AUDIO FEEDBACK FOR FORMATIVE ASSESSMENT PURPOSES IN TEACHING ABOUT ENGLISH LANGUAGE LEARNERS

Larisa A. Olesova
George Mason University

Luciana C. de Oliveira
University of Miami

INTRODUCTION

As asynchronous online courses continue to gain popularity, instructors and practitioners are increasingly looking for more effective formative assessment techniques to impact learning quality in distance education. One assessment technique, audio feedback, promises to increase the detail of formative assessment because instructors can deliver more comments on content in comparison to written feedback (Ribchester, France, & Wakefield, 2008).

Assessment in Online and Blended Learning Environments, pages 125–141
Copyright © 2015 by Information Age Publishing
All rights of reproduction in any form reserved.

In the field of distance education, audio feedback can strengthen an instructor's ability to establish more personalized communication with students (Ice, Curtis, Phillips, & Wells, 2007). Using audio feedback for assessment can enhance online presence, student engagement, and overall course satisfaction, which are very important for asynchronous online courses. Students receiving audio feedback in the form of assessment have described their experience as personal, enjoyable, complete, and clear (Kirschner, van den Brink, & Meester, 1991). The use of audio feedback assessment in asynchronous online courses increases retention of content and enhances learning community interactions. It is associated with the perception that the instructor cares more about the student (Ice et al., 2007; Olesova, Richardson, Weasenforth, & Meloni, 2011; Oomen-Early, Bold, Wiginton, Gallien, & Anderson, 2008).

This chapter discusses how audio feedback was used in asynchronous online courses when it was provided on a key assessment, specifically, students' case studies at the beginning of the semester, midway throughout the semester, and at the end of the semester. This chapter provides an overview of studies on how audio feedback was used in face-to-face and online courses. It discusses its pedagogical practice and role in assessment by showing how audio feedback was provided using Audacity and Adobe Professional software. Finally, the chapter discusses the benefits of using audio feedback in online courses and provides pedagogical recommendations for those who are interested in using audio feedback in their teaching practice.

LITERATURE REVIEW

Asynchronous online courses with their flexibility, interaction, and communication at any time and at any place may present drawbacks such as the lack of nonverbal cues in text-based communication (Cifuentes & Shih, 2001). It is known that text-based online communication can cause difficulties in students' understanding each other, interpreting words correctly, or understanding culture-specific references (Gunawardena & McIsaac, 2004). Students perceive text-based online communication as very restrictive; they cannot use body gestures or other nonverbal means for communication (Zhao & McDougall, 2008). Students need clarity of meaning to overcome misunderstanding, especially when it is associated with asynchronous text-based communication (Quinton & Smallbone, 2010). To overcome the limitations of text-based communication, the instructor's role in facilitating online interactions for successful online learning is important (Anderson, Rourke, Garrison, & Archer, 2001; Biesenbach-Lucas, 2003; Swan, 2003). Indeed, the instructor's role to provide guided instruction, encourage critical reflection, and give constructive feedback may enable students to overcome difficulties of text-based online communication (Biesenbach-Lucas, 2003). Yet, to increase both the verbal and nonverbal cues of asynchronous interactions, studies have proposed using asynchronous audio, specifically, instructional *audio feedback* (Ice et al., 2007; Oomen-Early et al., 2008).

Interest in using audio feedback in teaching started in the early 1960s (Tanner, 1962; McGrew, 1969; Coleman, 1972; Logan, Logan, Fuller, & Denehy, 1976; Moore, 1977). The first empirical studies on using audio feedback were conducted in the field of English composition in high school and revealed that using audio feedback was an effective technique to improve students' writing and to save teachers time (McGrew, 1969; Coleman, 1972). More recent studies (e.g., Berner, Boswell, & Kahan, 1996; Jelfs & Whitelock, 2000) have found that audio feedback positively affected students' motivation and self-confidence.

Audio feedback is defined as a technique in which instructors' comments and suggested changes to students' writing are recorded (Johanson, 1999; Syncox, 2003). One of the benefits of using audio feedback for assessment is that it puts the "act of listening under student control, allowing for listening at the students' own rate, and for repeated listening" (Boswood & Dwyer, 1995, p. 53). However, audio feedback requires more involvement and effort from instructors. They need time to become comfortable with recording audio feedback and students also need time to adapt to a new technology (Johanson, 1999). In addition, audio feedback cannot become an effective assessment by itself; it is more effective when it is employed with other assessment methods, for example, peer review (Johanson, 1999).

Studies on audio feedback for students in face-to-face environments have examined the effect of this technique on students' writing performance to determine whether it helps students understand teachers' comments appropriately. Studies have found that audio feedback is more personal and easier to understand because the instructor speaks directly to each student, adapting tone, inflection, and explanation to the particular student (Huang, 2000; Morra & Asís, 2009). Other studies have found that audio feedback is an effective technique in providing successful assessment because it might help students understand their writing gaps from audio feedback better than from written comments (Boswood & Dwyer, 1995; Johanson, 1999; Ribchester et al., 2008).

Studies on audio feedback provided on students' writing reveal that the technique can build the link between the revisions of a draft and the intended meaning of the writing to students. It allows the instructor to expand on the problem of understanding meaning "from a variety of different angles in the form of models and prompts" (Syncox, 2003, p.75). It gives instructors an opportunity "to offer *clearer* explanations about the function of the text in its social context, the relationship it crystallizes between writer and audience, the effectiveness of its thematic development, and its overall impact on the reader" (Boswood & Dwyer, 1995, p. 54).

Providing *clearer* explanation is very important in asynchronous online courses, as Swan (2003) explains, because real-time negotiation of meaning is impossible among instructors and students separated by space and time, making clarity of meaning even more imperative in online classes. In asynchronous online communication, both the tone and the format of the message are important; both need "to be relevant, responsive, accurate, and congruent with the learning task" (Bonnel, 2008, p. 292).

Audio feedback provided in asynchronous online courses is viewed as a technique where instructors record their comments regarding students' writing assignments, which students can listen to as they read along the instructional comments in the text (Ice, 2008). The central component of the audio feedback effect is that students may listen to previously recorded audio while they are reading the text to what it refers (Ice, 2008). One of the first studies on using audio feedback in online environments was conducted in the 1980s by Kelly and Ryan (1983). Later, Kirschner et al. (1991) conducted a qualitative experiment using audio feedback for writing assignments in distance education. Even though the researchers did not find significant differences in the amount of time spent in the preparation of the audio as well as in the students' final grades, they recommended examining whether the increase in the quality of the writing reported by other researchers also occurred in a distance education setting. Likewise, Sipple (2007) conducted another qualitative study to determine students' attitude toward audio and written commentary in developmental writing classes. The results of the study showed students positively perceived the impact of audio feedback on their revision practices. Furthermore, Rotheram (2007) analyzed using an MP3 recorder to give feedback on writing assignments and found that audio feedback could influence student learning powerfully because feedback was timely, perceived as relevant and meaningful, and suggested ways to improve writing. Moreover, Nortcliffe and Middleton (2007, 2008) investigated whether the iPod and the phone with audio feedback supported a meaningful and formative learning experience for the iPod generation. The researchers compared summative assessment results for using recorded audio feedback in assignments to that feedback in written format. The researchers reported that audio feedback through an iPod may significantly impact students' academic performance. The students found audio feedback helped them clarify how they could improve their writing submissions.

PEDAGOGICAL PRACTICE AND ROLE IN ASSESSMENT

The asynchronous online course English Language Development (EDCI 53000) was offered at Purdue University via Blackboard in the fall of 2011. The course is part of a series of courses that preservice and in-service teachers take to get an additional license in English language learning. In this online course, instructional audio comments were inserted or *embedded* in an Adobe Acrobat Professional document. This program allows instructors to record *audio feedback* and embed it into highlighted text. The students in this online course received a PDF file with *embedded audio feedback* as attachments via the Blackboard Assignment dropbox. The instructor provided *embedded audio feedback* in the form of discussion to help students improve their case study reports. In addition, *embedded audio feedback* was provided in the form of prompts or praise for some specific aspect of the report, directive information, and comments about details and understanding in the report.

Pedagogical practice is focused on providing instructional *embedded audio feedback* on a key assessment. In this online course, *embedded audio feedback* was provided for students who completed a case study. The case study assignment was a long-term observation of the English language development of an English language learner (ELL) in a classroom in Indiana schools at the beginning of the semester, midway through the semester, and at the end of the semester to determine changes in the ELLs' vocabulary and syntactic development in correlation with content knowledge (see the Appendix for rubrics for each of the case study reports).

Each student completed a report on each of these observations, culminating with a final report that discussed the observed changes and proposed a plan for future instruction of this ELL based on the assessment of the ELL's language development. Students related their observations to current research and assigned readings. To complete this field-based experience, students were situated in an approved elementary or secondary classroom. This field-based experience and work constituted 30% of the final grade for this course. Each student was expected to maintain a log of his or her activities during the field-based experience. Students were required to demonstrate the following criteria: (a) the successful integration of English language development techniques into teaching and learning; and (b) evidence of solid understanding of English language development issues in work with ELLs.

Students listened to previously recorded audio feedback while reading the text to what it referred. While listening to audio feedback on a case study report, students were able to understand their writing gaps and build the link between revisions of the case study report. Students used audio feedback three times during the semester for three case studies. Each feedback audio recording was approximately 2 minutes in length.

To reveal the role of embedded audio feedback in assessment, students were asked to provide their perceptions about embedded audio feedback. The majority of students found embedded audio feedback helpful and easier to understand because of clarity and details compared with written comments, which were hard to interpret. They liked embedded audio feedback because of the instructor's voice, personalization, and feeling of involvement. The students agreed that embedded audio feedback helped them understand what corrections they needed to make in their work. One of the students said that in previous online courses he or she has received grades but not an explanation other than the number of points per section on a rubric. Finally, the students enjoyed the embedded audio feedback and appreciated the instructor's comments on their assignment. For example, one of the students said, "I really enjoyed the oral comments that Dr. O. gave on assignments. They were insightful and helped me as I progressed throughout the course," or "I really appreciate the instructor's creativity in giving feedback. Audio feedback is an ingenious way to offer productive comments on our work."

Examples of Embedded Audio Feedback and Students' Reports

In this online course, audio feedback had embedded comments with instructional voice to provide in-depth and detailed instructional comments. First, the audio feedback was recorded using the free recording software Audacity (*www.audacity.com*). If it was needed, some necessary edits or revisions were made, for example, repetitions or long pauses during recording. Then, the file was saved as a .wav file to embed it to the Adobe Acrobat Professional document. To embed the audio feedback to the Adobe Professional document, the instructor filled out the grading rubric in a Microsoft Office Word document and saved as a PDF file.

As it was mentioned before, students submitted their case study report 1 at the beginning of the fall semester. The instructor provided audio feedback along with brief written comments explaining students' gaps and how they could be improved. This approach helped students find their gaps quickly and understand what they needed to improve for case study report 2. For example, one of the students submitted a short description of an ELL without support from literature and the instructor pointed out the gap in a brief written comment in the document. Then, the instructor recorded audio feedback with more in-depth explanation of how the student could improve case study 2 by adding more quotes from the teacher and the ELL he was observing. One of the requirements of this case study assignment was to incorporate actual classroom examples in the form of quotes from teacher and student to further explain the observations. The example of the part about an ELL student description in case study 1 is below.

EXAMPLE 1A. CASE STUDY 1, STUDENT A

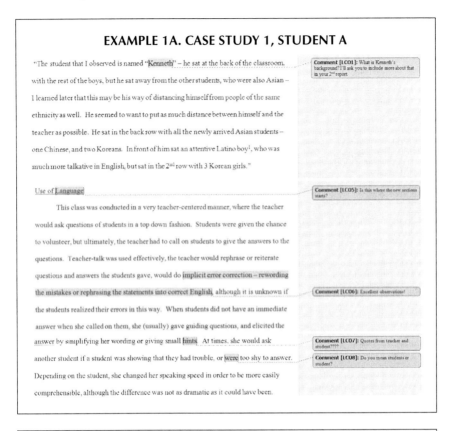

"The student that I observed is named "Kenneth" – he sat at the back of the classroom,

> **Comment [LCO1]:** What is Kenneth's background? I'll ask you to include more about that in your 2nd report

with the rest of the boys, but he sat away from the other students, who were also Asian –

I learned later that this may be his way of distancing himself from people of the same

ethnicity as well. He seemed to want to put as much distance between himself and the

teacher as possible. He sat in the back row with all the newly arrived Asian students –

one Chinese, and two Koreans. In front of him sat an attentive Latino boy[1], who was

much more talkative in English, but sat in the 2nd row with 3 Korean girls."

Use of Language

> **Comment [LCO5]:** Is this where the new section starts?

 This class was conducted in a very teacher-centered manner, where the teacher

would ask questions of students in a top down fashion. Students were given the chance

to volunteer, but ultimately, the teacher had to call on students to give the answers to the

questions. Teacher-talk was used effectively, the teacher would rephrase or reiterate

questions and answers the students gave, would do implicit error correction – rewording

the mistakes or rephrasing the statements into correct English, although it is unknown if

> **Comment [LCO6]:** Excellent observations!

the students realized their errors in this way. When students did not have an immediate

answer when she called on them, she (usually) gave guiding questions, and elicited the

answer by simplifying her wording or giving small hints. At times, she would ask

> **Comment [LCO7]:** Quotes from teacher and student????

another student if a student was showing that they had trouble, or were too shy to answer.

> **Comment [LCO8]:** Do you mean students or student?

Depending on the student, she changed her speaking speed in order to be more easily

comprehensible, although the difference was not as dramatic as it could have been.

EXAMPLE 1B. INSTRUCTIONAL EMBEDDED AUDIO FEEDBACK SCRIPT, CASE STUDY 1, STUDENT A

Hi Student A: I wanted to give you some feedback on your case study report #1. I thought that you did a wonderful job explaining the use of language of the ELL in the classroom, and you were able to pick up on some really interesting things about this ELL's identity. And I agree with you that you know, there is something really interesting going on with this ELL. I know that it will be an interesting case to continue to follow. It seems that he is really struggling with his identity. I can really see that you picked that up. That is not really easy to do, especially in a first observation like this one. So you know I am really glad that you are picking those things up. And also I think you did a very good job in your explanations in terms of the use of language. That was really good.

 I wanted to give you some feedback also on things for you to improve. First thing is in regard to your report itself. Please make sure that you include those sections that are on the assignment sheet: classroom, context, use of language, reflections and connections to readings. So, those sections really help when you are writing your report and also when we are reading your report because we want to make sure that you include everything that is required in the assignment.

Another thing that I wanted to mention was, well, like I said before, you did a great job in explaining what was going in the classroom, how the teacher was using language, but you didn't provide any quotes, actual quotes from the teacher or the student. And that is very, very important for that particular case, so for all of them for one, two, and three. So, you need to include not only what you observed and a discussion about what you observed, but you also need to provide evidence for what it is that you observed. In other words, if you say that was an implicit error correction, excellent, picking that up, was excellent. If you can provide an example of an actual quote that will strengthen your observation and that is the expectation for the assignment.

So when you do case study 2, please make sure that you include more quotes and you also discuss them in the way you were doing, like I said you did a great job in that.

I have added some more written comments on your report, so you can just look at those comments and let me know if you have any questions. I really enjoyed reading your report. I am looking forward to reading the next one.

Then, student A submitted case study report 2 describing the same ELL after listening to embedded audio feedback provided on case study report 1. The example of case study report 2 is below.

EXAMPLE 1C. CASE STUDY 2, STUDENT A

The ELL I am focusing on, Kenneth, sat in back, in his usual seat when the class started, and I think he would have liked to stay there, but the teacher specifically told him to come up to the 3rd row, saying to him "come and sit here! Can't have you talk!" He was sitting next to another Chinese student, Shao, so it is unknown if he usually talks to his friend in English or in Chinese, but it seems that Kenneth is prone to goofing off in this class, and Mrs. Streisand is trying to assert more control over him.

Kenneth's L1 is Chinese, but he has spent a lot of time in America, upwards of 6 years, and lived in South Dakota. In the previous class, Kenneth denied that he spoke Chinese at all, when prompted to speak with the new Chinese student, Shao, but this seems to be a coping mechanism for Kenneth – he does not let *anyone* know just how knowledgeable he is in English or in Chinese – Mrs. Streisand mentions that Shao, the new Chinese student, mentions that Kenneth knows more Chinese than he lets on, and knows more English than he admits to; this may be a way of avoiding responsibility in class, and giving him more freedom to goof off in classes. This seems to be the opposite of the ELL we saw in Valdes' research, Lillian, who often sat back and observed, but never accepted help, saying "I know" when students tried to help her. Kenneth seems to be less prideful, and doesn't mind "playing dumb" as long as it gives him less responsibilities in class. "

> Comment [LCO1]: excellent connection to the reading here

Use of Language

　　Much like the last class I had observed, the class started in a teacher-centered fashion, and Mrs. Streisand was giving open-ended questions in order to confirm students' knowledge about what they had been studying. She gives students the opportunity to volunteer answers, but the students tend to wait for her to call on specific students by name. Students that seem eager to volunteer answers make eye contact, or make themselves available to be called on by facing the teacher or raising their hands, but it does not seem like spontaneous bursts of language is encouraged in the classroom.

　　It seems the only language that is used in this classroom outside of the group work is direct responses to the questions, for example: "Who is Braham Bones?", and a student replies quietly with "rival", and the teacher recasts and expands upon the student's answer: "it's Ichabod's rival, is that what you said?". Even after the teacher has

> Comment [LCO4]: Good quotes

initiated the group work, she goes around to each group, and continues to ask them open ended questions, checking their vocabulary knowledge. This is how Mrs. Streisand can focus her attention on smaller groups, in a more informal interactive style, and give students one-on-one attention, in the same way she did during the previous observation. When the students were doing group work however, she used more teacher-talk than she had talking one-on-one. The teacher still uses teacher talk to elicit information from the students, asking open-ended questions like "What's a mooch?" and guiding questions like "What's a flirt? Is that what Katrina was? How did she act?", and focusing on a single group of students to give the answer, although she gives the question to the class at large raising her head and voice, and then repeating the question to the group of students that she wants to answer the question. Many students talk together to discuss what each of the answers are, through a lot of guessing and trial and error. The teacher does seem to work harder to get each group to interact and work together equally, and sometimes resorts to threats of "You're going to get a zero for participation if you don't help!" to persuade the students to continue working on their project and to volunteer answers to her questions.

The description in case study report 2 is more detailed with great connections to the weekly readings. It is clear that student A now understands how to describe the ELL, which helped improve his second report. The student was able to build connections between what was observed in the classroom with what was discussed and read in the course. Student A understood the expectations of the assignment better after the audio feedback.

Another example provided below shows that student B did not provide enough support and evidence for an ELL student description. It should be noted that providing a few quotes in the description of the ELL was the main problem among students in their first case study reports. One of the typical examples of using a few quotes in the first report to support statements is in example 2a of student B below. Example 2b is the script of instructional embedded audio feedback provided for case study 1 for student B. Example 2c shows improvements in case study 2.

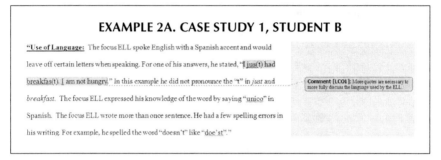

EXAMPLE 2A. CASE STUDY 1, STUDENT B

"<u>Use of Language:</u> The focus ELL spoke English with a Spanish accent and would leave off certain letters when speaking. For one of his answers, he stated, "I jus(t) had breakfas(t). I am not hungry." In this example he did not pronounce the "t" in *just* and *breakfast.* The focus ELL expressed his knowledge of the word by saying "unico" in Spanish. The focus ELL wrote more than once sentence. He had a few spelling errors in his writing. For example, he spelled the word "doesn't" like "doe'st"."

Comment [LCO1]: More quotes are necessary to more fully discuss the language used by the ELL.

EXAMPLE 2B. INSTRUCTIONAL EMBEDDED AUDIO FEEDBACK SCRIPT, CASE STUDY 1, STUDENT B

Hi Student B: I wanted to give you some feedback on your case study 1. I thought you did a good job in explaining the setup and the classroom context very well. In terms of your use of language I thought that that section provided some basic information about what was happening in the class. But it didn't really address some of the guiding questions that I had on the assignment sheet. So I would advise you to go back to the assignment sheet and look very carefully at those guiding questions, so that you could also provide some more examples of the language that the teacher used in the classroom instead of just describing the language, but more including maybe some quotes from the teacher to support what you were stating there.

The same for the English language learner, so I felt that your, that you have a focus ELL and you provided one quote from that focus ELL, so if you could provide at least maybe a couple more to show your points, to really explain how he was using language, and even if he wasn't using a lot of language, then the teacher was using most of the language so you know, kind of speculate, on why that was in that particular section, in the use of language section.

Under reflections and connections to readings I think you did a good job selecting quotes, quotes and points from Menyuk and Brisk. I would also advise you to whenever you include a quote you need to introduce it and comment on it. So, you commented on the quote but you didn't really introduce it, so that is going to be very important and especially pay attention to that for your next case study.

I have a lot of things to tell, except that perhaps in the section the use of language like I said you can incorporate more quotes and go a little bit more in-depth on the use of language by the teacher and the ELL, so that your case study will be richer.

And for the reflections and connections to readings for you to include again maybe a connection between what you observed and the readings, but also make sure that you introduce different quotes that you are using. And I felt that for your particular case, one aspect discussed in Menyuk and Brisk, the concept of code-switching, would have been really important to be discussed in that section. So you know be a little more careful in what you are selecting from the readings. So far what you selected was okay, I just felt that maybe code-switching could be included. So I think that is about it. If you have any questions you can always email me. Just let me know, and I am looking forward to reading your second case study report. Okay?

EXAMPLE 2C. CASE STUDY 2, STUDENT B

Use of Language: During the lesson, the teacher used simplified English when giving instructions and avoided idiomatic expressions. The teacher spoke slower during instruction than she did during informal interactions. She gave short and clear instructions. For example, she said, "In your red books, turn to page 98." The teacher asked the class, "What should you do before reading a story?" The teacher then said, "You should preview the story." The teacher also used visuals during the lesson. For example when the class was previewing the story, the teacher projected the story on the Smart Board and pointed at the pictures. The teacher used a lot of Spanish during this lesson since she had received a brand new student from Mexico two days before. For example, when the teacher explained to the class that they were going to preview the story by looking at the pictures, the teacher told the new student, "mira a las photos en la cuenta." The teacher asked the student if the word for story was "cuenta," and the student corrected her by saying that it was "cuento". During the lesson, the teacher often tried to explain some concepts in Spanish and asked other students in the class to translate for the new student. The teacher asked, "What's a folktale?" The students did not answer. The teacher explained, "A folktale is a story that is told over and over again." The teacher then asked the class, "Do you know any folktales?" The instructional assistant mentioned the story of "La llorona," and the teacher asked in Spanish if the students knew the folktale. The teacher asked, "Sabes el cuento la llorona?" The students talked amongst themselves to recall the story, often code-switching from English to Spanish. One student briefly explained the story to the teacher in English. After the explanation, the teacher asked the focus ELL to retell the folktale to the new student in Spanish, and the focus ELL translated the story for the student. The students clearly felt comfortable being

Comment [LCO1]: Good quotes throughout

able to code-switch in class. During the lesson, the teacher asked students to write down a question that they had about the first half of the story. The focus ELL had a few errors with syntax. The focus ELL wrote, "What in the pot". When I saw what he wrote, I asked him to read what he wrote aloud for me. He then noticed his error and self-corrected it to read, "What's in the pot", but did not include the question mark. The focus ELL also wrote, "Why he is taken it to the tall tree?" The student made an error in syntax when he wrote, "Why he is" instead of "Why is he". The student also had some issues with phonology because he wrote the word "taken" for "taking". For the last part of the story, the focus ELL was asked to read aloud. The focus student said, "He had in the shadows" instead of "He hid in the shadows." During the question and answer period, the same two students were answering questions in the class, and the focus ELL did not appear to be engaged in that part of the lesson. The teacher then asked for students to write down why they thought that the father was upset with his son. The focus ELL wrote, "He does't shar his big round pot to the people he is a selfish. It broke into peases." When the teacher talked about the word "selfish", another student code-switched to "egoista".

Student B had a problem of adding quotes to explain her observed ELL's use of language in the classroom in her first report. The instructor mentioned this gap in audio feedback with detailed explanation of how it could be improved for her second report. Case study report 2 shows that student B integrated quotes to support statements on how an ELL used language. Moreover, student B was able to integrate quotes in a way that it was easy to understand and see how language development could occur.

To summarize, it should be noted that comparing both reports helped instructors assess students' progress in the course. Providing more detailed feedback via audio helped generate thorough explanations to the most challenging issues students experienced in their first reports, such as incorporating more descriptions or more quotes to support their statements about their observed ELL's language development.

INSTRUCTOR'S PERSPECTIVES
ABOUT THE USE OF AUDIO FEEDBACK

The course instructor, Luciana, was excited to incorporate embedded audio feedback in this online course, as she had read and learned about its benefits in Larisa's dissertation study (Olesova, 2012). Therefore, when Larisa became Luciana's teaching assistant for this course, they both agreed that incorporating embedded audio feedback into the course would be a great idea. Although there were some perceived disadvantages, Luciana did not realize all of the benefits of audio feedback until she actually started to use it.

The main disadvantage of audio feedback was on the students' side. Some of the students were not able to open the embedded audio file because they did not realize that they had to double-click on the audio icon in the PDF. Once this got resolved, they were able to open it and thought the audio feedback was beneficial. This is just something to keep in mind as instructors start using embedded audio feedback with their students.

Using audio feedback has many advantages. Luciana felt more connected to the students. Because audio feedback requires the use of the instructor's voice to provide feedback, she felt that she was speaking directly to her students. This created an opportunity that is often not experienced in asynchronous online courses, unless the instructor uses synchronous chats and other resources to interact with students. Even though the feedback was recorded in advance and embedded into a PDF that was made available to students, she felt that she was more connected to them individually. The use of embedded audio feedback also seemed to increase her social presence in the online environment (see Richardson & Swan, 2003, for the importance of social presence in online environments).

Audio feedback took less time to create versus written feedback alone. Luciana often took double the amount of time to compose written feedback to students compared to how much time it took her to provide audio feedback. This enabled her to spend more time on other aspects of the course, which were beneficial for students as well. The process of recording the audio feedback was easy and fun to do. Sometimes providing feedback on student work can be an arduous task, but recording the feedback was not difficult.

Luciana also felt that she could see more improvements to students' reports because it seemed like students were able to understand her comments and suggestions better. In addition, she received many positive comments about the use of audio feedback in end-of-course evaluations, which supported the evidence that we already had of its benefits.

DISCUSSION AND RECOMMENDATIONS

This pedagogical practice of using embedded audio feedback on a key assessment in an asynchronous online course showed its effectiveness. Students who received embedded audio feedback were able to improve their case study reports (i.e., changes in the ELL's vocabulary and syntactic development in correlation with content knowledge). The instructor provided embedded audio feedback at the beginning of the semester on the first report, in the middle of the semester on the second report, and at the end of the semester on the final report. It was observed that each student who received individualized audio feedback was able to complete a report on classroom observations, to discuss the observed changes, and to propose a plan for future instruction of this ELL based on the assessment of the ELL's language development.

In addition, the instructor also observed that students were able to incorporate weekly readings into their second and final reports. They were also able to build the link between the revisions of a draft (Syncox, 2003). Therefore, embedded audio feedback was an effective technique in providing successful assessment; students in this online course were able to understand their writing gaps from audio feedback (Boswood & Dwyer, 1995; Johanson, 1999; Ribchester et al., 2008). In this online course, the instructor expanded on the problem of understanding meaning "from a variety of different angles in the form of models and prompts" (Syncox, 2003).

The following pedagogical implications can be recommended to those who plan to use embedded audio feedback on a key assessment in asynchronous online courses. First, embedded audio feedback can help students understand instructional comments on how to improve writing drafts better compared to written comments. Therefore, instructors are encouraged to provide embedded audio feedback to help students understand where their writing gaps are and how to improve their writing drafts.

The length of audio feedback is important. The audio file size should be small and show whether it is possible to use mono recording. This will allow students to download the file easily when the Internet connection is slow. It is recommended for instructors who intend to provide audio feedback to keep the audio feedback short with direct comments on the major points of the students' writing.

APPENDIX: RUBRICS

RUBRIC FOR CASE STUDY PART 1 AND 2 (10 POINTS/10%)

Criteria	Points Possible	Points Earned
Description of the classroom context is clear and nonjudgmental.	2	
Discussion of ways language is used is detailed, nonjudgmental, and supported by evidence and description.	3	
Direct quotes from participants are used to illustrate important points.	2	
Reflections and connections to readings are relevant and provide evidence of understanding of course material.	2	
Report is well written and complete.	1	
Total Possible:	**10**	**Total Earned:**

RUBRIC FOR CASE STUDY PART 3 (10 POINTS/10%)

Criteria	Points Possible	Points Earned
Description of the classroom context is clear and nonjudgmental.	1	
NEW: Description of focus ELL is complete.	2	
Discussion of ways language is used is detailed, nonjudgmental, and supported by evidence and description.	2	
Direct quotes from participants are used to illustrate important points.	1	
NEW: Observed changes and plan for future instruction of this ELL section identifies relevant changes and plans appropriate instruction for this ELL.	3	
Connections to the readings, activities, and concept maps from the course are relevant and provide evidence of understanding of course material.		
Report is well written and complete.	1	
Total Possible:	**10**	**Total Earned:**

REFERENCES

Anderson, T., Rourke, L., Garrison, D. R., & Archer, W. (2001). Assessing teacher presence in a computer conferencing context. *Journal of Asynchronous Learning Networks, 4*(1), 40–51.

Berner, A., Boswell, W., & Kahan, N. (1996). Using the tape recorder to respond to student writing. In G. Rijlaarsdam, H. van der Bergh, & M. Couzijn (Eds.), *Effective teaching and learning of writing* (pp. 339–357). Amsterdam: Amsterdam University Press.

Biesenbach-Lucas, S. (2003). Asynchronous discussion groups in teacher training classes: Perceptions of native and non-native students. *Journal of Asynchronous Learning Networks, 7*(3), 24–46.

Bonnel, W. (2008). Improving feedback to students in online courses. *Nursing Education Perspectives, 29*(5), 290–294.

Boswood, T., & Dwyer, R. (1995). From marking to feedback: Audio-taped response to student writing. *TESOL Journal, 5*(2), 20–23.

Cifuentes, L., & Shih, Y-C. D. (2001). Teaching and learning online: A collaboration between United States and Taiwanese students. *Journal of Research on Technology in Education, 33*(4), 456–474.

Coleman, V. B. (1972). *A comparison between the relative effectiveness of marginal-inter-linear-terminal commentary and of audio-taped commentary in responding to English composition.* Unpublished doctoral dissertation, University of Pittsburgh.

Gunawardena, C. N., & McIsaac, M. S. (2004). Distance education. In D.H. Jonassen (Ed.), *Handbook of research on educational communications and technology* (pp. 355–395), Mahwah, NJ: Erlbaum.

Huang, S. (2000). A quantitative analysis of audiotaped and written feedback produced for students writing and student' perceptions of the two feedback methods. Taiwan National Science Council, Taipei. (ERIC Document Reproduction Service No. ED448604)

Ice, P. (2008, April). *The impact of asynchronous audio feedback on teaching, social and cognitive presence.* Paper presented at the First International Conference of the Canadian Network for Innovation in Education, Banff, Alberta.

Ice, P., Curtis, R., Phillips, P., & Wells, J. (2007). Using asynchronous audio feedback to enhance teaching presence and students' sense of community. *Journal of Asynchronous Learning Networks, 11*(2), 3–25.

Jelfs, A., & Whitelock, D. (2000). The notion of presence in virtual environments: what makes the environment "real." *British Journal of Educational Technology, 31*(2), 145–153.

Johanson, R. (1999). Rethinking the red ink: Audio-feedback in the ESL writing classroom. Foreign Language Education Program, Texas University, Austin. (ERIC Document Reproduction Service No. ED 467865)

Kelly, P., & Ryan, S. (1983) Using tutor tapes to support the distance learner. *International Council for Distance Education Bulletin, 3,* 1–18.

Kirschner, P.A., van den Brink, H., & Meester, M. (1991). Audiotape feedback for essays in distance education. *Innovative Higher Education, 15*(2), 185–195.

Logan, H. L., Logan, N. S., Fuller, J. L., & Denehy, G. E. (1976). The role of audiotape cassettes in providing student feedback. *Educational Technology, 16*(12), 38–39.

McGrew, J. B. (1969). *An experiment to assess the effectiveness of the dictation machine as an aid to teachers in the evaluations and improvement of student compositions.* Report to Lincoln Public Schools, Lincoln, Nebraska (ERIC Document Reproductive Service No. ED 034776)

Moore, G. E. (1977). *Providing instructional feedback to students in education classes.* West Lafayette, IN: Purdue University. (ERIC Document Reproduction Service No. ED 173309)

Morra, A. M., & Asís, M. I. (2009). The effect of audio and written teacher responses on EFL student revision. *Journal of College Reading and Learning, 39*(2), 68–81.

Nortcliffe, A. L., & Middleton, A. (2007, September) *Audio feedback for the iPod generation.* Paper presented at the International Conference on Engineering Education, Coimbra, Portugal.

Nortcliffe, A. L., & Middleton, A. (2008). A three-year case study of using audio to blend the engineers learning environment. *Engineering Education: Journal of the Higher Education Academy Engineering Subject Centre, 3*(2), 45–57.

Olesova, L. (2013). *Feedback in online course for non-native-English-speaking students.* Newcastle upon Tyne, UK: Cambridge Scholars Publishing.

Olesova, L., Richardson, J., Weasenforth, D., & Meloni, C. (2011). Using asynchronous instructional audio feedback in online environments: A mixed methods study. *Journal of Online Learning and Teaching, 7*(1), 30–42.

Oomen-Early, J., Bold, M., Wiginton, K. L., Gallien, T. L., & Anderson, N. (2008). Using asynchronous audio communication (AAC) in the online classroom: A comparative study. *Journal of Online Learning and Teaching, 4*(3), 267–276.

Quinton, S., & Smallbone, T. (2010). Feeding forward: Using feedback to promote student reflection and learning – a teaching model. *Innovations in Education and Teaching International, 47*(1), 125–135.

Ribchester, C., France, D., & Wakefield, K. (2008). *"It was just like a personal tutorial": Using podcasts to provide assessment feedback.* Paper presented at the annual conference of HE Academy, Harrogate, UK.

Richardson, J. C., & Swan, K.P. (2003). An examination of social presence in online courses in relation to students' perceived learning and satisfaction. *Journal of Asynchronous Learning, 7*(1). Retrieved from http://sloanconsortium.org/jaln/v7n1/examining-social-presence-online-courses-relation-students039-percieved-learning-and-satis.

Rotheram, B. (2007) Using an MP3 recorder to give feedback on student assignments. *Educational Developments, 8*(2), 7–10.

Sipple, S. (2007). Ideas in practice: Developmental writers' attitudes toward audio and written feedback. *Journal of Developmental Education, 30*(3), 22–31.

Swan, K. (2003). Learning effectiveness: What the research tells us. In J. Bourne & J.C. Moore (Eds.), *Elements of quality online education: Practice and direction* (pp. 13–45). Needham, MA: Sloan Consortium.

Syncox, D. (2003). *The effects of audio-taped feedback on ESL graduate student writing.* Retrieved from ProQuest Digital Dissertations. (AAT EC53307)

Tanner, B. (1964). Teacher to disc to student. *English Journal, 53*(5), 362–363.

Zhao, N., & McDougall, D. (2008). Cultural influences on Chinese students' asynchronous online learning in a Canadian university. *Journal of Distance Education, 22*(2), 59–80.

CHAPTER 8

ASSESSMENT STRATEGY FOR SELF-PACED ONLINE LEARNING

Barbara E. Rowan
Pearson North America

Walter D. Way
Pearson North America

INTRODUCTION

Online education is growing at an astronomical rate, which means that online courses must be designed to deliver the same or better quality of education that an on-ground, face-to-face course can deliver. In Taylor, Parker, Lenhart, and Patten's (2011) study, college presidents (77%) reported that their institutions offer online courses with 62% predicting that in 10 years more than half of the textbooks used by undergraduate students will be entirely digital. Survey results showed that one in four college graduates have taken an online course; however, of students who have graduated in the last 10 years, nearly half have taken an online course. Furthermore, among college graduates who have taken an online course, 15% have earned a degree entirely online (Taylor et al., 2011). Online learning is now an integral

Assessment in Online and Blended Learning Environments, pages 143–155
143

component of all mainstream education and training environments. The new education gold standard is access to "high-quality, academically rigorous anywhere/anytime programs" (J. Flores, quoted in Rickard, 2010, p. 1). Thus, quality self-paced online learning is what educational environments seek.

Self-paced online courses are attractive to students, since they are able to start a course on demand, learn in any setting with an Internet connection, and work at their own pace to complete the course. This mode of learning is flexible and allows students to review the material as often as needed. Furthermore, the instruction provided in a self-paced online environment is consistent across students and institutions (eLearners.com, 2012; Malamed, n.d.; Radachy & Powers, 2009). Several studies have found that students prefer the self-paced version of a course, and that performance overall is not different from an instructor-led online course (e.g., Means, Toyama, Murphy, Bakia, & Jones, 2010; Russell, Kleiman, Carey, & Douglas, 2009). Nevertheless, there are a number of challenges with self-paced online courses that stem from the fact that there is no instructor present to lead students through the instructional process. Students who lack motivation, are procrastinators, or need additional academic assistance may not succeed in a self-paced online course (eLearners.com, 2012; Ironsmith, Marva, Harju, & Eppler, 2003; Radachy & Powers, 2009; Rhode, 2009). However, measuring student learning is a particular challenge to this mode of instruction.

For accurate measurement of student learning to occur within any course, but especially within a self-paced online environment, there must be a strong alignment between the course goals and the *learning outcomes*, that is, the explicit learning results that students are expected to demonstrate at the end of significant learning experiences (Spady, 1994). This process gives students what they need for meaningful learning, and gives creators of the content what they need to effectively develop the assessment strategy for the course.

The purpose of this chapter is to share an assessment strategy and technique that was developed specifically for self-paced online courses. The approach includes a variety of formative and summative assessment content that is aligned with explicitly stated learning outcomes and strategically deployed at particular intervals within the course. We illustrate this approach to online assessment in the context of a self-paced, online learning environment developed at Pearson, called *Propero*.

We have divided the chapter into four major sections. In the first section, we provide an overview of *Propero*, which includes a variety of components designed to deliver and support online learning, including lesson presentations, assessments, online tutoring support, and academic advising. Next, we discuss the general challenges with establishing and measuring learning outcomes in online self-paced courses and the specific assessment strategies and practices that have been introduced into *Propero*. The third section describes plans and strategies for using data-mining techniques and data analyses to improve *Propero*, and the larger promise of data analytics to improve online courses. The final section outlines a number of challenges and opportunities for using assessment techniques in online learning courses.

PROPERO

Propero was developed by expanding upon an existing instructor-led online course model. It was designed to be a self-paced version of an already successful, award-winning online course model, *CourseConnect*. The structure of the self-paced online course is essentially the same as the instructor-led version, with a few exceptions. Both the instructor-led and the self-paced courses were built by instructional designers using a backward design approach (Wiggins & McTighe, 2005). The process begins with the development of the course-level learning outcomes, which are written by subject-matter experts and instructional designers specifically for the course being developed. For many of the courses, the course outcomes are then aligned with national standards recognized by professional organizations. Expected learning outcomes specify the specific knowledge, practical skills, attitudes, higher-order thinking skills, and so on, that students are expected to develop, learn, or master during a course (Suskie, 2009). The learning outcomes specify observable and measurable actions on the part of the learner.

The hierarchy of the CourseConnect and *Propero* courses consists of about 8–12 course learning outcomes, written by the subject-matter experts and instructional designers, which are the overarching learning goals for the course. Specific lesson-level learning objectives fall under each course outcome, with each lesson objective relating to one and only one course outcome and to one and only one lesson. Each lesson is chunked into topics, with about three to five topics per lesson. The information within each lesson is segmented into topics based on research on chunking, which states that large amounts of information have to be organized in order for someone to be able to deal with it. Therefore, small, general pieces of knowledge are gradually composed together to form larger, specific pieces of knowledge. Thus, when presenting information in an online course, it is wise to present smaller amounts of information at a time, so a student can then make sense of the information and build up to the larger knowledge that the student is to learn (Mayer, 2011). Each of the previously mentioned lesson objectives are mapped to a topic. The content within the lesson is written to address each lesson objective, which indirectly addresses each of the course outcomes that relate to that lesson. In addition, each lesson contains assessments that measure each lesson objective and course outcome.

The instructional designers who create the courses use many other best practices for designing online courses. For example, the structure of each topic is identical to the other topics, regardless of the course. Students are first presented with an introduction to the topic. The lesson presentation, that is, the presentation that contains the information to be presented to the student within this topic, follows the introduction. Within this lesson presentation, instructional designers ensure that information is presented to students in an appealing way, presenting words and graphics rather than words alone. Graphics and their corresponding text are placed near each other so that students are able to determine what the graphic illustrates. Media is used only when it will help students build more accurate and effective mental models. In fact, well-designed multimedia can promote active cognitive processing even when learners seem to be inactive (Mayer, 2011). At the completion of the lesson presentation, the learner is presented with opportunities to check their understanding, that is, to practice the information just learned in the lesson presentation. Finally, the learner is presented with a review of the topic. Figure 8.1 illustrates the learning design of the CourseConnect and *Propero* online course, and highlights several best

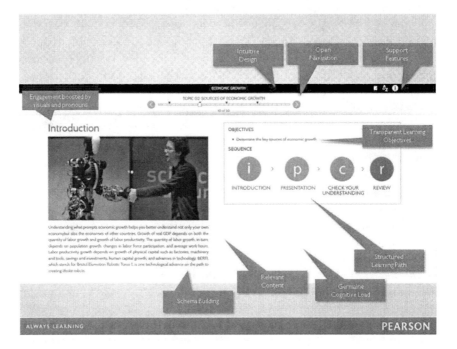

Figure 8.1 The visibility of the learning design used for *Propero* and *CourseConnect*.

practices that have gone into the creation of the instructor-led and self-paced online courses.

There are typically 12 lessons within each instructor-led and self-paced online course, and each lesson contains objectives that map to one and only one course outcome. Each time a student enters a lesson, the student is presented with the option of taking the Study Guide assessment, which is a short "pretest" of sorts that gives information about what the student knows and where the student should spend time studying. The student selects an answer for each item presented and also indicates the confidence level of the answer (*I am sure of this* versus *I don't know*). The study guide assessment can be taken multiple times and only exists to assist the student by providing feedback and a recommended study plan.

This is where the similarities between CourseConnect and *Propero* end. Because *Propero* is an instructor-free course, there is concern about students progressing through the course on their own. Previous studies indicate that students benefit from an instructor, mentor, or facilitator when working online (Glassmeyer, Dibbs, & Jensen, 2011; Radachy & Powers, 2009). For that reason, *Propero* students are offered free tutoring, which is accessible from within the course by following a link. This interaction with the tutors provides contact with someone who can verify that the student is progressing correctly, or can help the student get back on track.

Propero offers students a variety of support services, including academic counseling, referrals to instructors for additional help, and direct intervention when the student is doing poorly or has stopped visiting the course. These services are offered to help combat the higher dropout rate associated with self-paced online learning (eLearners.com, 2012; Radachy & Powers, 2009). In addition, students engaging in a *Propero* course have direct access to the eText, with links that will take the student to the specific section of the text covered by that particular lesson.

CHALLENGES WITH ASSESSMENT IN SELF-PACED ONLINE COURSES

Propero differs from its *CourseConnect* parent in its assessment strategy, as well. Because there is no instructor leading the course, several changes to the way assessment is normally conducted in an online course had to be made for *Propero*. Traditional online courses often include discussion prompts that require students to not only write a response but to also comment on other students' responses. In addition, traditional online courses include projects, papers, and other instructor-graded assignments. In the self-paced online course, there is no instructor to grade these projects or papers, and, since the courses are asynchronous, discussion prompts are of

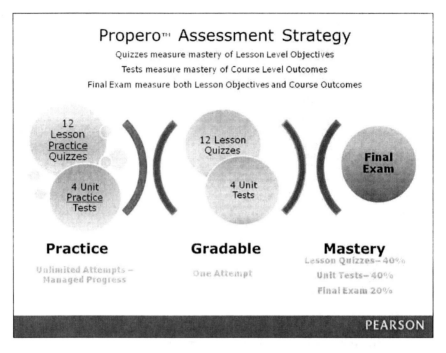

Figure 8.2 *Propero* assessment strategy.

limited value since students enrolled in the course will not likely be on the same lesson given a specific point in time. A new assessment strategy had to be adopted in order to measure student learning in the self-paced, online course. A graphical representation of the assessment strategy utilized in *Propero* is shown in Figure 8.2.

The assessment strategy used with *Propero* courses has been designed to follow best practices outlined in the *Standards for Educational and Psychological Testing* (AERA, APA, & NCME, 1999). These standards provide guidance to testing professionals in a variety of areas, including validity, reliability, test development, and administration. Table 8.1 presents a listing of specific standards that relate to the *Propero* assessment strategy. Specifically, the course structure and the assessment strategy have been developed based on best practices found in the literature. Documentation is in place to outline the assessment strategy and process used for item development. Experts external to the testing program have reviewed the test specifications and the item pool to provide evidence of content validity and to catch any items with bias or inappropriate language or terms. Furthermore, specific instructions are given to the students, and the instructions for item response are clear and understandable. Students are given the opportunity

TABLE 8.1 Standards for Educational and Psychological Testing That Relate to the Development of the Propero Assessment Strategy

Standard 3.1	Tests and testing programs should be developed on a sound scientific basis. Test developers and publishers should compile and document adequate evidence bearing on test development.
Standard 3.4	The procedures used to interpret test scores and, when appropriate, the normative or standardization samples or the criterion used should be documented.
Standard 3.5	When appropriate, relevant experts external to the testing program should review the test specifications. The purpose of the review, the process by which the review is conducted, and the results of the review should be documented. The qualifications, relevant experiences, and demographic characteristics of expert judges should also be documented.
Standard 3.6	The type of items, response formats, scoring procedures, and test administration procedures should be selected based on the purposes of the test, the domain to be measured, and the intended test-takers. To the extent possible, test content should be chosen to ensure that intended inferences from test scores are equally valid for members of different groups of test-takers. The test review process should include empirical analyses and, when appropriate, the use of expert judges to review items and response formats. The qualifications, relevant experiences, and demographic characteristics of expert judges should also be documented.
Standard 3.7	The procedures used to develop, review, and try out items and to select items from the item pool should be documented. If the items were classified into different categories or subtests according to the test specifications, the procedures used for the classification and the appropriateness and accuracy of the classification should be documented.
Standard 3.20	The instructions presented to test-takers should contain sufficient detail so that test-takers can respond to a task in the manner that the test developer intended. When appropriate, sample material, practice or sample questions, criteria for scoring, and a representative item identified with each major area in the test's classification or domain should be provided to the test-takers prior to the administration of the test or included in the testing material as part of the standard administration instructions.
Standard 5.5	Instructions to test-takers should clearly indicate how to make responses. Instructions should also be given in the use of any equipment likely to be unfamiliar to test-takers. Opportunity to practice responding should be given when equipment is involved, unless use of the equipment is being assessed.
Standard 5.6	Reasonable efforts should be made to ensure the integrity of test scores by eliminating opportunities for test-takers to attain scores by fraudulent means.
Standard 6.4	The population for whom the test is intended and the test specifications should be documented. If applicable, the item pool and scale development procedures should be described in the relevant test manuals. If normative data are provided, the norming population should be described in terms of relevant demographic variables, and the year(s) in which the data were collected should be reported.
Standard 7.4	Test developers should strive to identify and eliminate language, symbols, words, phrases, and content that are generally regarded as offensive by members of racial, ethnic, gender, or other groups, except when judged to be necessary for adequate representation of the domain.

to practice no-stakes formative items prior to taking summative assessments for a grade.

In addition, the assessment strategy for *Propero* was developed using best practices for assessment in higher education and in online and self-paced online courses. Documentation of the *Propero* Assessment Development Process is shown in Figure 8.3. Initially in the process, instructional designers and subject-matter experts develop the course-level learning outcomes. Then, the ID and the SME write the lesson-level learning objectives that relate to each course outcome. Once the structure of the course is complete, item writing can begin. Assessment specialists who are also subject-matter experts in the field develop the assessment items used in Propero specifically for each course. Training specific to *Propero* and its assessment strategy is required prior to item development. In all cases, the items written for Propero include immediate feedback to the students. All items written for *Propero* are subjected to a review for assessment and item quality, which is followed by expert reviews for content and bias. The review process is in place to ensure content is correct and to eliminate bias or offensive language. At the completion of the review process, the item pool is finalized and organized into the various assessment components, that is, practice measures or summative measures. Finally, the items written for *Propero* are evaluated by an outside organization to obtain independent documentation in support of content validity. In the world of online course development, time constraints require that assessment items be generated quickly. A benefit of the assessment development process for Propero is that high-quality items can be produced in a short period of time, without jeopardizing the validity of the measures.

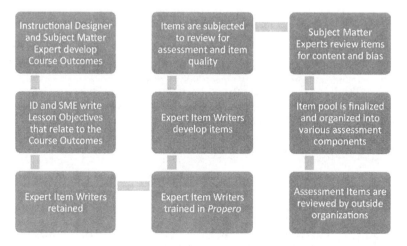

Figure 8.3 *Propero* assessment development process.

The measures used in *Propero* courses consist of items that are created to specifically measure either the lesson objectives or the course outcomes. Even though the items used in *Propero* are multiple-choice, items are developed using scenarios, showing graphs or charts, or using other situations that encourage students to apply the knowledge they have learned to the assessment item rather than just recalling facts. Item development is driven by the course outcomes and the lesson objectives, and students receive immediate item-level feedback on all assessment items within a *Propero* course. Student success on the measures in *Propero* indicates that students do in fact know what they are supposed to know, as outlined in the course description and outcomes.

The assessment strategy for *Propero* includes practice measures with unlimited attempts, quizzes, tests, and a final exam, each designed to specifically measure the lesson objectives or the course outcomes. Specifically, a student will enter the course, read the information from the text, and then work through the lesson presentation (LP), that is, the presentation of information to the student. These lesson presentations are written by subject-matter experts and instructional designers and provide multiple ways for a student to receive the information. The LPs include text, graphics, internal and external links to additional information, videos, graphs, and audio recordings. The LP is designed in a way to engage students in the learning process. Each lesson of the LP is divided into three to five topics, with the idea that presenting smaller chunks of information to students will assist them with learning the overall material presented in the lesson (Mayer, 2011). In addition, literature indicates that students must be reengaged about every 10 minutes in order to keep them focused on the instructional material, which is another benefit to presenting the information contained in the lesson presentation in smaller chunks (Brigham Young University Center for Teaching and Learning, n.d.). Within each topic, several Check Your Understanding (CYU) items are presented to the student. These are no-stakes practice opportunities for the student to use to determine knowledge retention at that point. These items can be multiple-choice, true/false, short answer, or matching, and all are auto-graded to provide immediate feedback to the student. The student can, based on the CYU scores, return to the topic for review or move on to the next topic. A screen capture of an LP from a Propero course can be found in Figure 8.4.

Once a student completes the LP for a lesson, the student is presented with a Quiz Practice for that lesson. This is an additional no-stakes opportunity for the student to determine knowledge of the material prior to taking higher-stakes, summative assessments. This Quiz Practice can be taken multiple times and students receive immediate feedback on each item; however, students are required to achieve a minimum score before going

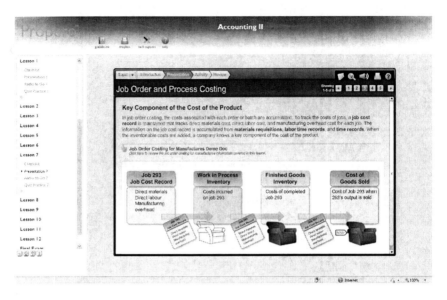

Figure 8.4   Screen capture from within *Propero* Accounting II course.

on to the higher-stakes assessments. Once the minimum score is reached, a student is permitted to take the Lesson Quiz, which is a graded assessment. This summative assessment contains items written to measure the lesson objectives covered by that particular lesson. Students know immediately how they performed on the Lesson Quiz.

Throughout the course at regular intervals, the student is required to take formative Test Practice assessments and summative tests. These formative and summative items are written to measure the course outcomes, thus providing measurement at the overall course level. As with the Quiz Practice, a student must achieve a minimum score on the Test Practice prior to being permitted to take the test for that section of the course. The grade earned on the test goes into the student's gradebook record. At the end of the course, the student will take a summative final exam comprised of items from the lesson level and the course level. Students receive immediate item-level feedback on all assessments within the *Propero* course.

The item pools for *Propero* are large enough to allow students formative opportunities to test their knowledge without compromising the pools used for summative assessment purposes. That is, the items in the formative quiz practice pools and the test practice pools are developed separately from those used for summative quizzes and tests. The items created for the practice measures are written following all guidelines and best practices of all item-writing in *Propero*. These practice items do not look any different than their summative assessment item counterparts. The final exam pulls items from the quiz and test summative pools, but not the formative pools. As item security is a concern for all online courses, several security features are present within *Propero*. All quizzes, tests, and final exams are kept secure. The item pools are large, and no one has access to the full item pools that are part of a *Propero* course. All assessments are timed in order to further preserve item security. In addition, during the summative assessments, the student's computer locks down automatically to prevent the student from accessing the course or the Internet for information related to the items.

The Use of Data for the Improvement of *Propero*

Data collection is important to the future of self-paced courses, and specifically for the future of *Propero*. Initial data collection has focused on student assessment results and persistence. Preliminary analyses indicate that students overall are proceeding successfully through the *Propero* courses. Among the first cohort of 73 students across all *Propero* courses offered, 20 students are still progressing, 38 have successfully completed a course with a 70% or higher cumulative percent earned, and 15 students have withdrawn from a course for various reasons. Of the 15 students withdrawing from a course, only three withdrew because they were failing the course, while eight withdrew for other reasons, including not being prepared for the level of the course, a dislike for or the inability to master the self-paced environment, or not being aware of the time it would take to complete the course. Four of these 15 students registered for a *Propero* course but never entered or accessed the course. These students were withdrawn from the course by the *Propero* administration. The median percent earned for the 38 students completing a *Propero* course was 81%. The median number of days to complete a course was 74.5 days, and students spent an average of 46 hours within the online course itself. Future research will be carried out to evaluate the *Propero* assessment strategy as an alternate to those strategies used in on-ground and instructor-led online courses. Additional analyses will ensure that only the best item pool is being used for measuring student learning and that the item pool is measuring what it claims to measure. Preliminary evaluation is promising; however, the numbers are far too small for a proper item analysis. Therefore, future plans with *Propero* assessments include analyses of student performance to document the quality of the items and assessments, and continued development to improve and replenish the item pools.

FUTURE DEVELOPMENTS AND RESEARCH

The self-paced online course is only one possible use for the *Propero* model presented in this chapter. In the future, this *Propero* self-paced model may also be used in other environments, even with instructor-facilitated courses. As technology advances, more sophisticated but still auto-graded assessment items will be used in *Propero* courses. Pearson plans to continue a larger global initiative of sharing assets from other groups. This would augment the items used in *Propero*, as well as provide enhancements to the course itself. Future research into the assessment strategy of *Propero*, the training given to the expert item writers, and the extensive review of the item pools will strengthen this self-paced online learning opportunity for students. The research results will inform the future direction of *Propero*.

CONCLUSION

The world of education is changing, and quality self-paced online instruction is a desired commodity. However, the assessment strategy used in a self-paced online course must differ from that used within the traditional online course. *Propero* is an effective self-paced online course option for students, one that has been positively evaluated by outside organizations. The assessment strategy used in *Propero* includes formative material to keep students engaged in the course and motivated to finish while also providing summative measures of student learning. Additional services are provided to *Propero* students, including tutoring, counseling, and direct intervention, in an attempt to assist students through the learning process. Furthermore, the assessment strategy presented for *Propero* would be affected for other online courses, even though led by an instructor. Additional research on the assessment strategy developed for self-paced online courses will drive its possible uses in the future.

REFERENCES

AERA, APA, & NCME. (1999). *Standards for educational and psychological testing.* Washington, DC: American Educational Research Association.

Brigham Young University Center for Teaching and Learning. (n.d.). *Helping the brain to learn.* Retrieved from http://ctl.byu.edu/teaching-tips/helping-brain-learn.

eLearners.com. (2012). *Self-paced education–Self-paced online courses.* Retrieved from http://www.elearners.com/online-education-resources/online-learning/self-paced-education.

Glassmeyer, D. M, Dibbs, R. A., & Jensen, R. T. (2011). Determining utility of formative assessment through virtual community: Perspectives of online graduate students. *Quarterly Review of Distance Education, 12*, 23–35.

Ironsmith, M, Marva, J., Harju, V., Eppler, M. (2003). Motivation and performance in college students enrolled in self-paced versus lecture-format remedial mathematics courses. *Journal of Instructional Psychology, 30*. Retrieved from http://freepatentsonline.com/article/Journal-Instructional-Psychology/112686161.html.

Malamed, C. (n.d.). Group or self-paced instruction? The eLearning Coach, Retrieved from http://theelearningcoach.com/elearning_design/group-or-self-paced-instruction/.

Mayer, R. E. (2011). *Applying the science of learning*. Boston, MA: Pearson Education.

Means, B., Toyama, Y., Murphy, R. Bakia, M., & Jones, K. (2010). *Evaluation of evidence-based practices in online learning: A meta-analysis and review of online learning studies*. Washington, DC: U.S. Department of Education. Retrieved from http://www2.ed.gov/rschstat/eval/tech/evidence-based-practices/finalreport.pdf.

Radachy, J., & Powers, C. E. (2009). Bridging the gap between facilitated and non-facilited online courses. *Learning Solutions Magazine*. Retrieved from http://www.learningsolutionsmag.com/articles/36/bridging-the-gap-between-facilitated-and-non-facilitated-online-courses.

Rhode, J. F. (2009). Interaction equivalency in self-paced online learning environments: An exploration of learner preferences. *International Review of Research in Open and Distance Learning*. Retrieved from http://www.irrodl.org/index.php/irrodl/article/view/603/1178.

Rickard, W. (2010). *The efficacy (and inevitability) of online learning in higher education*. Retrieved from http://www.pearsonlearningsolutions.com/assets/downloads/white-papers/Online%20Learning%20Whitepaper.pdf.

Russell, M. Kleiman, G. Carey, R., & Douglas, J. (2009). Comparing self-paced and cohort-based online courses for teachers. *Journal of Research on Technology in Education, 41*, 443–466.

Spady, W. (1994). *Outcomes based education: Critical issues and answers*. Arlington, VA: American Association of School Administration.

Suskie, L. (2009). *Assessing student learning: A common sense guide* (2nd ed.). San Francisco, CA: Jossey-Bass.

Taylor, P., Parker, K., Lenhart, A., & Patten, E. (2011). The digital revolution and higher education: College presidents, public differ on value of online learning. Retrieved from http://www.pewsocialtrends.org/2011/08/28/the-digital-revolution-and-higher-education.

Wiggins, G. P., & McTighe, J. (2005). *Understanding by design* (2nd ed.). Alexandria, VA: Association for Supervision and Curriculum Development.

SECTION II

BLENDED LEARNING AND ASSESSMENT

CHAPTER 9

STUDENT ASSESSMENT IN A BLENDED LEARNING ENVIRONMENT

A Triad Approach

Norman Vaughan
Mount Royal University, Canada

INTRODUCTION

The idea of blending different learning experiences has been in existence ever since humans started thinking about teaching (Williams, 2003). What has recently brought this term into the limelight is the infusion of Web-based technologies into the learning and teaching process (Allen & Seaman, 2010; Clark, 2003). These technologies have created new opportunities for students to interact with their peers, teachers, and content.

Blended learning is often defined as the combination of face-to-face and online learning (Sharpe, Benfield, Roberts, & Francis, 2006; Williams, 2002). Ron Bleed, the former Vice Chancellor of Information Technologies at Maricopa College, argues that this is not a sufficient definition for blended learning as it simply implies "bolting" technology onto a traditional course, using technology

Assessment in Online and Blended Learning Environments, pages 159–186
Copyright © 2015 by Information Age Publishing

as an add-on to teach a difficult concept or adding supplemental information. He suggests that instead, blended learning should be viewed as an opportunity to redesign the way that courses are developed, scheduled, and delivered through a combination of physical and virtual instruction, "bricks and clicks" (Bleed, 2001). The goal of this redesigned approach to education should be to join the best features of in-class teaching with the best features of online learning to promote active, self-directed learning opportunities for students with added flexibility (Garnham & Kaleta, 2002; Littlejohn & Pegler, 2007; Norberg, Dziuban, Moskol, 2011). This sentiment is echoed by Garrison and Vaughan (2008) who state that "blended learning is the organic integration of thoughtfully selected and complementary face-to-face and online approaches and technologies" (p. 148). A survey of e-learning activity by Arabasz, Boggs, and Baker (2003) found that 80 percent of all higher education institutions and 93 percent of doctoral institutions offer hybrid or blended learning courses.

Most of the recent definitions for blended courses indicate that this approach to learning offers potential for improving the manner in which we deal with content, social interaction, reflection, higher-order thinking and problem solving, collaborative learning, and more authentic assessment in higher education (Graham, 2006; Mayadas & Picciano, 2007; Norberg et al., 2011). Dziuban and Moskal (2013) further suggest that "blended learning has become an evolving, responsive, and dynamic process that in many respects is organic, defying all attempts at universal definition" (p. 4). For the purpose of this research study, blended learning is defined as the intentional integration of face-to-face and online learning experiences through the use of digital technologies (Figure 9.1).

There has also been a shift in the way teachers and researchers think about student learning in higher education over the last two decades. Instead of characterizing learning as an acquisition process based on teacher transmission, it is now more commonly conceptualized as a process of students actively constructing their own knowledge and skills (Barr & Tagg, 1995; DeCorte, 1996). Students interact with subject concepts, transforming

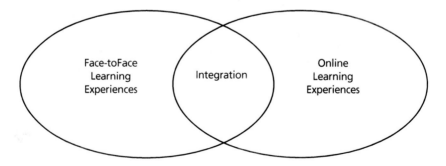

Figure 9.1   Campus-based blended learning approach.

and discussing them with others, in order to internalize meaning and make connections with what they already know. Terms like "learning-centered," which have entered the vocabulary of higher education, are one reflection of this new way of thinking. Even though there is disagreement over the precise definition of a learning-centered approach, the core assumptions are "active engagement in learning and learner responsibility for the management of learning" (Lea, Stephenson, & Troy, 2003, p. 323).

Despite this shift in conceptions of teaching and learning, a parallel shift in relation to assessment and feedback has been slower to emerge. In higher education, the assessment process is still largely controlled by and seen as the responsibility of teachers; and feedback is still generally conceptualized as a transmission process, even though some educational researchers have challenged this viewpoint (Sadler, 1998; Boud, 2000; Yorke, 2003). Teachers "transmit" feedback messages to students about what is right and wrong in their academic coursework, about its strengths and weaknesses, and students use this information to make subsequent improvements.

There are a number of problems with this transmission view of assessment and feedback. First, if the assessment process is exclusively in the hands of teachers, then it is difficult to see how students can become empowered and develop the self-regulation skills needed to prepare them for learning outside higher education institutions and throughout life (Boud, 2000). Second, there is an assumption that when teachers transmit feedback information to students these messages are easily decoded and translated into action. Yet, there is strong evidence that feedback messages are often complex and difficult to decipher, and that students require opportunities to actively construct an understanding of them (e.g., through discussion) before they can be used to regulate performance (Ivanic, Clark, & Rimmershaw, 2000; Higgins, Hartley, & Skelton, 2001). Third, viewing feedback as a cognitive process involving only transfer of information ignores the way feedback interacts with motivation and beliefs. Research shows that feedback both regulates and is regulated by motivational beliefs. For example, external feedback has been shown to influence how students feel about themselves (positively or negatively) and what and how they learn (Dweck, 1999). Fourth, as a result of this transmission view of assessment, the workload of teachers in higher education increases year by year as student numbers and class sizes become larger. One way of addressing this issue is to re-examine the nature of assessment feedback and who provides it (e.g., self, peer, and teacher), in relation to its effectiveness in supporting learning processes.

Self-Assessment

Alverno College (2006) defines self-assessment feedback as "the ability of students to observe, analyze, and judge their own performances on the basis of criteria and to determine how they can improve it" (p. 1). Akyol and Garrison (2011) have recently demonstrated how this notion of self-regulated learning or metacognition "in a blended course is a collaborative process where internal and external conditions are being constantly assessed" (p. 184). In addition, they have described three dimensions of metacognition, which involve the knowledge, monitoring, and regulation of cognition. The knowledge of cognition refers to awareness of self as a learner and includes entering knowledge and motivation associated with the inquiry process, academic discipline, and expectancies. The monitoring of the cognition dimension implies the awareness and willingness to reflect upon the learning process. And, the regulation of metacognition focuses on the action dimension of the learning experience. It involves the employment of strategies to achieve meaningful learning outcomes.

Two major criticisms of self-assessment in higher education are that students do not possess the necessary skills and experience to properly assess themselves and thus, this form of assessment is unreliable and simply leads to grade inflation (Rust, 2002). Conversely, others suggest that self-assessment is a key process for helping students to reflect, understand, and take action and responsibility for their learning (Brown, 2004).

Peer Assessment

According to the Foundation Coalition (2002), "peer assessment allows students to assess other students (their peers) in a course. Peer assessment can also provide data that might be used in assigning individual grades for team assignments" (p. 1). As French moralist and essayist Joseph Joubert attributed with the quote "to teach is to learn twice," in an effective blended course, all participants are both learners and teachers. The term "teaching" rather than "teacher" presence implies that everyone in the course is responsible for providing input on the design, facilitation, and direction of the teaching process.

A number of concerns have been raised about this assessment approach including students' lack of confidence in the process, their ability to provide meaningful feedback, and pressure from peers to provide positive feedback and grades (Langan & Wheater, 2003). These issues are countered by those who emphasize that peer assessment provides students with richer and more authentic opportunities to learn from their peers (e.g., view and critique each other's work) as well as potentially reducing teacher workload (Boud, 2007).

Teacher Assessment

Teacher assessment practices in higher education are often limited to high-stakes summative assessment activities such as midterm and final examinations

(Boud, 2000). The role of a teacher in a blended course is to provide ongoing and meaningful assessment feedback in order to help students develop the necessary metacognitive skills and strategies to take responsibility for their learning.

Thus, teachers in a blended course should place a greater emphasis on formative assessment practices (Alberta Assessment Consortium, 2002; American Association of Higher Education and Accreditation, 1996; Gibbs, 2006; Gibbs & Simpson, 2004; Gorsky, Caspi, & Trumper, 2006). Pask's (1976) conversation theory of learning suggests that learning takes place through our intrapersonal (inner voice) and interpersonal (external voice with others) conversations and that assessment feedback helps shape and regulate this dialogue in higher education courses. Nicol and Macfarlane-Dick (2006) have developed seven principles of good assessment feedback based on the work of Pask. Good feedback:

- Helps clarify what good performance is (goals, criteria, standards)
- Facilitates the development of self-assessment and reflection in learning
- Delivers high-quality information to students about their learning
- Encourages teacher and peer dialogue around learning
- Encourages positive motivational beliefs and self-esteem
- Provides opportunities to close the gap between current and desired performance
- Provides information to teachers that can be used to help shape teaching

A blended approach to learning combined with the use of collaborative digital technologies such as blogs, wikis, and other social networking applications in higher education can provide an opportunity to reinforce these principles of good assessment feedback. The term "Web 2.0" was coined by Tim O'Reilly in 2005 to describe the trend in the use of World Wide Web technology to enhance creativity, information sharing, and, most notably, collaboration among users. Brown and Adler (2008) add that the capabilities of these Web 2.0 tools have "shifted attention from access to information toward access to people" (p. 18). Through the use of a research study this chapter illustrates how a blended approach to learning and digital technologies can be used to create meaningful assessment activities for students in higher education.

METHODS OF INVESTIGATION

An action research (Stringer, 2007) approach was utilized to investigate how a blended approach to learning and digital technologies could support student assessment in higher education. Gilmore, Krantz, and Ramirez (1986) define such a framework as:

> Action research...aims to contribute both to the practical concerns of people in an immediate problematic situation and to further the goals of social science simultaneously. Thus, there is a dual commitment in action research to study a system and concurrently to collaborate with members of the system in changing it in what is together regarded as a desirable direction. Accomplishing this twin goal requires the active collaboration of researcher and client, and thus it stresses the importance of co-learning as a primary aspect of the research process. (p. 161)

This approach consisted of quantitative (pre- and post-course online surveys) and qualitative (online journal entries and post-course student interviews) research methods to collect and analyze data from students enrolled in a blended preservice teacher education course titled Current and Emerging Pedagogical Technologies. This is a second-year course where students explore and investigate the potential for integrating digital technologies into their future teaching practice through face-to-face and online learning activities.

DATA COLLECTION

Data were collected by an undergraduate student research assistant (USRA) during the fall 2010 semester. The USRA invited all students enrolled in the course to be part of this research project and a total of 22 students participated in this study (96% response rate). The project received institutional ethics approval and the students signed an informed consent form. The consent form offered the participants confidentiality and the ability to withdraw from the study at any time.

The data collection process began with a pre-course online survey (Appendix 9.1). The purpose of this survey was to identify students' initial perceptions about the value of self-reflection, peer feedback, and teacher assessment based on previous course experiences. The survey consisted of a mixture of Likert-scale and open-ended questions and the second version of the *Free Assessment Survey Tool* (*http://toofast.ca*) was used to administer an online version of the survey.

Throughout the semester the student participants were also asked to complete an online journal entry after each major assessment activity (a total of five assignments). These journal entries asked students to explain how they made use of self-reflection, peer review, and teacher assessment feedback to improve each of the course assignments ($n = 22$, 96% response rate). The *Majarha ePortfolio* system (*http://mahara.org*) was used to facilitate this online journaling process (Appendix 9.2).

At the end of the fall 2010 semester, the students were asked to complete a post-course online survey about their perceptions of self-reflection, peer feedback, and teacher assessment based on their blended course experience (*n* = 18, 78% response rate). This survey consisted of identical questions from the precourse survey (Appendix 9.3). Finally, the students were invited to participate in a 30-minute post-course interview with the USRA to discuss the course assessment practices as well as the preliminary survey and journal findings (Appendix 9.4). Four students volunteered to be interviewed and these interviews were digitally recorded and transcribed by the USRA.

DATA ANALYSIS

A constant comparative approach was used to identify patterns, themes, and categories of analysis that "emerge out of the data rather than being imposed on them prior to data collection and analysis" (Patton, 1990, p. 390). The pre- and post-course online survey along with the journal data were exported into Microsoft Excel for statistical and thematic analysis by the USRA and the course instructor. Comparisons were made between students' pre- and post-course survey responses. This data was correlated with the students' journal responses throughout the semester. At the end of the fall 2010 semester, a preliminary report was compiled and emailed to each of the student participants who were then invited to participate in a post-course interview to discuss the initial study findings. These interviews were digitally recorded and transcribed.

FINDINGS

The findings from this research study are highlighted with regard to student comments about how a blended learning approach and digital technologies could support self, peer, and teacher assessment practices and activities.

Self-Assessment

The precourse survey results indicated that students initially had a wide range of perceptions regarding the value of self-assessment feedback. One student indicated "I don't find it too important to me. I see by my grades how I am doing instead of evaluating myself" (Survey Participant 11) while another stated "I would rather get feedback from a teacher or a peer"

TABLE 9.1 Students' Perceptions of the Value of Self-Assessment Feedback

	High/Very High	Medium	Low/Very Low
Before Course	41%	45%	14%
After Course	59%	35%	6%

(Survey Participant 6). A number of students commented that they did not have much previous experience with self-assessment activities and thus, "I can sometimes have a hard time recognizing where I can improve when I'm self-evaluating" (Survey Participant 17).

During the course, students used digital technologies to support several self-assessment activities such as Audacity (*http://audacity.sourceforge.net*) for self-assessment narrations of project artifacts (e.g., digital stories created in *MS Photostory* (*www.windowsphotostory.com*), Google Blogger (*www.blogger.com/home*) for online journaling, and Google Sites (*https://sites.google.com*) for the creation of an ePortfolio. The students who participated in this study were asked to rate the value of self-assessment feedback before and after the course. The results are displayed in Table 9.1.

These results suggest that some students had a higher perception regarding the value of self-assessment at the end of the course but approximately one-third of the students were still ambivalent about the use of this type of assessment feedback. These findings were confirmed in the post-course interviews when students were asked to describe how they used self-assessment feedback to improve their coursework. One student stated that assessment was the responsibility of the course instructor and "Personally I didn't feel I needed to do it. . . . I don't really value my opinion on assignments once I've finished them" (Interview Participant 3). Conversely, another student described how self-assessment activities helped her internalize her learning: "I could see how I did things, what worked and what didn't. I could also see my goals and if I really got to where I wanted to be" (Interview Participant 1). This comment was echoed by Interview Participant 4, who indicated, "When I started to analyze and critique my own work, I started seeing areas for improvement. I always want to give myself a good self-evaluation so I made changes or modified certain parts of the assignment to feel comfortable about giving myself a fair but good evaluation."

Peer Assessment

The student participants expressed a number of concerns about peer assessment activities based on their previous course experiences in the precourse survey. These issues ranged from frustration, confusion, and academic loafing to intimidation with the process. For example, one student stated that "It was frustrating because it didn't really mean anything. The teacher re-marked the assignment anyway . . . " (Survey Participant 15). Another student was confused by the peer assessment process as "I didn't know if their feedback would be right or wrong" (Survey Participant 21). Several students commented about academic loafing: "I feel sometimes my classmates may not be paying attention and just give marks based on the hope that people will grade them lightly" (Survey Participant 5), and how the fear of intimidation limits the quality and honesty of the peer assessment: "Students are always intimidated when evaluating their peers in fear of giving them a bad mark" (Survey Participant 11).

Digital technologies were used in the course to support a variety of peer assessment activities. These activities included using Google Docs (*www.docs.google.com*) for peer review of student lesson plans. The group tools in the Blackboard Learning Management System (*www.blackboard.com*) to provide peer review of project artifacts (e.g., digital stories created in Microsoft Photostory [*www.windowsphotostory.com*]). Wikispaces (*www.wikispaces.com*) was utilized for the co-construction and peer editing of online discussion summaries and class notes. The students were also asked to rate the value of peer-assessment feedback before and after the course (Table 9.2).

Before the course, less than 20% of the students had a high perception of the value of peer assessment feedback; whereas, after the course, a very slight majority of students had a more positive perception of this form of assessment feedback. These results were tempered by the post-course interview results. One student indicated, "I can see how it would be useful but I found that my peers either gave me wrong feedback, like telling me to do it one way when clearly the assignment said to do it another way, or just told me something I already knew and was working on" (Interview Participant 1). Another student described how she used peer-assessment feedback "as a guideline for my work. It was nice to have someone review my work in the middle of the process because it let me know that I was on the right track" (Interview Participant 4). In addition, interview Participant 2 stated that "Any time we are able to have more eyes on something to add suggestions, it is worthwhile to take advantage of it."

TABLE 9.2 Students' Perceptions of the Value of Peer-Assessment Feedback

	High/Very High	Medium	Low/Very Low
Before Course	19%	62.0%	19.0%
After Course	53%	23.5%	23.5%

Teacher Assessment

In the precourse survey, students indicated they received a range of assessment feedback from their instructors, which was usually summative in nature. One student stated that "It all depends on the teacher" (Survey Participant 3) while another complained that "No one tells me anything and since I don't have the same teachers for each course, I don't really know how to improve my coursework" (Survey Participant 21). Several students stressed "that it is important to be able to adapt to requirements that others set for you" (Survey Participant 14).

Interactive technologies were used by the course teacher primarily to provide students with formative assessment feedback. For example, the teacher gave initial assessment comments and grades on all assignments in digital format (e.g., student lesson plans in Google Docs, digital stories in MS Photostory, WebQuests in QuestGarden [*http://questgarden.com*]). Students then had the opportunity to revise their assignments based on this feedback and resubmit final versions to their ePortfolios (e.g., Google Sites) for summative assessment. It appears that this emphasis on formative feedback impacted students' perceptions regarding the value of teacher assessment (Table 9.3).

These survey results indicate that almost all of the students involved in this study had a much higher perception of teacher assessment after the course. In the post-course interviews, the students explained how they used the teacher's formative assessment comments to improve their coursework. "The feedback allowed me to reexamine how I did something and then go back to review and make changes where necessary" (Interview Participant 2). For several students, this was the first time they had received formative feedback from a teacher and one student commented that " . . . having an instructor give you a first mark, and then being able to go back and revise was really helpful in improving my work" (Interview Participant 1). Another student emphasized how he "really liked the formative feedback from the instructor because it allows you to improve on similar assignments you might have to do again in the same class or maybe another course—sort of like a building-block approach to learning" (Interview Participant 4).

TABLE 9.3   Students' Perceptions of the Value of Teacher-Assessment Feedback

	High/Very High	Medium	Low/Very Low
Before Course	64%	36%	0%
After Course	94%	6%	0%

Student Recommendations

The student participants in this research study provided recommendations for how a blended learning approach and digital technologies could be used to design meaningful self, peer, and teacher assessment activities in their online journal assignment postings and the post-study interviews.

Self-Assessment

With regard to self-assessment practices, the students provided specific recommendations for how digital technologies could be used for grading rubrics and online journaling in higher education courses.

Rubrics. The Teaching, Learning, and Technology (TLT) Group (2011) defines a rubric as "an explicit set of criteria used for assessing a particular type of work or performance. A rubric usually also includes levels of potential achievement for each criterion, and sometimes also includes work or performance samples that typify each of those levels" (n.p.). The participants in this study indicated that rubrics can be useful for clarifying assignment and assessment expectations only when students are actively involved in their co-construction. In the post-study interviews, one participant stated that without student involvement, rubrics "can become simple checklists, a way to make sure that you've covered everything the teacher wants for the assignment rather than what you really wanted to do and learn" (Interview Participant 3). Unfortunately, this comment suggests that without student involvement, rubrics have the potential to support a surface rather than a deep approach to learning.

In terms of recommendations, the students suggested that several types of digital technologies could be used to support the co-construction of assessment rubrics. These included applications such as Rubistar (*http://rubistar.4teachers.org/index.php*), Teachnology (*www.teach-nology.com/web_tools/rubrics*), and Google Docs (*www.docs.google.com*). The students in this study preferred using Google Docs based on the simplicity and their familiarity with this tool. An example of a co-constructed assessment rubric for a lesson plan assignment is illustrated in Figure 9.2.

The study participants also recommended that students should have the opportunity to practice applying the co-constructed rubric to previous completed coursework and that students should have the ability to add one unique grading component or criteria (e.g., creativity).

In addition, digital technologies in a blended course can be used to provide a variety of options for students to self-assess themselves. For example, students can use Audacity (*http://audacity.sourceforge.net*), an open-source audio tool, to create self-assessment narrations of how they achieved the various learning outcomes outlined in the rubric. The use of self-assessment

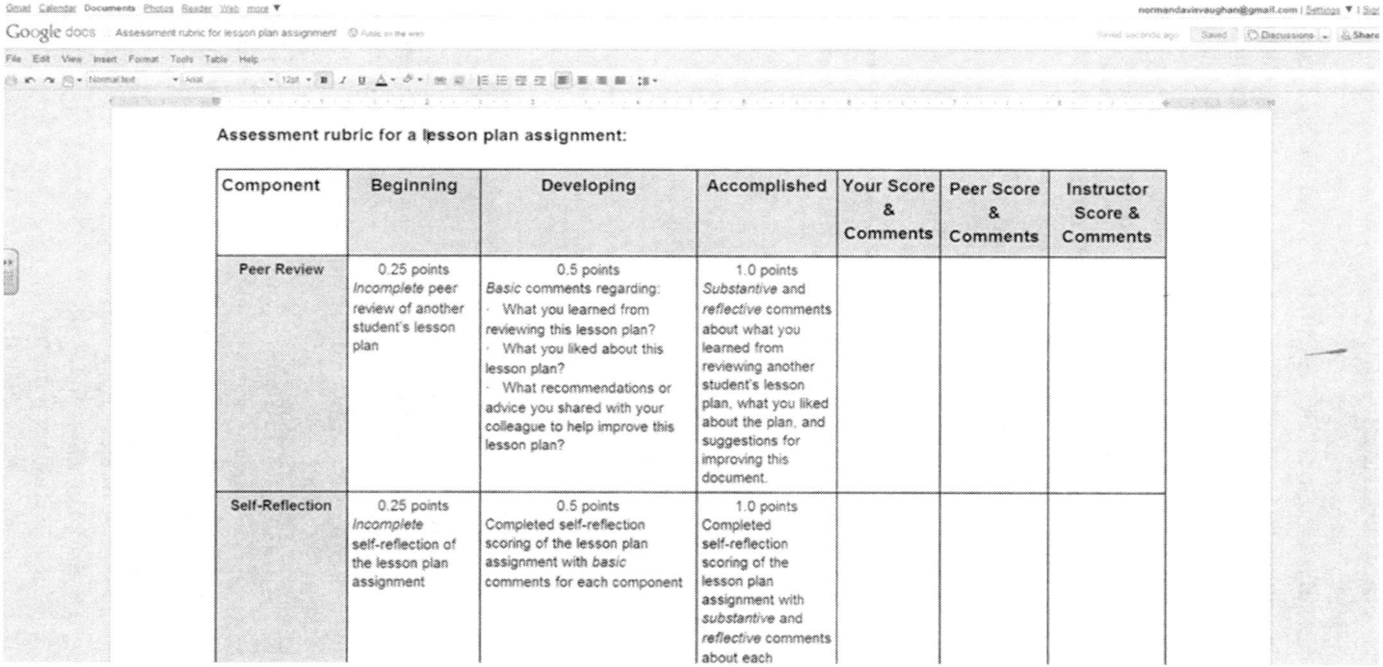

Assessment rubric for a lesson plan assignment:

Component	Beginning	Developing	Accomplished	Your Score & Comments	Peer Score & Comments	Instructor Score & Comments
Peer Review	0.25 points *Incomplete peer review of another student's lesson plan*	0.5 points *Basic comments regarding:* · What you learned from reviewing this lesson plan? · What you liked about this lesson plan? · What recommendations or advice you shared with your colleague to help improve this lesson plan?	1.0 points *Substantive and reflective comments about what you learned from reviewing another student's lesson plan, what you liked about the plan, and suggestions for improving this document.*			
Self-Reflection	0.25 points *Incomplete self-reflection of the lesson plan assignment*	0.5 points Completed self-reflection scoring of the lesson plan assignment with basic comments for each component	1.0 points Completed self-reflection scoring of the lesson plan assignment with *substantive and reflective comments about each*			

Figure 9.2 Assessment rubric for a lesson plan assignment (http://tinyurl.com/lessonplanrubric).

audio feedback can be a powerful way for students to internalize their learning (Ice, Curtis, Phillips, & Wells, 2007).

Online Journals. Students in professional programs such as Teacher Education and Nursing are often required to maintain either a course or program journal. Online blogging tools such as WordPress (http://wordpress.org) and Google's Blogger (www.blogger.com) are commonly being used to support this type of self-assessment activity.

Students in this study indicated online journals can be useful for self-reflection but that too often they can become a "boring and repetitive activity when I am simply being asked to reply to a set of teacher-directed questions. Usually, I just post what I think the teacher wants to hear, not what I'm really thinking" (Interview Participant 2). Again, without student involvement, this type of self-assessment activity can reinforce a surface rather than a deep approach to learning.

The study participants strongly recommended that students should have much greater control over their online journal postings. They suggested that there should be more opportunities for "freedom of expression rather than conforming to a teacher set structure" (Interview Participant 1). The students involved in this study proposed that their online journal assignment should be focused on processed-oriented postings that led to a final product such as an end-of-semester self-reflection paper, and that this paper could be assessed using a co-constructed rubric in Google Docs.

Peer Assessment

The student participants suggested a variety of ways that peer assessment activities could be enhanced through the use of digital technologies in the post-study surveys and interviews. They indicated the biggest barrier to completing this type of peer activity, outside of class, was finding a common time and place to meet. The students suggested that digital technologies could potentially be used to overcome this challenge. For example, the group areas in learning management systems such as Blackboard could be used to communicate and share documents about the peer assessment process for individual and group projects. These group areas usually consist of asynchronous (e.g., email and discussion board) and synchronous (e.g., chat) communication tools along with a file exchange function.

The students also indicated that during the course they had been impressed with how easy it was to provide peer review feedback on written assignment by sharing Google Docs (Figure 9.3). This application allowed them to control who had commenting and editing privileges for their documents. In addition, online journal applications such as Blogger could be used to provide peer review feedback on individual project work and wiki tools such as Wikispaces (*www.wikispaces.com*). The history files of a wiki

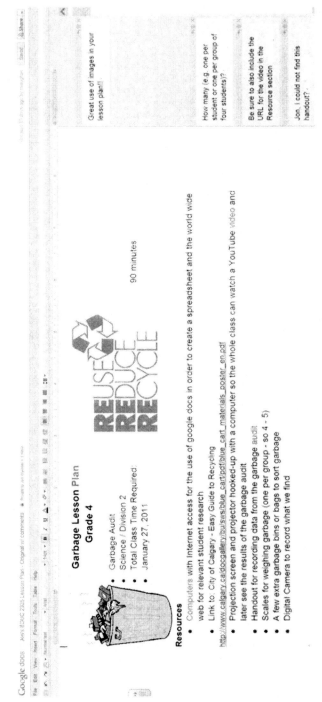

Figure 9.3 Peer review of a writing assignment in *Google Docs*.

summary clearly demonstrate the contribution and critique that was made by each member of the group.

A number of students involved in this study were also taking an introductory biology course. They commented on how the teacher in this course was using the University of California at Los Angeles' Calibrated Peer Review (*http://cpr.molsci.ucla.edu*) tool to teach them how to provide constructive feedback to their peers on the laboratory manuscript assignments for the course. The biology teacher also used personal response systems (e.g., clickers) for study group quizzes and discussion prompts. Crouch and Mazur (2001) describe how clickers can be used to support a form of peer instruction. The process begins with the teacher posing a question or problem. The students initially work individually toward a solution and "vote" on what they believe is the correct answer by selecting the desired numbered or lettered response on their clicker. The results are then projected for the entire class to view. For a good question, there is usually a broad range of responses. Students are then required to compare and discuss their solutions with the person next to them in the classroom in order to come to a consensus. Another "vote" is taken but this time only one response or clicker per group can be utilized. In most circumstances, the range of responses decreases and usually centers around the correct answer. As an alternative to this process, this biology teacher also had groups of students generate the quiz questions in advance of the classroom session.

While the student participants appreciated the ability of a blended learning approach and digital technologies to provide increased flexibility and communication opportunities to complete peer assessment activities, outside of the classroom, they had several concerns. First, a number of students expressed concern about their lack of experience with peer assessment in the post-study interviews. They strongly recommended that teachers should "provide guidance and a class orientation on how to give each other meaningful feedback" (Interview Participant 4). Another student suggested that there should be "opportunities for oral and written feedback" (Interview Participant 2). He thought that digital technologies were being used primarily to provide written peer feedback and that in a blended course students should also be learning how to provide oral feedback to each other. This comment was echoed by a student who suggested that teachers should "provide class time to begin and conclude peer assessment activities" (Interview Participant 1). She believed that this combination of face-to-face and online interaction would help to build trust and accountability for the peer assessment process.

Teacher Assessment

The student participants provided several suggestions about how digital technologies could be used to support these practices. The first idea was to have teachers use collaborative writing tools such as Google Docs to provide formative assessment feedback at checkpoints or milestones for individual or group projects. This would allow students to receive teacher feedback throughout the process of constructing the project rather than just focusing on summative assessment feedback for the final product.

The students also encouraged teachers to take a portfolio approach to assessment. This would involve students receiving a second chance or opportunity for summative assessment on their course assignments. For example, students would initially submit and receive teacher assessment for each of the required course assignments. Throughout the semester, students would have the opportunity to revise these assignments, based on the initial teacher feedback, and then post them to their course or program portfolios for final summative assessment by the teacher. There is a range of e-Portfolio tools that can support this process, ranging from the LiveText (*https://www.livetext.com*) commercial application to the free Google Sites (*http://sites.google.com*) tool.

In addition, digital technologies can be used to support external expert assessment opportunities. For example, students can publically share critiques of academic articles by using blogging tools such as WordPress and Blogger. The authors of these articles can then be invited to post comments about these critiques to the students' blogs. External experts can also provide assessment feedback on individual or group presentations through the use of Web-based video technologies. These types of presentations can be video-recorded and either streamed live (e.g., Livestream [*www.livestream.com*]) or posted to a video-sharing site such as YouTube. The external experts can then provide assessment feedback in either synchronous (e.g., real-time audio) or asynchronous (e.g., online discussion forums) formats to the students. Figure 9.4 illustrates a video recording of an individual student presentation that has been posted to YouTube.

Besides providing ideas on how blended learning and digital technologies could be used to support teacher assessment activities, the student participants in the interview sessions also had three recommendations for faculty members. The first recommendation was that teachers should "focus on providing students with ongoing formative assessment feedback rather than on just summative midterm and final examination comments" (Interview Participant 2). The second was that teachers should strive to "provide oral feedback in addition to their written assessment feedback. For example, teachers could request that students meet with them during virtual office hour sessions to orally debrief about assignments through the use of synchronous communication tools such as Skype or Adobe Connect" (Interview Participant 4). Finally, Interview Participant 3 emphasized, "Let us provide instructors with more feedback on their assignments and teaching practice throughout the semester, not just at the end" and he recommended Angelo and Cross's (1993) book *A Handbook of Classroom Assessment Techniques for College Teachers* to facilitate this process.

0:09 / 1:14   360p

Figure 9.4   Example of a video recording of student presentation posted to *YouTube*.

CONCLUSION

The preservice teacher education students who participated in this research study were also asked to describe how they combined the use of self, peer, and teacher assessment feedback to improve their coursework. One student commented, "I used the self-reflection for checking my work and making sure I had everything I needed. I used peer review for a different perspective on my work and I used instructor feedback to understand how I could improve my work" (Interview Participant 4). Another student stated, "Self-reflection showed me what I liked about my work and what needed to be improved, peer feedback gave comments on what could be done better, and then instructor feedback gave ideas on how the assignment could be fixed up to get a better mark" (Interview Participant 2). In addition, there were numerous comments in the student online journals about how blended learning and digital technologies helped them integrate these three forms of assessment into a triad approach (Figure 9.5).

For example, students were using rubrics, blogs, and online quizzes to provide themselves with self-reflection and feedback on their course assignments. Students received further feedback on their coursework from their peers through the use of digital technologies such as wikis and clickers. Finally, teachers and in some cases external experts reviewed students'

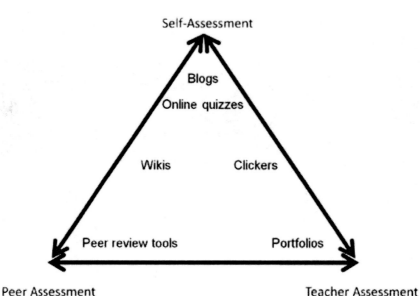

Figure 9.5 Using digital technologies to support a triad approach to assessment.

ePortfolios and used video technologies to observe student performance, diagnose student misconceptions, and provide additional formative assessment feedback.

In conclusion, the research study presented in this chapter has demonstrated that self, peer, and teacher assessment activities in a blended course should be an integrated process rather than a series of isolated events in order to help students develop their own metacognitive skills and strategies.

APPENDIX 9.1
Precourse Student Online Survey Questions

Important Note: The purpose of this survey is to gather student responses that will help inform the types of assessment practices used in the Mount Royal College Education Program. Participation in this survey is voluntary and your responses will be kept confidential. Nonparticipation in this study will not jeopardize student progress in this EDUC2325: Understanding Current and Emerging Pedagogical Technologies course or the Education Program. Completion of the questionnaire below will constitute informed consent in this *How do students make use of self-assessment, peer assessment, and teacher assessment feedback to improve their academic coursework?* study. This study has been approved by the Mount Royal Human Research Ethics Board (HREB).

Name: _____

A: Self-Assessment Feedback

Alverno College (2001) defines self-assessment feedback as the ability of students to observe, analyze, and judge their own performance on the basis of criteria and determine how they can improve it.

1. What kind of previous experience do you have with self-assessment activities (i.e., journals, learning logs, portfolios)?

2. How did you make use of this self-assessment feedback to improve your academic coursework (e.g., strategies, processes)?

3. Based on your previous experience, how would you rate the value of this self-assessment feedback?

   1 (very low)   2 (low)   3 (medium)   4 (high)   5 (very high)

4. Why?

B: Peer Assessment Feedback

Peer review is a process used for checking the work performed by one's equals (peers) to ensure it meets specific criteria.

1. What kind of previous experience do you have with peer assessment activities (i.e., groupwork, presentations, papers)?

2. How did you make use of this peer assessment feedback to improve your academic coursework (e.g., strategies, processes)?

3. Based on your previous experience, how would you rate the value of this peer assessment feedback?

    1 (very low)   2 (low)   3 (medium)   4 (high)   5 (very high)

4. Why?

C: Teacher Assessment Feedback

Teacher assessment feedback on student work.

1. What kind of previous experience do you have with teacher assessment activities and feedback (i.e., midterms, papers, final exams)?

2. How did you make use of this teacher assessment feedback to improve your academic coursework (e.g., strategies, processes)?

3. Based on your previous experience, how would you rate the value of this teacher feedback?

    1 (very low)   2 (low)   3 (medium)   4 (high)   5 (very high)

4. Why?

D: Integration of Self-Assessment, Peer Assessment, and Instructor Assessment Feedback

1. Do you have previous experience integrating all three forms of assessment feedback to improve your academic coursework? (Yes/No)

2. If yes, please explain how you have integrated all three forms of assessment to improve your academic coursework (e.g., strategies, processes).

APPENDIX 9.2
Online Journal Entries

After each of the five major assessment activities in the EDUC2325 course, the study participants will be asked to respond to the following questions in their online journals in the *Mahara ePortfolio* system.

1. How did you make use of self-assessment, peer assessment, and teacher assessment feedback to improve the course assignment?

2. Which type of assessment feedback was *most valuable?* Why?

3. Which type of assessment feedback was *least valuable?* Why?

APPENDIX 9.3
Post-Course Student Online Survey Questions

Important Note: The purpose of this survey is to gather student responses that will help inform the types of assessment practices used in the Mount Royal College Education Program. Participation in this survey is voluntary and your responses will be kept confidential. Nonparticipation in this study will not jeopardize student progress in this EDUC2325: Understanding Current and Emerging Pedagogical Technologies course or the Education Program. Completion of the questionnaire below will constitute informed consent in this *How do students make use of self-assessment, peer assessment, and teacher assessment to improve their academic coursework?* study. This study has been approved by the Mount Royal Human Research Ethics Board (HREB).

Name: _____

A: Self-Assessment Feedback

Alverno College (2001) defines self-assessment feedback as the ability of students to observe, analyze, and judge their own performance on the basis of criteria and determine how they can improve it.

1. What kind of self-assessment activities did you utilize in the EDUC2325 course (e.g., journals, learning logs, portfolios)?

2. How did you make use of this self-assessment feedback to improve your academic work in the EDUC2325 course (e.g., strategies, processes)?

3. How would you rate the value of this self-assessment feedback in the EDUC2325 course?

   1 (very low), 2 (low), 3 (medium), 4 (high), 5 (very high)

4. Why?

B: Peer Assessment Feedback

Peer assessment is a process used for checking the work performed by one's equals (peers) to ensure it meets specific criteria.

1. What kind of peer assessment activities did you utilize in the EDUC2325 course (e.g., groupwork, presentations, papers)?

2. How did you make use of this peer assessment feedback to improve your academic work in the EDUC2325 course (e.g., strategies, processes)?

3. How would you rate the value of this peer assessment feedback in the EDUC2325 course?

    1 (very low), 2 (low), 3 (medium), 4 (high), 5 (very high)

4. Why?

C: Instructor Assessment Feedback

Teacher assessment feedback on student work.

1. What kind of teacher assessment activities and feedback did you receive in the EDUC2325 course (e.g., midterms, papers, final exams)?

2. How did you make use of this teacher assessment feedback to improve your academic coursework (e.g., strategies, processes)?

3. Based on your previous experience, how would you rate the value of this teacher feedback?

    1 (very low)   2 (low)   3 (medium)   4 (high)   5 (very high)

4. Why?

D: Integration of Self-Assessment, Peer Assessment, and Teacher Assessment Feedback

1. Did you integrate all three forms of assessment feedback to improve your academic work in the EDUC2325 course? (Yes/No)

2. If yes, please explain how you integrated all three forms of assessment to improve your academic work in the EDUC2325 course (e.g., strategies, processes)?

APPENDIX 9.4
Post-Course Student Interview Questions

Based on your experience and review of the survey results for the EDUC2325 course, please share your thoughts on the following questions.

A: Self-Assessment Feedback

Alverno College (2001) defines self-assessment feedback as the ability of students to observe, analyze, and judge their own performance on the basis of criteria and determine how they can improve it.

1. General comments on the types of self-assessment activities and feedback that students report are currently taking place in the EDUC2325 course (e.g., journals, learning logs, portfolios)?

2. Do you agree with the benefits and/or value that students report from these types of self-assessment activities? Please explain why or why not.

3. Conversely, what are your thoughts on the challenges or drawbacks that education students have identified about self-assessment feedback?

4. Additional recommendations for improving the quality and opportunities for self-assessment feedback in the EDUC2325 course?

B: Peer Assessment Feedback

Peer assessment is a process used for checking the work performed by one's equals (peers) to ensure it meets specific criteria.

1. General comments on the types of peer assessment activities and feedback that students report are currently taking place in the EDUC2325 course (e.g., groupwork, presentations, papers)?

2. Do you agree with the benefits and/or value that education students have identified about peer assessment feedback? Please explain why or why not.

3. Conversely, what are your thoughts on the challenges or drawbacks that education students have identified with peer review assessment?

4. Additional recommendations for improving the quality and opportunities for peer assessment feedback in the EDUC2325 course?

C: Teacher Assessment Feedback

Teacher assessment feedback on student work.

1. General comments on the types of teacher assessment activities and feedback that students report are currently taking place in the EDUC2325 course (e.g., midterms, papers, final exams)?

2. Do you agree with the benefits and/or value that education students have identified about teacher assessment feedback? Please explain why or why not.

3. Conversely, what are your thoughts on the challenges or drawbacks that education students have encountered with teacher assessment feedback?

4. Additional recommendations for improving the quality and opportunities for teacher assessment feedback in the EDUC2325 course?

D: Integration of Self-Assessment, Peer Assessment, and Instructor Assessment Feedback

1. General comments on how students report that they are using all three forms of assessment feedback to improve your academic work in the EDUC2325 course?

2. Please explain in detail how you integrated all three forms of assessment to improve your academic work in the EDUC2325 course (e.g., strategies, processes)?

REFERENCES

Akyol, Z., & Garrison, D. R. (2011) Assessing metacognition in an online community of inquiry. *Internet and Higher Education, 14*(3), 183–190.

Alberta Assessment Consortium (2002). *About classroom assessment.* Retrieved from http://www.aac.ab.ca/final2002.doc.

Allen, I. E., & Seaman, J. (2010). *Class differences: Online education in the United States, 2010.* Online Learning Consortium. Retrieved from http://onlinelearning-consortium.org/publications/survey/class_differences.

Alverno College (2001). *Assessment essentials: Definition of terms.* Retrieved from http://depts.alverno.edu/saal/terms.html.

American Association of Higher Education and Accreditation (1996). *Nine principles of good 'practice for assessing student learning.* Retrieved from http://www.niu.edu/assessment/Manual/media/9Principles.pdf.

Angelo, T. A., & Cross, K. P. (1993). *A handbook of classroom assessment techniques for college teachers.* San Francisco, CA: Jossey-Bass.

Arabasz, P., Boggs, R., & Baker, M. B. (2003). Highlights of e-learning support practices. *Educause Center for Applied Research Bulletin, 9.* Retrieved from https://net.educause.edu/ir/library/pdf/ERB0309.pdf.

Barr, R. B., & Tagg, J. (1995) A new paradigm for undergraduate education. *Change, 27*(6), 13–25. Retrieved from http://critical.tamucc.edu/~blalock/readings/tch2learn.htm.

Bleed, R. (2001). A hybrid campus for a new millennium. *Educause Review, 36*(1), 16–24.

Boud, D. J. (2000). Sustainable assessment: rethinking assessment for the learning society. *Studies in Continuing Education, 22*(2), 151–167. Retrieved from http://www.education.uts.edu.au/ostaff/staff/publications/db_28_sce_00.pdf.

Boud, D. J. (2007). *Rethinking assessment for higher education: Learning for the longer term.* London, UK: Routledge.

Brown, J. S., & Adler, R. P. (2008). Minds on fire: Open education, the long tail, and learning 2.0. *Educase Review, 43*(1), 17–32.

Brown, S. (2004). Assessment for learning. *Learning and Teaching in Higher Education, 1*(1), 81–89. Retrieved from http://www2.glos.ac.uk/offload/tli/lets/lathe/issue1/articles/brown.pdf.

Clark, D. (2003). *Blend it like Beckham.* Epic Group PLC. Retrieved from http://www.epic.co.uk/content/resources/white_papers/blended.htm.

Crouch, C. H., & Mazur, E. (2001). Peer instruction: Ten years of experience and results. *American Journal of Physics, 69*(9), 970–977.

DeCorte, E. (1996). New perspectives on learning and teaching in higher education. In A. Burgen (Ed.), *Goals and purposes of higher education in the 21st century* (pp. 112–132). London: Jessica Kingsley.

Dweck, C. (1999) *Self-theories: their role in motivation, personality and development.* Philadelphia, PA: Psychology Press.

Dziuban, C. D., & Moskal, P. D. (2013). Blended learning: A dangerous idea? *Internet and Higher Education, 18*, 15–23.

Foundation Coalition. (2002). *Peer assessment and peer evaluation.* Retrieved from http://www.foundationcoalition.org/publications/brochures/2002peer_assessment.pdf.

Garnham, C., & Kaleta, R. (2002). Introduction to hybrid courses. *Teaching with Technology Today, 8*(6). Retrieved from http://www.uwsa.edu/ttt/articles/garnham.htm.

Garrison, D. R., & Vaughan, N. D. (2008). *Blended learning in higher education.* San Francisco, CA: Jossey-Bass.

Gibbs, G. (2006). How assessment frames student learning. In C. Bryan & K. Clegg (Eds.), *Innovative Assessment in Higher Education* (pp. 23–36). London, UK: Routledge.

Gibbs, G., & Simpson, C. (2004) Conditions under which assessment supports students' learning? *Learning and Teaching in Higher Education, 1,* 3–31.

Gilmore, T., Krantz, J., & Ramirez, R. (1986). Action based modes of inquiry and the host-researcher relationship. *Consultation, 5*(3), 160–176.

Gorsky, P., Caspi, A., & Trumper, R. (2006). Campus-based university students' use of dialogue. *Studies in Higher Education, 31*(1), 71–87. Retrieved from http://old.oranim.ac.il/Docs/CSHE_A_139217.pdf.

Higgins, R., Hartley, P., & Skelton, A. (2001). Getting the message across: The problem of communicating assessment feedback. *Teaching in Higher Education, 6*(2), 269–274.

Ice, P., Curtis, R., Phillips, P., & Wells, J. (2007). Using asynchronous audio feedback to enhance teaching presence and students' sense of community. *Journal of Asynchronous Learning Networks, 11*(2), 3–25.

Ivanic, R., Clark, R., & Rimmershaw, R. (2000). What am I supposed to make of this? The messages conveyed to students by tutors' written comments. In M. R. Lea & B. Stierer (Eds.), *Student writing in higher education: New contexts* (pp. 47–65). Buckingham, UK: Open University Press.

Langan, M. A., & Wheater, C. P. (2003). Can students assess students effectively? Some insights into peer-assessment. *Learning and Teaching in Action, 2*(1). Retrieved from http://www.celt.mmu.ac.uk/ltia/issue4/langanwheater.pdf.

Lea, S. J., Stephenson, D., & Troy, J. (2003) Higher education students' attitudes to student-centred learning: Beyond "educational bulimia." *Studies in Higher Education, 28*(3), 321–334.

Littlejohn, A., & Pegler, C. (2007). *Preparing for blended e-learning: Understanding blended and online learning (connecting with e-learning).* London, UK: Routledge.

Mayadas, F. A., & Picciano, A. G. (2007). Blended learning and localness: The means and the end. *Journal of Asynchronous Learning Networks, 11*(1), 3–7.

Nicol, D. J., & Macfarlane-Dick, D. (2006). Formative assessment and self-regulated learning: a model and seven principles of good feedback practice. *Studies in Higher Education, 31*(2), 199–218.

Norberg, A., Dziuban, C. D., & Moskal, P. D. (2011). A time-based blended learning model. *On the Horizon, 19*(3), 207–216.

O'Reilly, T. (2005). *What is Web 2.0?* O'Reilly Network. Retrieved from http://oreilly.com/web2/archive/what-is-web-20.html.

Pask, G. (1976). *Conversation theory: Applications in education and epistemology.* Amsterdam: Elsevier.

Patton, M. Q. (1990). *Qualitative evaluation and research methods* (2nd ed.). Newbury Park, CA: Sage.

Rust, C. (2002). The impact of assessment on student learning: How can the research literature practically help to inform the development of departmental assessment strategies and learner-centred assessment practices? *Active Learning in Higher Education, 3*(2), 145–158.

Sadler, D. R. (1998) Formative assessment: revisiting the territory. *Assessment in Education, 5*(1), 77–84.

Sharpe, R., Benfield, G., Roberts, G., & Francis, R. (2006). *The undergraduate experience of blended e-learning: A review of UK literature and practice.* London, UK: Higher Education Academy. Retrieved from http://www.heacademy.ac.uk/resources/detail/teachingandresearch/Undergraduate_Experience

Stringer, E. T. (2007). *Action research* (3rd ed.). London, UK: Sage.

Teaching, Learning, and Technology (TLT) Group. (2011). *Rubrics: Definition, tools, examples, references.* Retrieved from http://www.tltgroup.org/resources/flashlight/rubrics.htm.

Williams, C. (2002). Learning on-line: A review of recent literature in a rapidly expanding field. *Journal of Further and Higher Education, 26*(3), 263–272.

Williams, J. (2003). Blending into the background. *E-Learning Age Magazine, 1.*

Yorke, M. (2003) Formative assessment in higher education: moves towards theory and the enhancement of pedagogic practice. *Higher Education, 45*(4), 477–501.

CHAPTER 10

CONTINUOUS FORMATIVE ASSESSMENT DURING BLENDED AND ONLINE INSTRUCTION USING CLOUD-BASED COLLABORATIVE DOCUMENTS

Norman Herr, Mike Rivas, Tae Chang, and John M. Reveles
California State University Northridge

Marty Tippens
Woodbury University

**Virginia Vandergon, Matthew A. d'Alessio
and Dorothy Nguyen-Graff**
California State University, Northridge

INTRODUCTION

Blended and online learning environments provide instructors with significant challenges regarding the engagement and assessment of learners. How

Assessment in Online and Blended Learning Environments, pages 187–214
Copyright © 2015 by Information Age Publishing
187

can teachers engage learners and assess their understanding in remote settings? Furthermore, how can instructors perform formative assessment to adjust their instruction to meet the immediate needs of distant learners? The Continuous Formative Assessment (CFA) model helps teachers create an environment that engages learners and provides opportunities for instructors to monitor student progress through continuous formative assessments so they can modify instruction to maximize learning in blended and online environments.

Schools and universities have been encouraged to develop a "culture of assessment" to provide evidence on the effectiveness of instructional programs (Weiner, 2009). Although the emphasis on assessment has produced a wealth of literature, legislation, initiatives, reforms, and professional development, the vast majority has focused on assessment *of* learning (summative assessment) rather than assessment *for* learning (formative assessment). Formative assessment is generally defined as a process used by teachers that provides feedback by which they can adjust ongoing teaching and learning to improve achievement during the process of instruction (Popham, 2008). What makes formative assessment "formative" is that it is immediately used to make adjustments to instruction to meet the needs of the learners during the construction of understanding (Shepard, 2005).

Formative assessment is not a new concept, and any teacher who adjusts his or her teaching during instruction on the basis of evidence of student understanding and performance is employing formative assessment (Popham, 2008; Shepard, 2005). Traditional formative assessment techniques such as student questioning or quizzes are limited in how many students are assessed or can be difficult to analyze during class. The challenge is even greater in online environments where there is limited interaction with students. How does one accurately assess student comprehension and performance during a class session, particularly in blended and online settings?

A promising response to this question is found in new collaborative cloud-based document technologies. Such technologies provide the opportunity to instantly collect and analyze large sets of data from multiple students, groups, and class sections with speed and accuracy, regardless of the physical location of students. The CFA instructional model employs these technologies to create environments that mirror collaborative professional research communities in which colleagues evaluate each other's work and ideas on a continual basis. Similarly, teachers create blended and online classroom activities in which students analyze whole-class data using collaborative cloud-based spreadsheets, documents, wikis, and presentations. These activities help students gain an understanding that the learning enterprise requires collaboration, independent verification, and peer review. This chapter introduces a range of collaborative cloud-based activities through which educators can continuously monitor student ideas and adjust their instructional practice to enhance student learning.

LITERATURE REVIEW / CONCEPTUAL FRAMING

To understand *formative assessment* and its role in online and blended instruction, it is helpful to contrast it with *summative* and *interim assessments.* *Summative assessments* are generally "high-stakes" tests that are used to determine student grades and class- or schoolwide performance. Summative assessments are used to measure mastery of predetermined content or standards and are the backbone of accountability systems at all academic levels. Student grades, college admission, scholarships, graduation, and school rankings are all determined primarily by summative assessments. Summative assessments play a critical role in accountability systems and inform local, statewide, and national educational policies (Perie, Gong, Marion, & Wurtzel, 2007).

Although summative assessments are invaluable for accountability, they cannot be used to diagnose gaps between student knowledge and the intended curriculum at a time when instructional adjustments can be made to benefit student learning. Summative assessments inform stakeholders concerning what students did or did not learn, but do not provide information that will change instruction to benefit current students. Educators therefore employ *interim assessments* throughout instruction to provide such information. Interim assessments, also known as medium-cycle assessments, are administered throughout a course to provide information to diagnose problems and provide information on how instruction can be changed to best meet student needs. Interim assessments take many forms, such as quizzes and reports, and may factor into final grades and school or system assessments. Interim assessments provide students with practice for summative tests and provide teachers with information necessary to adjust future instruction (Perie et al., 2007; Pinchok & Brandt, 2009).

Although summative and interim assessments provide invaluable information and help establish an environment of accountability, they do not provide instructors or students with the information necessary to improve teaching and learning during the actual instruction. By contrast, *formative assessments* are embedded in instruction and are directly linked to teaching and learning *as it occurs.* Formative assessments identify gaps in understanding and can be used by teachers and students to make adjustments to improve student learning *as it occurs.* Formative assessments can be frequent and provide teachers and students with timely feedback on progress (Black & Wiliam, 1998, 2009; Shepard, 2005).

There is much research to show that formative assessments can be used to improve student learning success. Meta-studies analyzing the findings of numerous investigators concluded that formative assessments provide "moments of contingency" (Black & Wiliam, 2009, p. 10), critical points where learning changes direction depending on an assessment. Well-designed formative assessments provide information to make instructional modifications in real time to address student needs (Black & Wiliam, 2009; Shepard, 2005). There are numerous techniques that can be used for formative assessment including hand raising (in response to specific questions), hand signals (to measure levels of self-reported understanding), choral responses (in which students are invited to respond simultaneously to teacher-posed questions), think–pair–share (in which teachers assess student understanding as student groups share with the class), quick-writes (in which students make journal entries in response to specific prompts), exit cards (in which students submit questions or answers as they leave class), self-assessments (in which students check their own understanding by working problems or answering questions in class), and quizzes (in which teachers pose questions to test student understanding) (Bernackic, Ducettee, Majerichb, Stulla, & Varnumd, 2011; Fluckiger, Vigil, Pasco, & Danielson, 2010; Jahan, Shaikh, Norrish, Siddqi, & Qasim, 2013; Youssef, 2012). All of these techniques have proven valuable in traditional classroom settings, but many of these still do not provide the instructor with an immediate assessment of student needs.

For example, the instructor gathers cards and reads them after class or grades quizzes after class. Formative assessments have been shown to be particularly valuable with lower-performing students. Learning deficiencies can be identified early in the learning cycle, allowing instructors to make teaching modifications before lower-performing students are left behind (Athanases & Achinstein, 2003). Numerous textbook publishers produce online quizzes to provide students and instructors immediate feedback, and such products can be very effective in helping identify gaps in students' understanding (Hoon, Chong, & Binti Ngah, 2010). Formative assessment is an iterative "joint productive activity" in which students assemble and interpret knowledge and present their understanding to their teachers who then adjust instruction to optimize learning. This process is repeated throughout learning units (Ash & Levitt, 2003).

Bandura (1997) and Zimmerman (2002) suggested that formative assessments permit students to express themselves and develop a sense of self-efficacy, a key requirement for the development of autonomous learning strategies. Polanyi (1967) and Schön (1987) emphasized the formative and reflective purpose of student discourse and encouraged an open community of learners where ideas and opinions are exchanged so that students can co-construct their understanding. The CFA model provides an environment where such discourse can take place, but unlike traditional instruction where certain students dominate and others are passive, all students are on an equal footing since all have access to the same document for their contributions. A discussion of the underlying theories on which the CFA model is built as well as practical instruction for implementation and findings from ongoing research follows.

FORMATIVE ASSESSMENT AND TECHNOLOGY

Online education has grown dramatically in recent years and is expected to continue growing in the years to come. In his 2010 State of the Union address, President Barack Obama suggested that technology will play an increasingly significant role in America's plan to increase the number college graduates while decreasing the cost of education. The President encouraged the growth of online education to attract more students to college, particularly those from populations underrepresented on traditional brick-and-mortar campuses (Sturgis, 2012). The growth of online and blended education has been accompanied by a growing concern regarding the quality of online education (Hirner & Kochtanek, 2012). Although it is easy to see how formative and interim assessments can be used to measure student understanding in online and blended classes, it is more difficult to see how formative assessments may be employed to directly inform instructional strategies and pacing.

The first electronic solution to formative assessment was the audience response system developed in the early 1970s (Simmons & Elsberry, 1988). William Simmons, an executive at IBM, reflected on the lack of productivity in corporate meetings. Only one person could talk at a time and each decision required a formal vote. Executives often did not speak their mind because of the desire for conformity with the opinions of their superiors. Simmons worked with Theodore Gordon of the Futures Group to design and develop an electronic audience response system. Simmons applied this technology in corporate meetings and found he got not only greater engagement but also more honest feedback. Simmons (Simmons & Elsberry, 1988) found that he could instantly get information on the group's true consensus.

Today there are many audience response systems, also called "student" or "classroom" response systems, in use in educational settings, including dedicated "clickers," computer software, and smartphone apps that aggregate student inputs (Kay & LeSage, 2009). Such systems track individual responses, display polling results, confirm understanding of key points, and gather data for reporting and analysis. These handheld dedicated systems allow students to input responses to questions posed by their instructor.

The instructor receives immediate statistics on student performance on true–false, multiple-choice, and short-answer questions. Studies have shown improved student participation, attendance, and learning with the use of student response systems (Beatty & Gerace, 2009; Bennett & Cunningham, 2009; Buchanan, 2001; Chevalier, 2011; Gok, 2011; Peat & Franklin, 2002). Such systems not only provide information for teachers, they increase accountability for students (Kaleta & Joosten, 2007). Although student response systems have been shown to be a valuable formative assessment tool, current systems do not provide adequate means for free-response questions. They have limited input capabilities and cannot receive complex text, audio, video, or graphic responses that can be used to assess higher levels of understanding. Some uses also require assessments to be prepared in advance, limiting the ability of the teacher to make a spontaneous assessment.

Most student response systems require instructors to create multiple-choice and short-answer questions prior to class. Although such systems have the advantage of providing detailed and immediate statistics on student understanding, they fail to give any insight into the thinking of the student and the reason for their understanding. To circumvent the limitations of handheld student response systems, researchers at the Colorado School of Mines (CSM) developed free Web-based software called InkSurvey that enables students to use pen-based mobile technologies to respond to the open-format questions of their instructor, with diagrams, equations, graphs, and proofs (Kowalski & Kowalski, 2013). The instructor instantly receives student responses and thereby gains real-time insight into student thinking and can immediately reinforce correct understandings and address misconceptions as they develop. InkSurvey has been used successfully in college physics and engineering classes with enrollments exceeding 60 students. Researchers determined that when interactive engineering computer simulations were coupled with real-time formative assessment data collected with InkSurvey, students achieved large and statistically significant learning gains regardless of their learning styles (Kowalski & Kowalski, 2013).

The formative assessment techniques mentioned so far have been shown to be effective in traditional face-to-face classrooms, but can they be used in synchronous or asynchronous online or blended classes? Indeed, many of the techniques mentioned so far can be replicated using cloud-based collaborative resources. Reviews of the literature show that interactive online formative assessments can foster a learner-centered focus and enhanced learner engagement (Gikandi, Morrow, & Davis, 2011). Online feedback systems that are integrated into the student's online learning space have been shown to improve student engagement and performance (Chen & Chen, 2009; Hatziapostolou & Paraskakis, 2010; van Gog, Sluijsmans, Joosten-ten Brinke, & Prins, 2010). Interactive computer-marked assignments and conventional tutor-marked assignments have been shown to help students keep up-to-date in their studies (Jordan, 2009). Others have experimented with social networking to promote peer-to-peer collaboration and formative assessment (Blue & Tirotta, 2011) and some have shown that blogs can be used as a student-based formative assessment tool to cultivate reflective peer-to-peer learning (Olofsson, Lindberg, & Hauge, 2011). Others have shown that anonymous electronic feedback systems can be beneficial in stimulating instructors to make changes to improve the delivery of online courses (Berridge, Penny, & Wells, 2012). Collectively, such studies have indicated that Web-based formative feedback can be instrumental in improving the student learning experience.

The Need for New Formative Assessment Methods

As mentioned previously, schools and universities are encouraged to develop a "culture of assessment" to provide evidence on the effectiveness of instructional programs (Weiner, 2009). Summative assessments provide information after the fact. They tell you what students did or did not master, but they do not provide the information necessary to make changes in instructional or learning strategies while learning is occurring. Although summative assessments may provide powerful incentives for student learning, they do not inform teaching while it is occurring and therefore do not allow instructors and students to alter their approaches to optimize the learning environment. Many teachers agree that formative assessment is very important, but traditional techniques provide incomplete pictures of student understanding. For example, a "show of hands" only tells the instructor the percentage of students who think they understand, and not the percentage that truly understand nor the level of their understanding. Though many of the existing technological solutions work well for preplanned assessment, they do not fluidly allow instructors to create follow-up prompts in real time that modify their instruction in response to student needs.

Educators have grappled with this problem for many years and have adopted a variety of techniques in an attempt to perform continuous formative assessments. For example, in the "modeling method" of physics instruction student teams summarize their models and evidence on a small whiteboard that is easily displayed to the entire class. The whiteboard serves as a focus for the team's report and ensuing class discussions (Hestenes, 2010; Wells, Hestenes, & Swachkhamer, 1995). While this approach has been used effectively, it does not produce a lasting record of students' thinking that can be referred to later. Students' work disappears as soon as the whiteboard is erased. One solution is to have students put their responses on paper to be turned in, as in a quick-write (Clidas, 2010; Rief, 2002) or in a notebook/ journal that students maintain during the course (Roberson & Lankford,

2010).Both of these produce a lasting record, but the logistical challenges of assessing and maintaining them make it difficult for teachers to use them effectively (Ruiz-Primo, Li, Ayala, & Shavelson, 2004).

As we move to blended learning and synchronous online learning, which combines computer-mediated activities with traditional face-to-face classroom methods, we need to think of new ways to use the best of current assessment tools. These environments create a number of new possibilities for formative assessment that allow teachers to quickly see meaningful student responses and adjust teaching based on their needs. There is a need for techniques that provide continuous formative assessment that can be used in traditional, blended, and online learning contexts.

CONTINUOUS FORMATIVE ASSESSMENT

The authors have developed a teaching technique that employs synchronous collaborative web-based documents to perform continuous, real-time formative assessments of students' understanding so that educators can adjust their instruction to address the immediate needs of their students regardless of whether they are in traditional or online settings. The continuous formative assessment (CFA) model has the potential to engage *all* learners *all* of the time as they provide feedback, data, quick-writes, and analyses in response to instructor prompts. Using this model, teachers have the opportunity to observe all student contributions as they are made.

The CFA model has been made possible by the development of free collaborative Web-based spreadsheets, documents, presentations, and drawings (Herr et al., 2012a, 2012b; Herr & Rivas, 2010; Herr, Rivas, Foley, Vandergon & Simila, 2011a, 2011b; Rivas & Herr, 2010). Online tools such as Google Docs or Windows Office Live allow teachers to develop online documents and share editing privileges with their students. The shared documents provide a platform for formative assessment as both the teacher and the student have immediate access. For example, in a blended classroom in which students have computers or tablets, or in an online synchronous lesson, teachers can use a shared online spreadsheet to record students' responses. Teachers enter student names in column one and pose a question in the header of column two (Figure 10.1). Students respond to the question in the cell next to their name, providing the teacher with instant information regarding current student understanding of the lesson. This process can be repeated throughout the class, allowing teachers to assess their students continuously. The spreadsheet becomes a lasting artifact of student thinking and can be analyzed later or referred to by both the teacher and the students.

	A Initials	B Pressure equation	C Pressure is...	D predictions of the candle / flask	E how do you collapse a tank car?	F How high?
1						
2	CV	P=F/A	force	the flame will go out	heat water inside, let it evaporate, then seal off tank	10m
3	DF	f/a	weight weighing down on you	flame will go out	heat water inside	10m
4	SA	p=f/a	gravity	water turn to vapor, then flame go out if available oxygen is burned/used up	water inside and heated tank with cold surroundings	10m
5	GG	p=f/a	force over a specific area	some liquid will rise and candle will go out	lower pressure inside. heat water inside and let it evaporate into vapor, seal	10m
6	HE	P =force of a unit volume	force	flame will go out, water level will increase on the outside, level on inside will be less	change in temperatrure closed to open container	10 m
7	NG	P = F/A	Force pushed onto lower pressure to raise to high pressure	pressure inside drops as steam condenses - Outside pressure pushes water up	Have water inside tank, heat, seal the hose attached to tank with cooler temperature water	32 m
8	HH	p=f/a	pressure is a force	the water is going to go up a little into the flask and put the flame out	heat up water inside and then seal the tank	10 m
9	JK	p=f/a	the force on an object	candle will create steam, the water will rise and put out the candle	heated water inside of the tank, then sealed and cooled the tank	10m
10	LO	p=f/a	ratio of force distribution	the water will rise and put out the fire	put water inside and then heat it up and seal it	100 m
11	TY		force on a given area	candle flame goes out, gas pushes water level up	heated water in open tank then seal	10m
12	SS	force per area	a force	the water level should rise in the flask.	same way as the can	10 m
13	SR	p=f/a	force on something	candle will go out	lower pressure inside the tank, higher pressure outside	10m
14	FR	P=F	pressure is a force	The heat from the candle will make it buoyant/ flame goes out	evaporate a small amt of water then seal the tank	10m
15	DW	P=F/A	force per unit area	Flask will get smoky, then flame will go out, then water will rise	Fill with steam, seal and wait	10 meters

Figure 10.1 Example of an electronic quick-write in which a teacher asks students to respond to prompts which are typed in the top row of a spreadsheet. Each student uses the row with their initials.

Although many companies now offer online documents, Google offers the most comprehensive suite of free resources, and so we now discuss their offerings in more detail. In 2006 Google acquired Upstartle, the software company that introduced the first Web-based word processor. In addition, Google acquired rights to the first Web-based spreadsheet from 2Web Technologies (Google Press Center, 2006). In 2007, Google developed the first Web-based presentation program (Bodis, 2007) and introduced all three as a free development suite known as Google Drive. Any individual who opens a free Google account has an automatic link to Google Drive (formerly called Google Docs). Users can develop documents, spreadsheets, and presentations online using any modern browser, or can import them from a wide range of formats. Google documents are automatically saved to Google servers whose actual location or name is not needed. These documents are described as being located "in the cloud." As with related wiki technologies, a revision history is associated with each document so users can review, revise, and/or reverse editorial changes.

Cloud-based documents allow for the type of collaboration and sharing environment for productive student learning communities (Falkner & Falkner, 2012). Teachers and students can work on the same file as they coauthor reports, creative writing, and other documents. As students collaborate, each can see which revisions have been made by their colleagues, and can reverse or restore changes by selecting options in the revision history. Rather than working on original files and sending copies for peers to work on, all students work directly on the original so there is no confusion about the current status of the document. Such Web-based development resources preclude the need for expensive software, since all one needs is a free downloadable Web browser.

Collaborative cloud-based document technology creates new opportunities for formative assessment involving laboratory science experiences. While ideal science laboratory experiences should help *develop scientific reasoning* and an *understanding of the complexity and ambiguity of empirical work* (National Research Council, 2006), many laboratory experiences that students receive do not assist in the achievement of these goals. Web-based documents can provide an opportunity for students to understand the complex and collaborative nature of empirical research as they collect and analyze data from multiple lab groups, classes, or schools (Herr et al., 2011b; Herr & Rivas, 2010). Data collection can be simplified by survey tools, such as Google Forms, that link directly to online Google Spreadsheets. Teachers or students can develop forms online and then invite students to input their findings. Spreadsheets are created from the data, with records (rows) representing the lab groups and fields (columns) representing answers to specific questions. Links to survey forms and their associated spreadsheets can be provided by copying document addresses to email messages, blogs, newsgroups, or websites. Students reply to the online forms, and together build a single spreadsheet file that is shared by all.

Within moments, an entire class can input their data, generating a table with as many records as there are laboratory groups, and as many fields as there are questions on the form. These datasets can be analyzed with built-in online tools and "mashup gadgets" (Web application hybrids), or downloaded to each group for analysis with traditional tools such as Microsoft Excel. The instructor can easily analyze all contributions on a single screen, regardless of the physical location of the contributors. This provides the opportunity for formative feedback and possibly peer feedback, as the results are apparent to all. For example, an online instructor can collect observational weather data from his or her students and then analyze it in light of weather station reports of temperature, pressure, and dew point. As class is conducted in a medium such as Google Hangouts (a free video-conferencing application) or Collaborate (Blackboard's tool for synchronous online instruction), both the instructor and all of the students can continuously monitor all student data, which is plotted on a Google Spreadsheet. This monitoring allows a new level of formative assessment for data collection, as many errors can be identified and corrected before it's too late (d'Alessio & Lundquist, 2013).

Many classroom experiments call for the measurement or calculation of specific values, such as the density of water, the molar volume of a gas, the wavelength of a laser's light, or the percentage of root tip cells in mitosis. Students may notice that their values differ from those of other lab teams and thereby gain an understanding of the value of descriptive statistical measures, such as mean and standard deviation, when analyzing experimental data. As students graph class data using Web-based spreadsheet tools, they may note bell-shaped distributions and gain a more intuitive understanding of the normal curve and basic descriptive statistics. Bimodal distributions may indicate the use of two different techniques while random distributions may indicate flaws in experimental design or implementation. By analyzing class datasets, students learn the complexity of the natural world and see the need for standardizing procedures and controlling for confounding variables. Thus, collaborative Web-based technologies can be employed to provide continuous formative assessment of laboratory techniques (Herr et al., 2010a, 2010b). Many science educators shy away from online and blended learning environments because they believe that such environments do not provide realistic laboratory experiences and lack the community that is so important to scientific research. The CFA model can address many such concerns by bringing students together online to conduct collaborative investigations.

Web-based documents can be employed to help students learn aspects of the nature of science and gain experience working in large teams. Scientists work in research laboratories that are part of larger networks and associations, and share their findings with their peers through journals and conferences. In the traditional college or school science classroom, only the instructor reviews student work. Web-based document technology provides students the opportunity to work cooperatively in the collection of data, analysis, and assessment of peer data.

Web-based document technologies (e.g., Google Documents, Spreadsheets, Forms, and Presentations) provide an environment for collaboration, but online instructors must develop appropriate activities and lessons if they plan to capitalize on the opportunities the technology affords. For example, an investigation may ask students to find the relationship between mass, length, and the period of a pendulum. Students in an online or blended physics class can submit the results from experiments performed at home to a collaborative form or spreadsheet. Relationships that are invisible with the few data points collected by a single lab group become clear with the addition of whole class data. If each group measures the period of a pendulum using different weights and lengths, then students will have large datasets to analyze. Using *spreadsheet curve-fitting* technology, students can find the equations that best fit the class data. By analyzing whole class data, students can determine that the period of a pendulum is independent of mass, but directly dependent upon the square root of the length of the pendulum. Such conclusions can be made quickly when working with whole class data, but may take a long time if each lab group must independently generate all of the necessary data. Pooled data makes it easier to find mistakes and correct them during the activity. Rather than waiting for the final lab report, teachers and students can assess data as it is input into the cloud-based spreadsheet where mistakes will often show up as outlying points. By performing a formative assessment on student data immediately upon input, the instructor can save students much wasted time trying to interpret flawed data.

TECHNIQUES FOR CONTINUOUS FORMATIVE ASSESSMENT

All of the following techniques use collaborative online resources. In each case, the instructor sets up a document on which students simultaneously enter data, or a folder to which students simultaneously upload documents. The instructor establishes sharing privileges so that students can access these resources using their email login and passwords. By making such resources private, the instructor can identify the contributions made by each student. In addition, the instructor can analyze the revision history to see a chronology of changes made by specific students. The following techniques are possible with both computers and mobile communication devices such as phones and tablets.

CFA Technique 1: Online Quick-Write

The electronic quick-write is perhaps the most useful of all of the CFA techniques. The instructor sets up a spreadsheet such that student initials, names, or ID numbers are in column one. He or she then starts asking questions and provides a brief title at the top of the adjacent column. The instructor can tell when students start to type because their cells turn gray. Once they press the enter key, their entry appears in the appropriate column. Figure 10.1 shows the first few rows and columns of a quick-write that was made for a particular class. The first column shows that all but one of the students (row 14) knew the mathematical definition of pressure. The instructor then asked the students to complete the sentence, "Pressure is. . . ." In this open-ended environment, students produced a variety of responses (column C), which indicated that they did not truly understand the formula that they had just accurately written.

By examining the data in columns B and C, the instructor is able to do a quick formative assessment regarding students' understanding of pressure. Namely, students seem to "know" the formula for pressure, but do not know how to express the formula in words. Being able to ask open-ended questions enables more complex questions requiring students to demonstrate understanding. This provides a "moment of contingency" at which the instructor needs to illustrate how to turn algebraic equations into sentences and thus help students understand the meaning of this and future equations. Without this formative assessment tool, it is quite possible that the instructor could continue teaching, assuming that students truly understood the concept of pressure.

In column D, students are asked to make a prediction regarding what will happen when a flask is inverted on top of a burning candle that is standing in a tray of water. This question was asked as a follow-up to a similar activity where students observed soda cans spontaneously collapsing under atmospheric pressure when steam inside the empty cans condensed. A quick survey of column D shows the instructor that only one student (row 7) seems to make the connection between the two phenomena. The instructor is then prompted to show a video of a railroad tank car that collapses under normal atmospheric pressure. In column E, we see that nearly everyone is making a correct prediction, which is most simply described in row 15. Finally, the instructor assesses his or her students' knowledge of atmospheric pressure by asking a question in which they must determine the height to which air pressure can push a column of water in an evacuated tube. At this point, the instructor sees only two errors (rows 7 and 10) and decides that it is appropriate to move to the next level of understanding regarding pressure.

With CFA, instructors open a single spreadsheet document and simply add multiple worksheets to it. If each worksheet is dated, the instructor has a comprehensive picture of student understanding for each day of instruction. Eventually students stop raising their hands to answer questions, and automatically enter their responses in the spreadsheet. The instructor can quickly scan the spreadsheet for blanks. Any blank indicates that the student was either off task or unable to answer the prompt. In a normal classroom, students often defer to the "good students" who offer verbal responses. The instructor gets only one data point to go on, and it is generally data from one of the best students in the class who is willing to raise his or her hand in order to contribute.

The online quick-write provides instructors the opportunity to get student responses on many questions in a single period. This technique works very well in online environments and provides the instructor with immediate data regarding the engagement and understanding of all participants, regardless of their physical location.

CFA Technique 2: Collaborative Presentation

Instructors can assess student understanding by assigning each an individual page in an online presentation and watching the presentation develop in response to a teacher prompt. Figure 10.2 shows a presentation that was made when trying to illustrate the concept of order of magnitude in measurements. Students were assigned an order of magnitude and were to find a photo of an object at that scale. The collaborative presentation differs from the collaborative spreadsheet in that each student is assigned a unique page rather than a unique row in a spreadsheet. These pages can accommodate not only text responses, but also audio and video files.

CFA Technique 3: Collaborative Diagram Album

Teachers often ask students to diagram the subjects being discussed in class. The whiteboard methods used by Hestenes (2010) and others provide a way of quickly sharing student-generated diagrams. To see students work in an online or blended setting, the teacher can ask students to use smartphones to scan their drawings and upload them to the class folder in the cloud. In Figure 10.3, students were asked to draw an apparatus for measuring the wavelength of a laser beam. After each student completed their

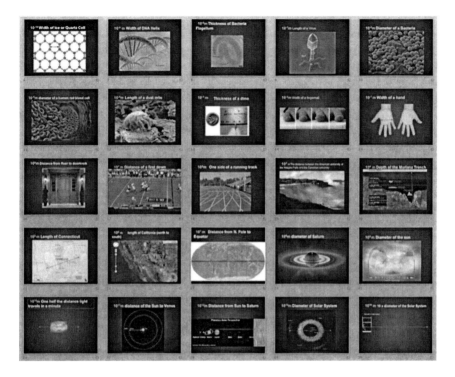

Figure 10.2 Slides from a collaborative presentation. Each student added one slide to illustrate an order of magnitude of size.

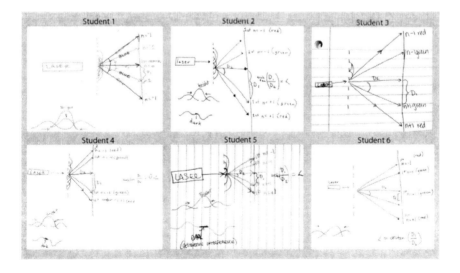

Figure 10.3 Student drawings collected simultaneously in a cloud-based shared folder.

drawing on paper, they scanned it and entered it into the shared folder. When the instructor clicks on the folder, he or she can review the contributions of all students simultaneously, and can bring student work up for illustration. With collaborative albums, teachers can monitor the thought processes of their students in real time. Unlike the whiteboard approach, the students' work is not erased when the next question is asked and can be used when students are spread around the world.

CFA Technique 4: Collaborative Photo/Movie Album

As previously demonstrated, the CFA model can use any type of media, at any time, from any part of the world. In technique 3, the instructor set up a collaborative album into which students deposited scans of diagrams made with pencil or pen and paper. Sometimes, photographs or movies are more telling than diagrams or text. Using technique 4, students can take photographs or movies on their smartphones and send them to a shared folder. For example, Figure 10.4 shows the movies made by students trying to illustrate the motions shown by the graphs. Some students made movies using their fingers, while others use a mouse, a toy car, or their entire body. Once the movies are collected, the instructor plays them back to the students in his or her online class and they evaluate their accuracy using an online quick-write. In addition to harvesting movie data, the instructor can also get photographs from his or her students. Figure 10.5 illustrates a shared album into which students deposited a variety of photographs of science-related topics they had seen in their communities or travels. A quick glance at the thumbnails in the album allows the online instructor to do a formative assessment on their success in meeting this requirement.

CFA Technique 5: Collaborative Data Plotting

One of the challenges of online learning is that it is difficult to learn from one's peers. You can't just look over their shoulder while they are doing an activity or experiment to get ideas, nor can you hang around after class to discuss techniques and strategies. Fortunately, cloud-based collaborative documents allow you to meet with your peers in cyberspace. Figure 10.6 shows the data collected by numerous students in a physical science class. Students were tasked with the goal of determining the factors that cause something to sink or float in water. Students assemble block combinations that vary in volume and mass and then determine if they sink or float in water. The instructor has prepared an online spreadsheet with cells for each lab group. As they enter the mass and volume of

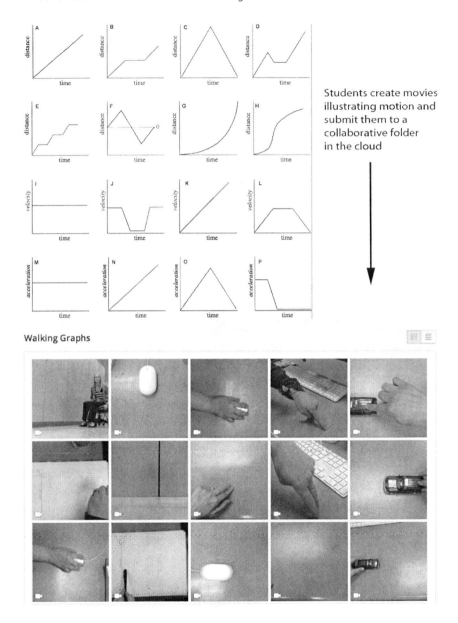

Students create movies illustrating motion and submit them to a collaborative folder in the cloud

Walking Graphs

Figure 10.4 Collaborative movie album. Movies submitted by students to illustrate movements corresponding to graphs.

Figure 10.5 Online collaborative photo album. Photos students submitted to illustrate subjects of scientific interest in their community.

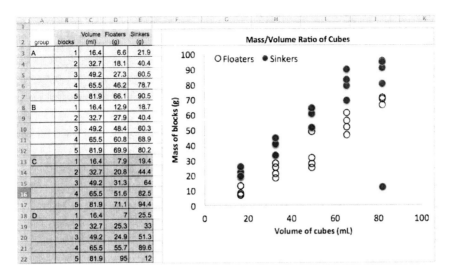

		Volume (ml)	Floaters (g)	Sinkers (g)
group	blocks			
A	1	16.4	6.6	21.9
	2	32.7	18.1	40.4
	3	49.2	27.3	60.5
	4	65.5	46.2	78.7
	5	81.9	66.1	90.5
B	1	16.4	12.9	18.7
	2	32.7	27.9	40.4
	3	49.2	48.4	60.3
	4	65.5	60.8	68.9
	5	81.9	69.9	80.2
C	1	16.4	7.9	19.4
	2	32.7	20.8	44.4
	3	49.2	31.3	64
	4	65.5	51.6	82.5
	5	81.9	71.1	94.4
D	1	16.4	7	25.5
	2	32.7	25.3	33
	3	49.2	24.9	51.3
	4	65.5	55.7	89.6
	5	81.9	95	12

Figure 10.6 Collaborative spreadsheet. Students submit their data to online spreadsheet and make interpretations based on pooled data.

floaters or sinkers, marks are plotted on the graph. The graph develops a clear pattern when the data points of each individual or lab group are reported. Eventually, students see a clear line between sinkers and floaters and infer that anything above this line will sink in water and anything below this line will float in water. As is intended, they deduce that the mass-to-volume ratio of the blocks determines whether they float or sink, and the dividing line between the two objects represents the mass-to-volume ratio of the fluid in which they are placed. Thus, students discover the concept of density by discovery rather than by direct instruction. As students see their data plotted, they may also see some outliers and come to question the quality of such data. Outliers generally indicate something important or simply bad data. In this case, the student reversed the mass and volume measurements, and once they saw their error, they quickly corrected it. Thus, students can perform formative assessments on the quality of their own data and draw conclusions based on their own data as well as the data of their peers.

RESEARCH QUESTIONS

The CFA model presented in this chapter raises a variety of interesting questions related to the effectiveness of formative assessment in online and blended learning environments.

1. *Instructor Formative Assessment:* To what degree do instructors adjust their instruction to meet student needs when employing CFA compared to traditional models of instruction?
2. *Student Formative Assessment:* What effect does the CFA model have in motivating students to apply formative self-assessments such as self-monitoring and self-correcting?
3. *Accountability/Engagement:* To what degree are students engaged in the instructional process by the use of CFA compared to traditional models of instruction?
4. *Student Learning:* What effect does the CFA model have on student learning?

METHODOLOGY/APPROACH

To address these research questions, researchers are performing mixed-methods studies using survey instruments, observations from third-party researchers, and interviews with teachers and students. A preliminary survey was delivered online in computer-equipped classrooms at the end of the fall semester of 2012. The participants were students in three courses at California State University, Northridge, in which CFA was employed on a daily basis throughout the semester. Most survey questions were given in the Likert-scale format. Seven of the nearly 100 questions in the survey were free response. The questions asked students to compare the effectiveness of the CFA pedagogy with other methods that they had received at the university with respect to accountability, engagement, metacognition, social learning, and intent to employ similar techniques in their own instruction. Fifty-one of 70 students completed the voluntary survey that included additional questions related to program evaluation (response rate = 73%). The students were graduates of one of the following three courses: Website Development for Teaching Science (a masters degree course for in-service science teachers), Methods of Teaching Science (a credential course for pre-service science teachers), and Computers in Instruction (a credential course for secondary school teachers, regardless of field). Twenty-one respondents were in-service teachers enrolled in a master's-degree program in secondary science education and 30 were preservice secondary school credential students representing a variety of disciplines. Fifteen of the respondents were male and 36 were female. Ethnicity demographics of the participants were not recorded in the survey.

We are currently engaged in additional research efforts to clarify the effectiveness of the CFA pedagogy in promoting effective formative assessment. Independent researchers are making observations, conducting surveys, and interviewing professors, teachers, and students in university and secondary school courses in which CFA is employed.

RESULTS/FINDINGS

A variety of studies are currently in process to address the research questions we have proposed. We shall discuss preliminary findings, but look forward to the results of the ongoing research to provide more comprehensive answers. Students were asked to compare how accountable they felt to their instructor during instruction. They were asked to compare the course they had taken in which CFA was employed with all other courses they had taken at the university. For example, in the first question (Figure 10.7), students were asked to evaluate how accountable they felt to their instructor during instruction by responding to a five-point scale with values ranging from "much less accountable" to "much more accountable" compared to all other university classes they had taken. The top two values were combined to indicate respondents' general response. Figures 10.7 and 10.8 show the results of the survey. Participants reported substantial benefits of the CFA model for the dimensions identified in our research questions:

1. *Instructor Formative Assessment*: Six professors at California State University, Northridge (representing the departments of chemistry, geology, biology, and secondary education) have employed the CFA technique. Personal discussions with these professors indicate that all believe that CFA provides them with valuable information regarding the level of student understanding, allowing them to modify lessons to maximize student engagement and learning.
2. *Student Formative Assessment*: Seventy-four percent of respondents said that they were more mentally engaged in the instructional process as a result of the CFA approach, and 85% said that they were more likely to catch their own errors. These early results suggest that, in a class employing CFA techniques, students display an increased propensity to self-monitor and self-correct and are subsequently taking more responsibility for their own learning during instruction.
3. *Accountability/Engagement*: The initial study showed that 77% of respondents felt more accountable to the instructor, 71% felt more accountable to peers, 75% felt more accountable for their own learning, and 74% felt that they were more mentally engaged as a result of the CFA approach.
4. *Student Learning*: Eighty-nine percent of respondents thought that more learning would occur if they used CFA in their own secondary school classrooms, and 96% said they intend to use the CFA model in their own instruction. This self-reported data is supported by research from colleagues at the Colorado School of Mines working with a CFA tool known as InkSurvey (as described previously).

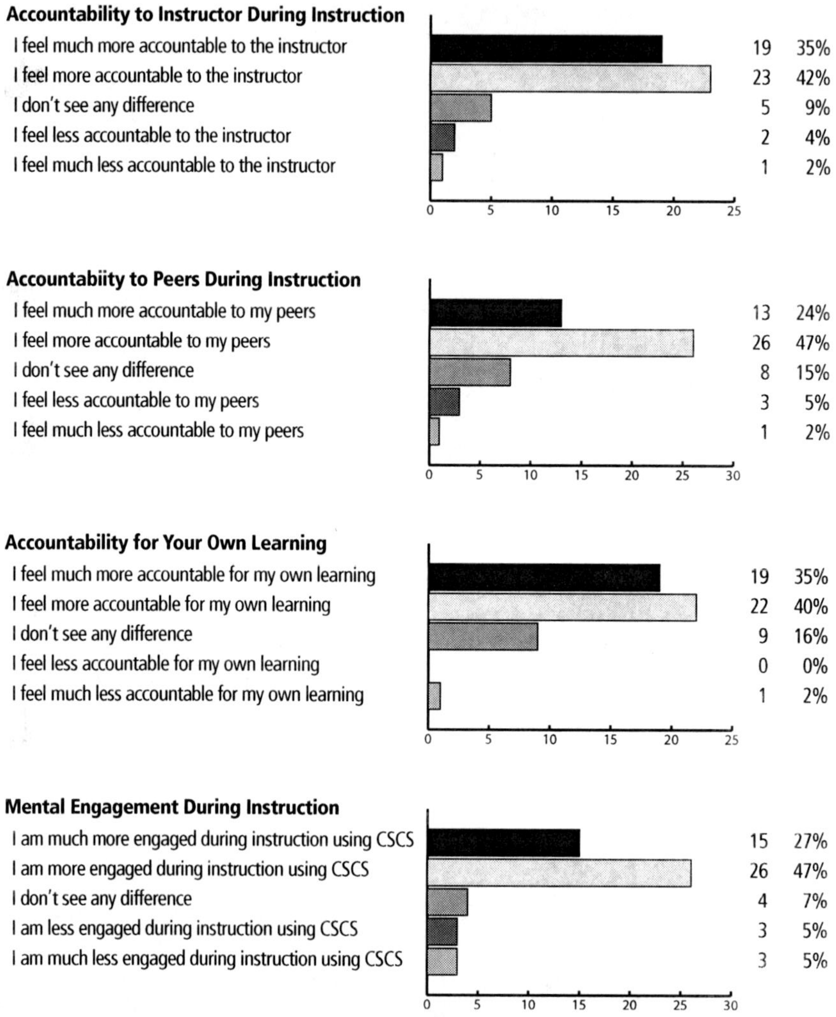
Accountability to Instructor During Instruction
I feel much more accountable to the instructor 19 35%
I feel more accountable to the instructor 23 42%
I don't see any difference 5 9%
I feel less accountable to the instructor 2 4%
I feel much less accountable to the instructor 1 2%
0 5 10 15 20 25
Accountabiity to Peers During Instruction
I feel much more accountable to my peers 13 24%
I feel more accountable to my peers 26 47%
I don't see any difference 8 15%
I feel less accountable to my peers 3 5%
I feel much less accountable to my peers 1 2%
0 5 10 15 20 25 30
Accountability for Your Own Learning
I feel much more accountable for my own learning 19 35%
I feel more accountable for my own learning 22 40%
I don't see any difference 9 16%
I feel less accountable for my own learning 0 0%
I feel much less accountable for my own learning 1 2%
0 5 10 15 20 25
Mental Engagement During Instruction
I am much more engaged during instruction using CSCS 15 27%
I am more engaged during instruction using CSCS 26 47%
I don't see any difference 4 7%
I am less engaged during instruction using CSCS 3 5%
I am much less engaged during instruction using CSCS 3 5%
0 5 10 15 20 25 30

Figure 10.7 Survey of participants' perspectives of the effectiveness of CFA with respect to accountability and engagement in comparison with all other university courses in which CFA is not used.

Catching and Correcting Your Errors

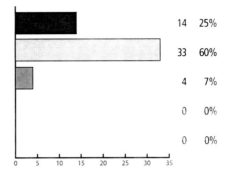

I am much more likely to catch my errors when I see data from my peers	14	25%
I am more likely to catch my errors when I see data from my peers	33	60%
There is no difference	4	7%
I am less likely to catch my errors when I see data from my peers	0	0%
I am much less likely to catch my errors when I see data from my peers	0	0%

Learning From Peers

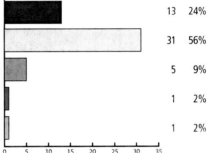

I have learned much more from my peers using CSCS than if this pedagogy was not used	13	24%
I have learned more from my peers using CSCS than if this pedagogy was not used	31	56%
CSCS has not affected how much I learn from my peers	5	9%
I have learned less from my peers using CSCS than if this pedagogy was not used	1	2%
I have learned much less from my peers using CSCS than if this pedagogy was not used	1	2%

Potential Use of CSCS in Your Classrooms

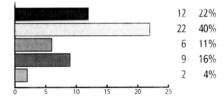

I would use it everyday	12	22%
I would use it an average of couple of times a week	22	40%
I would use it an average of one a week	6	11%
I would use it an average of once a month	9	16%
Never	2	4%

Potential Effect of CSCS in Your Classrooms

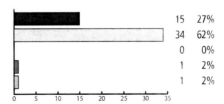

Significant improvement in student learning	15	27%
Improvement in student learning	34	62%
No difference in student learning	0	0%
Decline in student learning	1	2%
Significant decline in student learning	1	2%

Figure 10.8 Survey of participants' perspectives of the effectiveness of CFA in helping them catch errors and learn from peers. Survey of participants' perspectives on the potential for use and effectiveness of CFA in their own future classrooms.

DISCUSSION AND IMPLICATIONS

The CFA model is well suited for online and blended learning environments. Online learning has always been suspect because instructors have been unable to measure the level of student engagement nor verify that the individual answering summative assessments is the individual enrolled in the class. The CFA model has been shown to enhance accountability, providing a window into student engagement and a profile of student thinking during synchronous online or in-person instruction.

The CFA model helps establish an environment that resembles more closely the professional learning environment in which colleagues share their ideas with each other and provide feedback and critique. An instructor can elect to make some or all of student contributions visible to the entire class. In such an environment, students can evaluate their ideas and contributions in light of those of their peers, just the way professionals share their findings and provide critiques of their colleagues' work.

Preliminary data from pre-service teachers indicates tremendous enthusiasm for the CFA model, and dramatic improvements in collaborative online technologies suggest that these strategies will continue to grow in popularity. The move away from traditional print resources toward computer-based learning suggests an increasing familiarity with the technologies that support CFA. For example, South Korea announced that it intends to replace textbooks with tablets by 2015 (Kim & Jung, 2010). This trend is expected to grow worldwide, and with it will come increased understanding of and access to the technologies necessary for CFA.

CONCLUSIONS, RECOMMENDATIONS, AND FUTURE RESEARCH

The CFA model provides a mechanism by which instructors of online and blended courses can assess the learning of their students during synchronous instruction. As instructors analyze student data, they have an opportunity to adjust their instruction to immediately meet student needs. As a result of increased accountability and engagement, it is anticipated that students will perform better and be less likely to fall behind or drop out of online and blended courses. Although there are a variety of research initiatives underway at the university where this pedagogy was developed, it is clear that more research needs to be done in other institutions and settings.

REFERENCES

Ash, D., & Levitt, K. (2003). Working within the zone of proximal development: Formative assessment as professional development. *Journal of Science Teacher Education, 14*(1), 23–48.

Athanases, S., & Achinstein, B. (2003). Focusing new instructors on individual and low performing students: The centrality of formative assessment in students: A pilot study. *Instructors College Record, 105,* 1486–1520.

Bandura, A. (1997). *Self-efficacy: The exercise of control.* New York, NY: Freeman.

Beatty, I. D., & Gerace, W. J. (2009). Technology-enhanced formative assessment: A research-based pedagogy for teaching science with classroom response technology. *Journal of Science Education and Technology, 18*(2), 146–162.

Bernackie, M. L., Ducettee, J. P., Majerichb, D. M., Stulla, J. C., & Varnumd, S. J. (2011). The effects of formative assessment pre-lecture online chapter quizzes and student-initiated inquiries to the instructor on academic achievement educational research and evaluation: *An International Journal on Theory and Practice, 17,* 253–262.

Bennett, K. R., & Cunningham, A. C. (2009). Teaching formative assessment strategies to preservice teachers: Exploring the use of handheld computing to facilitate the action research process. *Journal of Computing in Teacher Education, 25,* 99–105.

Berridge, G. G., Penney, S., & Wells, J. A. (2012a). eFACT: Formative assessment of classroom teaching for online classes. *Turkish Online Journal of Distance Education, 13*(1), 68–78.

Black, P., & Wiliam, D. (1998). *Inside the black box: Raising standards through classroom assessment.* London, UK: King's College London.

Black, P., & Wiliam, D. (2009). Developing the theory of formative assessment. *Educational Assessment, Evaluation and Accountability, 21,* 5–31.

Blue, E., & Tirotta, R. (2011). The benefits & drawbacks of integrating cloud computing and interactive whiteboards in teacher preparation. *Techtrends: Linking Research and Practice to Improve Learning, 55*(3), 31–39.

Bodis, A. (2007). *Our feature presentation.* Official Google Blog. Retrieved from http://googleblog.blogspot.com/2007/09/our-feature-presentation.html.

Buchanan, T. (2001). The efficacy of a world wide web mediated formative assessment. *Journal of Computer Assisted Learning, 16*(3), 193–200.

Chen, C.-M., & Chen, M.-C. (2009). Mobile formative assessment tool based on data mining techniques for supporting web-based learning. *Computers and Education, 52*(1), 256–273.

Chevalier, J. (2011). *Teachers' perception of handheld response systems as a tool for formative assessment in high school classrooms.* Ann Arbor, MI: ProQuest.

Clark, I. (2011). Formative assessment: Policy, perspectives and practice (EJ931151). *Florida Journal of Educational Administration and Policy, 4*(2), 158–180.

Clidas, J. (2010). A laboratory of words. *Science and Children, 48*(3), 60–63.

d'Alessio, M. A., & Loraine L. L. (2013). Computer supported collaborative rocketry: Teaching students to distinguish good and bad data like an expert physicist. *The Physics Teacher, 51*(7), 424–427.

Falkner, K., & Falkner, N. J. (2012). Supporting and structuring "contributing student pedagogy" in Computer Science curricula. *Computer Science Education, 22*(4), 413–443.

Fluckiger, J., Vigil, Y., Pasco, R., & Danielson, K. (2010). Formative feedback: Involving students as partners in assessment to enhance learning. *College Teaching, 58*(4), 136–140.

Gikandi, J. W., Morrow, D., & Davis, N. E. (2011). Online formative assessment in higher education: A review of the literature. *Computers & Education, 57*(4), 2333–2351.

Gok, T. (2011). An evaluation of student response systems from the viewpoint of instructors and students. *Turkish Online Journal of Educational Technology, 10*(4), 67–83.

Google Press Center. (2006). Google press center: Google announces limited test on google labs: Google Spreadsheets. Retrieved from http://googlepress. blogspot.com/2006/06/google-announces-limited-test-on-google_06.html

Hatziapostolou, T., & Paraskakis, I. (2010). Enhancing the impact of formative feedback on student learning through an online feedback system. *Electronic Journal of e-Learning, 8*(2), 111–122.

Herr, N., Foley, B,. Rivas, M., d'Alessio, M., Vandergon, V., Simila, G., Nguyen-Graff, D. & Postma, H. (2012a, March). Employing collaborative online documents for continuous formative assessments. *Proceedings of the Society for Information Technology and Teacher Education (SITE)*. Austin, TX.

Herr, N., Foley, B., Rivas, M., d'Alessio, M., Vandergon, V., Simila, G., Nguyen-Graff, D. & Postma, H. (2012b, October). Using cloud-based collaborative documents to perform continuous formative assessment during instruction. *Proceedings of AACE E-Learn Conference*. Montréal, Canada.

Herr, N. & Rivas M. (2010, October). Teaching the nature of scientific research by collecting and analyzing whole-class data using collaborative Web-based documents. *Proceedings of the Association for the Advancement of Computing in Education*. Orlando, Florida.

Herr, N., Rivas, M., Foley, B., Vandergon, V. & Simila, G. (2011a, January). Computer supported collaborative education: Strategies for using collaborative Web-based technologies to engage all learners. *Proceedings of the 9th Annual Hawaii International Conference on Education*. Honolulu, Hawaii.

Herr, N., Rivas, M., Foley, B., Vandergon, V. & Simila, G. (2011b, January). Using collaborative Web-based documents to instantly collect and analyze whole class data. *Proceedings of the 9th Annual Hawaii International Conference on Education*. Honolulu, Hawaii.

Hestenes, D. (2010). Modeling theory for math and science education. In R. Lesh, P. L. Galbraith, C. R. Haines, & A. Hurford (Eds.), *Modeling students' mathematical competencies* (pp. 13–41). New York, NY: Springer.

Hirner, L., & Kochtanek, T. (2012). Quality indicators of online programs. *Community College Journal of Research and Practice, 36*(2), 122–130.

Hoon, T., Chong, T., & Binti Ngah, N. (2010). Effect of an interactive courseware in the learning of matrices. *Educational Technology and Society, 13*(1), 121–132.

Jahan, F., Shaikh, N., Norrish, M., Siddqi, N., & Qasim, R. (2013). Comparison of students' self-assessment to examiners assessment in a formative observed structured clinical examination: A pilot study. *Journal of Postgraduate Medical Institute, 27*(1), 94–99.

Jordan, S. (2009). Online interactive assessment in teaching science: A view from the Open University. *Education in Science, 231,* 16–17.

Kaleta, R., & Joosten, T. (2007). Student response systems: A University of Wisconsin System study of slickers. *EduCause Center for Applied Research Research Bulletin, 10,* 4–6.

Kay, R. H., & LeSage, A. (2009). A strategic assessment of audience response systems used in higher education. *Australasian Journal of Educational Technology, 25*(2), 235–249.

Kim, J. H. Y., & Jung, H. Y. (2010). South Korean digital textbook project. *Computers in the Schools, 27*(3–4), 247–265.

Kowalski, F., & Kowalski, S. (2013). *The effect of student learning styles on the learning gains achieved when interactive simulations are coupled with real-time formative assessment via pen-enabled mobile technology.* Report for 2011 HP Catalyst Grant and by the National Science Foundation (Grant No. 1037519).

National Research Council. (2006). *America's lab report: Investigations in high school science.* Washington, DC: National Academies Press.

Olofsson, A. D., Lindberg, J. O. & Hauge, T. E. (2011). Blogs and the design of reflective peer-to-peer technology-enhanced learning and formative assessment (EJ930914). *Campus-Wide Information Systems, 28*(3), 183–194.

Peat, M., & Franklin, S. (2002). Supporting student learning: The use of computer–based formative assessment modules. *British Journal of Educational Technology, 33*(5), 515–523.

Perie, M., Marion, S., Gong, B., & Wurtzel, J. (2007). *The role of interim assessments in a comprehensive assessment system.* Washington, DC: The Aspen Institute.

Pinchok, N., & Brandt, W. C. (2009). *Connecting formative assessment research to practice: An introductory guide for educators.* Naperville, IL Learning Point Associates.

Polanyi, M. (1967). *The tacit dimension.* New York, NY: Anchor Books.

Popham, W. J. (2008). *Transformative assessment.* Alexandria, VA: Association for Supervision and Curriculum Development.

Rief, L. (2002). Quick-writes lead to literacy. *Voices from the Middle, 10*(1), 50–51.

Rivas, M., & Herr, N. (2010, January). The use of collaborative web-based documents and websites to build scientific research communities in science classrooms. *Proceedings of the 8th Annual Hawaii International Conference on Education.* Honolulu, Hawaii.

Roberson, C., & Lankford, D. (2010). Laboratory notebooks in the science classroom. *Science Teacher, 77*(1), 38–42.

Ruiz-Primo, M. A., Li, M., Ayala, C., & Shavelson, R. J. (2004). Evaluating students' science notebooks as an assessment tool. *International Journal of Science Education, 26*(12), 1477–1506.

Schön, D. (1987). *Educating the reflective practitioner.* San Francisco, CA: Jossey-Bass.

Shepard, L. A. (2005). Formative assessment: Caveat emptor. Paper presented at the The Future of Assessment: Shaping Teaching and Learning ETS Invitational Conference, New York.

Simmons, W. W., & Elsberry, R. (1988). *Inside IBM: the Watson years (a personal memoir),* Pennsylvania, PA: Dorrance.

Sturgis, I. (2012). The online frontier. *Diverse: Issues in Higher Education, 29*(3), 16–19.

Van Gog, T., Sluijsmans, D. M. A., Joosten-ten Brinke, D., & Prins, F. J. (2010). Formative assessment in an online learning environment to support flexible on-the-job learning in complex professional domains. *Educational Technology Research and Development, 58*(3), 311–324.

Weiner, W. (2009). Establishing a culture of assessment. *Academe Online.* Retrieved from http://www.aaup.org/article/establishing-culture-assessment#.VBEHUy5dW6w.

Wells, M., Hestenes, D., & Swackhamer, G. (1995). A modeling method for high school physics instruction. *American Journal of Physics, 64*, 114–119.

Youssef, L. S. (2012). Using student reflections in the formative evaluation of instruction: a course-integrated approach. *Reflective Practice, 13*(2), 237–254.

Zimmerman, B. J. (2002). Becoming a self-regulated learner: An overview. *Theory into Practice, 41*(2), 64–70.

CHAPTER 11

BLENDED LEARNING AND ASSESSMENT THROUGH DYNAMIC DIGITAL PORTFOLIOS

The E-Scape Approach

Kay Stables
University of London, United Kingdom

Osnat Dagan
Beit Berl College, Israel

Dan Davies
Cardiff Metropolitan University, United Kingdom

INTRODUCTION

Portfolios that document the outcomes of learning have been highlighted as valuable tools to support authentic, performance-based assessment. Of particular value are the insights they afford to learning that has taken place

Assessment in Online and Blended Learning Environments, pages 215–234
Copyright © 2015 by Information Age Publishing
All rights of reproduction in any form reserved.

over time, including through project-based learning (PBL; Barak, 2011; Chang Barker, 2005; Mason, Pegler, & Weller, 2004). With the introduction of digital tools, e-portfolios present greatly enhanced opportunities for linking evidence to judgment. A standard view of portfolios, both paper based and digital, is that they provide a repository for work that has been done, creating a space for recording and reflecting and for presenting an ongoing archive of evidence of learning. Through research undertaken in the Technology Education Research Unit (TERU) at Goldsmiths, University of London, for the UK Assessment of Performance Unit (Kimbell, Stables, Wheeler, Wozniak, & Kelly, 1991) we explored a different type of portfolio, one that captures evidence "on task," dynamically. Through this approach we created the concept of an "unpickled" portfolio (Stables & Kimbell, 2000; Kimbell, 2006; Kimbell & Stables, 2008): a portfolio that captures evidence of process-based performance during short, focused assessment tasks. We saw these portfolios as learners' working documents that allowed us to see evidence of thinking, ideas, action, and reflection in real time. Originally these portfolios were paper based. More recent research (Kimbell et al., 2004, 2009) has demonstrated the value of moving to digital portfolios. In particular, we have found immense positive impact on learning and assessment through capturing assessment evidence using mobile devices and digital tools that support drawing, writing, audio recording, and still and moving image.

Working with an SME (Sherston Software Ltd.), the research team in TERU created an e-learning system that supports both formative and summative assessment. The system operates in active learning environments and dynamically captures evidence as learners document their work using mobile technologies such as phones, netbooks, tablets, and laptops. The documentation that is captured synchronizes directly to a learner Web space. This approach has developed into "e-solutions for creative assessment in portfolio environments"—the e-scape project (Kimbell et al., 2009).

Through this chapter, we illustrate how this approach can support assessment of learning through a seamless blending between online and offline work, within and beyond classroom settings. Through the system, learners and teachers can access the portfolios at school or at home, providing and responding to formative feedback directly in the portfolio. In this way, the system enables blended learning that is practice based, capturing dynamically the evidence of learning as it occurs. In addition, this evidence is available through a Web space for summative assessment and can be accessed by a range of assessors at the same time. The elements of the system are detailed below.

THE CHALLENGE OF AUTHENTIC ASSESSMENT
FOR SUMMATIVE AND FORMATIVE PURPOSES

Traditional assessment approaches, typified by written tests, are not effective for assessing process- or performance-based capabilities. It would not be logical, for example, to assess the capability of a soccer player to score goals by asking them to take a written test. Historically, dating at least as far back as the emergence of crafts guilds in medieval England, there have been "practical tests" to assess a person's ability to perform practice-based skills (Hanson, 1993). While these tests provide a more authentic approach to assessing performance, they have typically shown what people can do, but not why they have done it. The tests have not made visible the thinking taking place while the practice is underway, as educators have become more conscious of the importance of assessment in the learning process. This has highlighted the reality that where written tests provide no insight into practice and practice tests provide no insight into thinking, the tests are increasingly seen as inadequate. Neither provides insight into the learning that has, or is, taking place.

This was the problem that the original TERU team faced when commissioned by the UK government to assess a population of 10,000 15-year-olds on their capability as design and technologists (Kimbell et al., 1991). The research that was undertaken opened up issues of authenticity in performance-based assessment: authenticity of process, authenticity of context and activities, and authenticity of evidence and judgement. The resulting research tool (the "unpickled" portfolio) was the paper-based portfolio described above through which learners documented their designing, and the thinking behind it, in response to a contextually based design challenge. The evidence generated enabled holistic assessment of capability. This early project validated our approach to performance-based assessment in a summative context and formed the basis of future developments. The e-scape project has taken the concept into a digital world while maintaining the authenticity created by the original.

Conceptual Framing

Behind the e-scape approach there are certain key concepts:

- Learning and development processes are not linear, but are based on an iteration of action and reflection.
- Authentic, performance-based, assessment can have pedagogic value in that the learner can evidence their capability *through* a learning process.

- Holistic, rather than atomized, judgments provide greater authenticity when assessing performance-based capability.

Our view of process was developed through the early APU project in which we rejected linear views of process that prescribed and managed design activity. Our research enabled us to create and validate a model that characterized how designing starts with an ill-formed, hazy idea that is progressed through a series of active and reflective processes that gradually bring clarity to the developing outcome. This model is shown in Figure 11.1.

Good learning and teaching depend on sound assessment judgments. These may be made either summatively, to inform on overarching achievement and attainment, or formatively, to inform next steps in learning. In the context of process-based learning, while it is possible to focus exclusively on summative assessment, there is added value if the learning is ongoing through the assessment task or project. Balancing the teacher's assessment intentions with the learner's process intentions creates a pedagogic model of assessment that can be seen as "win–win." We have described this elsewhere as a system that is like a double-sided looking glass that reflects back, metacognitively, what has been achieved or attained, alongside what has been learned (Stables & Kimbell, 2007). This pedagogic model is embedded in the e-scape system.

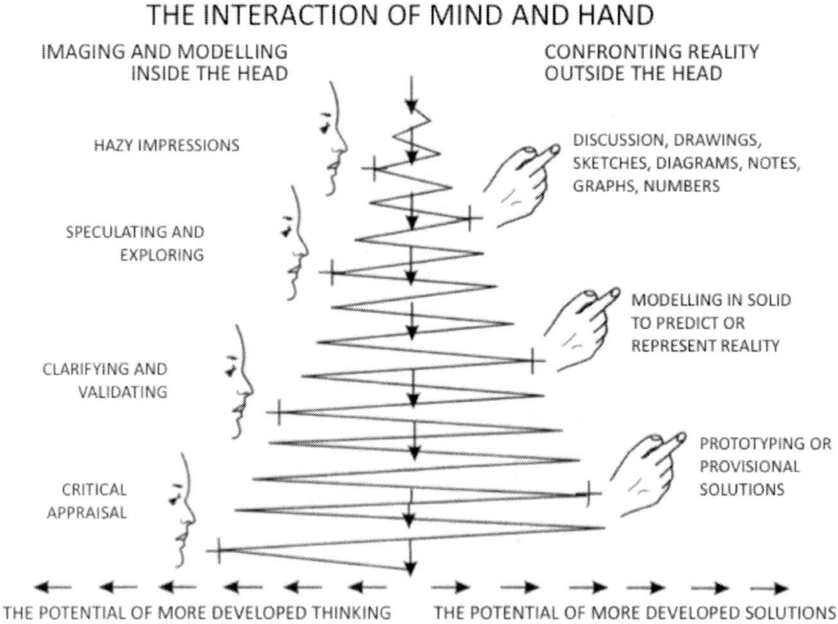

THE INTERACTION OF MIND AND HAND

Figure 11.1 The APU model of assessment (Kimbell et al., 1991, p. 20).

The Elements of the System

The e-scape system was initially developed in the context of Design and Technology (a UK school subject) and has now been explored across a range of disciplines and with primary (elementary), secondary (high school), and tertiary (university) learners. In summary, learners use a mobile digital device with e-scape's integrated capture tools installed as a digital project notebook. The learners' capabilities are assessed through the "trace-left-behind" as they document their process (Kimbell et al., 2009). The complete system is made up of four combined technologies:

- An activity authoring tool that enables teachers or examiners to design, author, and share e-scape activities using a set of online tools accessed through a standard browser.
- An activity management system that enables teachers to run the e-scape activities on class sets of mobile devices.
- A portfolio viewer that enables teachers, learners, and assessors to view the learners' portfolios of evidence using a standard Web browser.
- A "pairs engine" that enables a system of comparative judging to be managed.

The portfolio that emerges through the system contains a photo storyline of the learners' real design models along with the reflections of the learners and their peers. As such, it provides insight into the learner's cognitive journey (Kimbell & Stables, 2008; Hope, 2001). This allows teachers, assessors, and the learners themselves to gain insight into the learning that has and is taking place (Kimbell, 2006). Being Web based, the portfolio enables assessment to be undertaken remotely and asynchronously by a range of assessors, making the system particularly useful for national assessment systems and for comparative judgment (Pollit & Crisp, 2004).

The combination of the model of process with the anticipation of a pedagogical thrust to the assessment activity has resulted in assessment activities that can be diagnostic, support formative judgments, and provide guidance on next steps in learning. Through the story of learning told through the whole portfolio, holistic summative judgments can be made. This latter possibility enables assessment based on Adaptive Comparative Judgment (ACJ), a statistically reliable assessment method that also opens up opportunities to democratize assessment (Kimbell, 2007, 2009). Below, we offer three case studies to illustrate how e-scape has been used in different contexts.

THE CASE STUDIES

The e-scape approach has been trialed in a range of settings, age groups, and subject areas. We have chosen three case studies that illustrate the approach in distinctive ways:

- Summative "controlled" assessment that can be used for high-stakes assessment, illustrated through the school subject of Design and Technology in secondary (high school) settings
- Summative assessment of primary (elementary school) scientific and technological enquiry skills
- Formative and summative assessment of project-based learning across a range of school subjects in junior and senior high schools

Case Study 1: Learning and Assessing Design and Technology (D&T)

The original e-scape project was commissioned in 2004 by the (now defunct) English Qualifications and Curriculum Authority (QCA). The requirement was for the development of a new approach to assessing Design and Technology at GCSE that would make innovative use of a digital portfolio-based system both for the documenting of project work and for its assessment. The research questions were concerned with four overarching dimensions of the potential of the system as an assessment tool: technological, pedagogic, manageability, and functionality. The overarching intention of the funders was to have a system that could be used for "controlled assessment"—assessment of project work carried out under controlled conditions—for national GCSE examinations at age 16 (the General Certificate of Secondary Examinations). Initially a number of digital tools were explored, including digital pens, digital voice recognition, and personal digital assistants (PDAs), the latter being replaced by smartphones as the research progressed. It was specified that each assessment activity should last for 6 hours, spread across two mornings. The focus of the main design task trialed was designing pill dispensers that met the needs of a specific client group.

The activity was structured using the system's inbuilt "authoring tool" (Figure 11.2) that controlled:

- The overall duration of the activity
- The time sequence of subtasks that build up the overall portfolio
- The response mode of learners (e.g., drawing/writing/photo/audio/video)

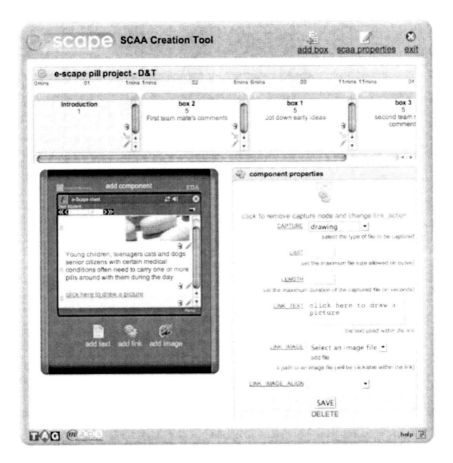

Figure 11.2 The e-scape authoring tool.

- The degree of flexibility in the timing of subtasks (controlled and flexible)
- The resource materials to be embedded (e.g., texts/images)

The 6-hour activity was broken into a series of 23 subtasks through which learners:

- Generated initial ideas
- Received peer feedback from two "critical friends"
- Reflected on the needs of their client group
- Undertook and reflected on further development
- Accounted for the major inspiration of their ideas
- Prototyped their ideas

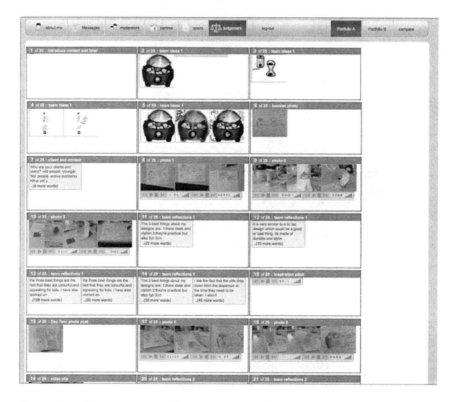

Figure 11.3   The structure of the e-scape portfolio.

- Received further peer feedback
- Created a short "walk-through" video that presented their ideas through their prototype

As they wrote, drew, modeled, photographed, videoed, and annotated the development of their ideas, the Web-based portfolio was simultaneously created through a continuous synchronizing process. Figure 11.3 provides an overview of the layout of the portfolio that, in the Web browser, is interactive. This means that clicking on thumbnails of photographs brings them to full size, while audio files can be played by clicking on their link. The resulting portfolios numbered 352 and were drawn from learners across 16 schools, chosen to provide a regional spread across England (North East, North West, Midlands, South West, and South East). The portfolios were assessed holistically using the ACJ system referred to above.

Most of the teachers who had run the assessment activities also took part in the comparative judging, alongside other experts in the field. The judging process, managed by the pairs engine, based on Thurstone's (1927) law of comparative judgment further developed by Pollit and Crisp (2004), presents judges with pairs of portfolios to scrutinize and assess holistically, based on criteria of capability derived through earlier research (Kimbell et al., 2004). Having assessed the work within the two portfolios, each judge identifies which of the pair they consider to be better. The system continues to send pairs of portfolios to a team of judges (in the case of our trial, 28 in total) until a reliable rank order has been formed. In our trial each judge made 130 paired comparisons. The rank that emerged from the process had very high interjudge reliability (0.95), indicating that as a system that produces a rank of performance, it is extremely effective. However, the benefits of the system went far beyond this when the comments of the judges (largely teachers) are taken into account. In addition to finding the system easy, fast, and practical (not having boxes of exam scripts or portfolios to carry around), they also felt the system to be fairer as decisions were being made by multiple judges, not by a single examiner.

They also considered that involving the learners in a similar process would be beneficial. This idea was explored further by a small-scale trial. The trial took one class of 15-year-old learners who had taken part in the assessment activity and trained them to become assessment judges. The learners then assessed a sample of e-portfolios through a parallel process to the main judging, as described above. The trial demonstrated that the learners were very reliable judges. In addition, the learners themselves confirmed that the opportunity to view and judge the work of their peers was extremely informative in developing their own understanding of designing.

This pedagogic value of the system was echoed in other findings that emerged from the questionnaires completed by participants. Learners consistently told us that they found the handheld devices fun and easy to use. They considered that the approach was good for developing their ideas and for designing. In a free response question, the features most commonly identified as being among the best were the general ease of use of the system, the camera tool, the portability of the device, and the new and different way of working they experienced. The features that were disliked were typically technical issues such as system crashes, slow Internet, or limitations of certain digital tools. The teachers responded on two fronts: the ease of managing the system and their views of how the learners responded. For both the feedback was good. Teachers were confident about using the system and, in use, found it easy to set up and to manage. They also commented that they felt the learners' performance was better than expected and cited the "pacey timings," the "variety of response modes," and the "clear targets" as contributing to this.

Case Study 2: Assessing Scientific Enquiry on Primary Classrooms

Teacher assessment has become more important in primary science education in England since the discontinuation of the Standard Attainment Tests (SATs) that all 11-year-old learners took in this subject until 2009. Since this date, learner performance data in science reported to the English government by each primary school has relied entirely on teacher assessment undertaken in the classroom. This arguably provides a more valid picture of children's scientific enquiry skills than a paper-and-pencil test. However, observations of science investigations in progress face the problem that the teacher cannot be everywhere at once. While the teacher is listening in on one group to provide formative feedback or collect summative evidence, elsewhere in the class there may be some significant learning going on that has been missed. Such learning is not always captured in the "write-up" of the investigation either. Some children who can think well scientifically have difficulty in expressing their ideas in writing. For many children—and teachers—the reliance on written evidence for assessment is the least attractive aspect of science, particularly at the upper primary level (ages 9–11).

In response to this challenge for teacher assessment, the Centre for Research in Early Scientific Learning (CRESL) at Bath Spa University decided to work with a group of specialist teachers in science, D&T, and ICT in eight primary schools to develop e-scape tasks to assess 11-year-old learners' scientific and technological enquiry skills. The approach taken built upon the findings of part of the *e-scape* project that sought to develop e-portfolio assessment of science at age 15 (Davies, 2009). The model of assessment used was an improvement on standard approaches to primary classroom assessment of enquiry skills in that it captured learners' decisions made about experimental design *at the time* rather than retrospectively, and that it allowed learners to record their ideas and findings using a variety of modes (voice recordings, diagrams, direct data entry, video) as relevant to the stage of the investigation.

The e-scape system was used for three main purposes:

- To develop tasks that were designed to engage learners in stimulating enquiry
- To manage the running of the tasks in the classroom
- To facilitate the assessment of the resulting learner e-portfolios

In this study learners used netbooks with touch-sensitive screens to record their work, offering the standard range of multimodal response tools available within the e-scape system. In total the project teachers produced

10, 3-hour online assessment tasks covering the science topics of forces, electricity, materials, the human body, microorganisms, light, and sound. Each involved an element of designing and, in some cases, making:

1. Rugby Activity—Learners considered the physical attributes that a rugby player needs, then they investigated some of these factors and finally "designed" the ideal rugby player.
2. Static Electricity—Factors that affect static electricity were investigated in response to an orientation activity that asked learners to rub a balloon against their hair.
3. Shadows Activity—A video clip of shadow puppetry and a concept cartoon provided the stimulus for learners to investigate shadow formation.
4. Changing Sounds—After exploring a collection of musical instruments, the factors affecting pitch of notes in one instrument were investigated further.
5. Paper Spinners—A range of factors that affect the time a paper spinner takes to fall were tested.
6. Dissolving Task—A video clip of sugar dissolving in tea was the starting point for learners to investigate the factors that affect the time it takes for sugar to go into solution.
7. Electrical Circuits—The brightness of lamps in different electrical circuits was the focus of this activity.
8. Electricity Investigation—A similar task to that above except the focus was specifically on changing the thickness of wire in the circuit.
9. Friction—Factors that affect the grip of shoe soles were investigated.
10. Sticky Tape—The final task completed by all schools investigated the "stickiness" or strength of a range of tapes.

Evaluation judgements were made in five areas:

- The reliability of running the e-scape system in the primary classroom
- The extent to which 9- to 11-year-olds found the e-scape system a stimulating way to engage with scientific enquiry
- Comparison between the e-scape system and paper-based approaches to recording learner responses
- The reliability and validity of assessments of learner portfolios made by the project participants using the e-scape "pairs comparison" approach
- The usefulness of the e-scape software in making criterion-referenced assessments

Data were collected by conducting classroom observations of the system in operation, interviewing teachers, reviewing e-portfolios generated by learners, analyzing statistics generated by the ACJ process, and conducting a participant questionnaire.

The findings from this case study suggest that an e-scape approach to the assessment of scientific and technological enquiry has the potential to be authentic and reliable, and that it may even have a positive effect on current pedagogy. The pairs judging process for 154 learner e-portfolios demonstrated a high degree of reliability between the judgments made by the 17 teachers and tutors involved. Seven hundred and twenty pairs judgments were made (an average of 42 judgments per judge), resulting in a rank order with a reliability coefficient of 0.88 from just over nine judgments per portfolio, which would be likely to rise to 0.9 or higher with further judging rounds. Teachers' reflections on the process of designing an e-scape assessment task illustrated how they understood its iterative nature in that changes made to the activity inevitably had an impact on the portfolios produced. They noted, having worked through a series of comparative pair judgments, that "task design would need to have clearer understanding of what aspects were to be assessed." Other comments illustrate the impact of the e-scape approach on teachers' practice and are mainly focused on the multiple response-mode possibilities for learners. This was seen as a strength in two main ways: as motivational and as empowering for children with limited conventional writing skills. In terms of running the activity in the classroom using netbooks, teachers focussed on the motivational nature of the technology and the potential this provided for enhancing learning.

The assessment tasks written by teachers during the project can claim greater authenticity than the widely criticized and discontinued SATs (Harlen, 2007). This authenticity as an assessment task did, however, come at the expense of manageability in the classroom. In particular, the tasks took much longer than anticipated for the children to complete—a feature noted by several of the teachers—since the open-ended nature required learners to make decisions that subsequently proved to be mistakes. Although learning from these mistakes was valuable, the danger of children not completing tasks or not achieving as highly as they might in a more directed activity was a source of anxiety for the teachers. They were, however, willing to incorporate the notion of e-portfolios into their assessment approaches and to make use of the authoring tool structure to scaffold enquiry tasks using action and reflection steps. This demonstrates a positive version of the "backwash" effect of assessment into pedagogy and the curriculum (Harlen & Deakin Crick, 2002). Traditional approaches to assessment can reduce the amount of practical science in the classroom (Wyse, McCreery, & Torrence, 2008) while adopting the e-scape approach appears to prioritize practical enquiry.

Case Study 3: Assessment in My Palm—e-Scape in Project-Based Learning

Due to increasing concerns about the existing assessment system in Israel, the Ministry of Education added problem solving, critical thinking, research, and performance as skills to be assessed in matriculation examinations in several subjects. The skills are assessed through portfolios that document PBL undertaken in the final year of high school. This assessment contributes to the final examination grades. Before this development, learners typically undertook projects and made products before documenting their work at the end of the process. As a result, assessment was based on portfolios of work that did not reflect the learners' thinking and performance skills developed through the whole process.

The e-scape system was identified as an appropriate approach to explore to address the situation. World ORT (WO) introduced this idea to Israel by sponsoring Assessment in My Palm (AMP), a pilot project to examine the suitability of the e-scape system for the Israeli education system (Dagan, 2011). The aims of the pilot were:

- To assess learners' thinking and documenting skills
- To encourage learners' reflective abilities through the documentation of their project, as part of their learning skills
- To enhance formative assessment as well as summative holistic assessment and peer assessment

The AMP project explored the use of e-scape to provide the schools with both technological and pedagogic support in documenting PBL in a blended learning environment. As it was important to explore this approach to assessment in PBL across junior and senior high schools, not just in the matriculation year, teachers and learners from a range of subjects and school years were involved. This resulted in projects being undertaken in various subjects.

Six schools were chosen to participate in the pilot, with a number of teachers being involved in each school. The schools expressed their intent to be a part of the project and committed themselves to use the e-scape system. Each school received a set of netbooks, the e-scape software, and teacher training and tutoring throughout the year.

During the 2 years of the AMP pilot, each one of the six schools chose the subjects that would be taught and the length of each project. Using the authoring tool, teachers designed their own tasks in subjects as varied as Biology, Design & Technology, Electronics, Civic Studies, Photography, Art, Geography, English as a Second Language, and multidisciplinary studies.

In this pilot the focus was on the school's internal development of tasks and on local assessment done by the teachers. The teachers used e-scape for both summative and formative assessments, guiding and tutoring the learn-ers' progress during the process by giving blended feedback and support both through the software and face to face in the classroom. At the end of each project they gave their summative assessment according to the criteria of the subject matter.

THE IMPLEMENTATION PROCESS

The implementation process had two components. At the outset the teach-ers received training on using e-scape in both pedagogical and technical aspects. This involved them experiencing the software both as learners and as teachers. Once the activities were underway, a tutor from WO met each teacher or group of teachers twice a month to assist with the design and development of the projects; to help with the technological aspects; and to accompany the teachers during their lessons. The tutoring was essential for the teachers while implementing new technology, new pedagogical ap-proaches, and new methods of blended learning and assessment.

The teachers used e-scape to design and develop authentic tasks based on the demands of their curriculum. All the tasks were task-centered in the sense that the learners took them from the starting point to a change in the made-world (Kimbell & Stables, 2008) or to an understanding of the scientific world. Four projects are discussed here to illustrate the breadth of projects undertaken.

School 1: Light the Candle

This task for the ninth grade (14-year-old) learners lasted five lessons. The learners were asked to design and make a decorative candle for the Hanukah candlestick that reflected their interpretation of environmental issues and the preservation of the world. They worked in groups of three to four learners, each group designing a candle and together designing the whole Hanukah candlestick. The learners documented their work using the dynamic e-portfolio.

School 2: Design and Make a Bridge

This assignment was designed for seventh-grade learners. It was set in Science and Technology as part of the National Curriculum and lasted be-tween six to eight 90-minute lessons. The learners were asked to follow the design process and to design and make their own bridge over the Jordan

River, while integrating laws from physical science. Each group of two to three learners had to design their own bridge.

School 3: The Road Around the City

This assignment was developed for an interdisciplinary project that included science, geography, ecology, and even law for ninth-grade learners. The project focused on the planned introduction of a ring-road around a large town. It lasted 7 months and was divided into weekly assignments, with learners working in small groups. During the research process the learners worked at school and at home and even traveled to different places along the route of the proposed road to interview stakeholders, recording their interviews with audio and video tools. The research was collected into the dynamic portfolios and used as the basis for defining a problem and developing a solution. Each week teachers gave formative assessment through the e-scape system and at the completion of the project also gave summative assessments. The final project outcome was a presentation by the learners of their ideas to the town council and planners.

School 4: Integrating Science and Technology

One school used the system for independent small-group projects in ninth-grade science classes. Each group of learners had to identify a problem and solve it through scientific inquiry. The projects were highly diverse. For example, in one project the learners built a model of the nervous system that could be used to explain ADHD. In another, the learners explored balance by analyzing different shapes and structures of bicycle frames to establish which frame was the best for doing "wheelies" on the bikes. Everything was documented through the e-scape portfolio, including the videos of the "wheelies" experiments and their analysis. Each year the teacher invites external experts to assess the projects; the projects completed using e-scape gained the highest scores ever from these experts. The teacher's view was that this was partly because the range of appropriate modes of documenting their work increased the learners' understanding and their ability to articulate that understanding.

THE EVALUATION OF THE AMP PILOT PROJECT

The evaluation was based on questionnaires and interviews with teachers and learners. The questionnaires were completed in year 1 of the project and the interviews at the ends of Year one and year 2. The interviews were conducted by researchers from TERU.

For the six schools the project was implemented, it was a big change to use the notebook computers and the new software and to introduce new assessment and pedagogical approaches. Teachers reported that the e-scape approach enabled them to reflect on, and assess, the learners' real-time performance, including by providing online feedback to the learners along the way. They found that it helped them to create effective interactions between the learner and his or her thinking processes, between the learner and the teacher, between the learner and their teammates, and between the learner and the assessor. In schools where e-scape was used to document a detailed and rich account of extended projects, the teachers indicated very positive feedback, citing the combined value of the evidence of learning within the portfolios but also the way that the approach helped the learners to talk about their work.

There were a range of technical, organizational, and pedagogical difficulties (Dagan, 2011), but despite these, the learners, the teachers, and the head teachers in all the schools found the AMP project useful, challenging, and innovative. Teachers found that the e-scape approach helped learners' working methods as it taught them how to create a portfolio that showed the process of their project and their reflections on it. This resonates with the findings of the original Assessment of Performance Unit (APU) project that found that supporting learners' performance through an assessment activity made the process more apparent to both teachers and learners (Kimbell & Stables, 2008, p. 95). Teachers found that the software required them to be more precise in the instructions they built into the task and that this supported the development of their pedagogical skills. They also commented that learner motivation was high, despite the technical difficulties encountered. Learners with special educational needs benefitted greatly because they had the opportunity to use the multifunctionality of the technology (e.g., to record or use video instead of writing) and they received a task that was organized in smaller, more manageable steps.

Learners said that the best things about e-scape were that it was fun to use, a different way of learning, a good (and safe) way of documenting project work, and generally a "comfortable" way to work. They found everything about their projects and their learning more organized, both for themselves and for the teachers. Part of this was the ability to see the whole of their task at once, both on the mobile devices and through the Web-based portfolio. They enjoyed learning from each other, thinking together, discussing their work, and collaborating. The emphasis on articulating and documenting their thinking seemed to have moved working as a group to a new level. They particularly liked the use of video to track their own progress and found it very useful for self-assessment as they looked back over their work. They also considered that the approach was a good way to be assessed as they felt that their teachers had a better understanding of what they had done.

DISCUSSION

PBL takes place in a range of settings and often not in traditional classrooms. For example, in D&T the setting is often a workshop or studio, in science a laboratory, whereas in geography it may involve fieldwork. Conversely, traditional use of computers in education has been in computer labs or ICT suites. Mobile technologies have provided the opportunity to bring together the value of using digital tools in a broad range of learning environments. It is this opportunity that the e-scape system has exploited, as had been shown through the case studies. In all three cases learners of different ages and working in different subject disciplines were able to capture the evidence of their thinking and actions through a portfolio that blended digital and physical worlds. They found it a fun and motivating way to work and, importantly, that the tools were good for developing their ideas and for organizing a portfolio that showed their learning.

However, e-scape has gone further than just providing a mobile learning tool. It has also made possible an assessment system that captures evidence in real time and that allows this evidence to be created using a far greater range of tools than would be anticipated in traditional "examination" rooms. The range of communication tools included within the system has allowed learners with quite different learning styles to convey their ideas and their thinking in more appropriate ways—and in the process enabling assessors to gain far greater understanding of the learners' achievements and attainments. As one teacher from the AMP project explained:

> I have 14 pupils in the group, all of whom have special needs; all have difficulties with some part of their learning. When I told them they were going to work with computers in the biology lessons they were very excited. They felt that it would give them a chance to succeed and that they could work without my help. For them the computer is something friendly, not at all frightening. For them to take pictures and to type and write on the computer is not as difficult as writing from the blackboard. (AMP Year 2 interviews)

In addition, the Web-based dimension to the system has enabled the portfolios to be accessed easily by teachers and learners while the activity is in progress, and by assessors once it is completed. Teachers and learners across the case studies have welcomed the mix of online reflection and feedback with physical action and collaboration. This was expressed clearly by a learner from the AMP project:

It was good that we could see all of our work we had done in one place. And it was important to be able to go back and look at what we have done and to do it again, if it could be made better or to think about what we have done so that we can move on. The teacher was able to see what work we had done. It wasn't possible to hide behind anything, compared with bits of paper, and the teacher was better informed as to what we have done. (AMP Year 1 interviews)

The assessment potential has been further increased through the use of comparative judgment. Evidence from this being carried out in authentic, performative assessment settings has provided insight into the statistical reliability of such an approach and its consequent value on large-scale, high-stakes assessment. In addition, comparative judgment provides opportunities for professional sharing of the judgment process, including with the learners themselves when they are included as "judges." In the different case studies teachers took different roles, but all were positive about the pedagogic potential of e-scape and in both case study 2 and 3 the findings showed that working with the teachers while developing tasks had developed teachers' pedagogy.

FURTHER RESEARCH

Although the projects in the case studies are now completed, developments exploring the potential of the digital portfolios and the adaptive comparative judgment continue in a range of settings. Further background on the project and case studies has been documented through a special edition of the *International Journal of Technology and Design Education* (Volume 22.2). The team is currently considering new research exploring the potential of combining the approach with that of learning analytics to explore ways in which levels of semi-automation can be introduced into assessment and feedback for individual learners that will also provide larger datasets. In addition, the current e-scape system has been commercialized as "Live Assess" and is soon to be launched as an iPad application.

Digital technologies provide important opportunities for learning and assessment, but devoid of practical, performative, and hands-on activity in physical environments they support a distorted story of achievement and attainment. The e-scape approach offers a way of transcending this distortion by offering an authentic blending of the virtual and the real worlds of learning, teaching, and assessment.

REFERENCES

Barak, M. (2011). Fostering learning in the engineering and technology class: from content-oriented instruction to a focus on cognition, metacognition and motivation. In M. Barak & M. Hacker (Eds.), *Fostering human development through engineering and technology education* (pp. 35–55). Rotterdam, The Netherlands: Sense Publishers.

Chang Barker, K. (2005). ePortfolio for the assessment of learning. Vancouver, BC, Canada: FuturEd Consulting Education Futurists Inc.

Dagan, O. (2011). *Assessment in My Palm—A pilot project in Israel.* Paper presented at the Perspective on Learning in Design & Technology Education conference, London.

Davies, D. (2009). *Digital portfolio assessment of secondary students' scientific enquiry skills: The e-scape project.* Paper presented at the Contemporary Science Education Research: Learning and Assessment conference (Proceedings of ESERA 2009), Ankara, Turkey.

Hanson, F. A. (1993). *Testing, testing: Social consequences of the examined life.* Berkley: University of California Press.

Harlen, W. (2007). The quality of learning: Assessment alternatives for primary education *Primary Review Research Survey, 3/4.* Cambridge, UK: University of Cambridge, Faculty of Education.

Harlen, W. (2008). Science as a key component of the primary curriculum: A rationale with policy implications. *Perspectives on Education 1 (Primary Science),* pp. 4–18.

Harlen, W., & Deakin Crick, R. (2002). A systematic review of the impact of summative assessment and tests on students' motivation for learning (EPPI-Centre Review, version 1.1). *Research Evidence in Education Library.* (Vol. Issue 1). London, UK: EPPI-Centre, Social Science Research Unit, Institute of Education.

Hope, G. (2001). Taking ideas on a journey called designing: A model for explaining design drawing to young children. *Journal of Design and Technology Education, 6*(3), 197–201.

Kimbell, R. (2006). Innovative performance and virtual portfolios: A tale of two projects. *Design and Technology Education: An International Journal, 11*(1), 18–30.

Kimbell, R. (2007). E-assessment In project e-scape. *Design and Technology Education: An International Journal, 12*(2), 66–76.

Kimbell, R. (2009). Performance portfolios ... problems, potentials and policy. In A. Jones & M. de Vries (Eds.), *International handbook of research and development in technology education* (pp. 509–524). Rotterdam, The Netherlands: Sense Publishers.

Kimbell, R., Miller, S., Bain, J., Wright, R., Wheeler, T., & Stables, K. (2004). *Assessing design innovation: A research and development project for the Department for Education and Skills (DfES) and the Qualifications and Curriculum Authority (QCA).* London, UK: Goldsmiths University of London.

Kimbell, R., & Stables, K. (2008). *Researching design learning: issues and findings from two decades of research and development.* Berlin, Germany: Springer.

Kimbell, R., Stables, K., Wheeler, T., Wozniak, A., & Kelly, A. V. (1991). *The assessment of performance in design and technology.* London, UK: SEAC/HMSO.

Kimbell, R., Wheeler, T., Stables, K., Shepard, T., Martin, F., Davies, D., ... Whitehouse, G. (2009). *E-scape portfolio assessment: A research and development project for the Department of Children, Families and Schools, phase 3 report* (p. 169). London, UK: Goldsmiths, University of London.

Mason, R., Pegler, C., & Weller, M. (2004). E-portfolios: An assessment tool for online courses. *British Journal of Educational Technology, 35*(6), 11.

Pollitt, A., & Crisp, V. (2004). *Could comparative judgements of script quality replace traditional marking and improve the validity of exam questions?* Paper presented at the annual conference of the BERA, UMIST Manchester, UK.

Stables, K., & Kimbell, R. (2000). The unpickled portfolio: pioneering assessment in design and technology. In R. Kimbell (Ed.), *Design and Technology International Millennium Conference* (pp. 195–202). London, UK: Design and Technology Association.

Stables, K., & Kimbell, R. (2007). Evidence through the looking glass: Developing performance and assessing capability. In L. Taxén (Ed.), *The 13th International Conference on Thinking* (pp. 175–182). Norrköping, Sweden: Linköping University Electronic Press.

Thurstone, L. L. (1927). A law of comparative judgement. *Psychological Review, 34,* 273–286.

Wyse, D., McCreery, E., & Torrance, H. (2008). The Trajectory and Impact of National Reform: curriculum and assessment in English primary schools. *Primary Review Research Survey 3/2.* Cambridge, UK: University of Cambridge, Faculty of Education.

CHAPTER 12

STRATEGIES FOR SUCCESS

Using Formative Assessment to Build Skills and Community in the Blended Classroom

Anupama Arora, Shari Evans, Catherine Gardner, Karen Gulbrandsen, and Jeannette E. Riley
University of Massachusetts Dartmouth

INTRODUCTION

The University of Massachusetts Dartmouth has been engaged in a blended learning initiative, focused on faculty development and student learning, since 2009. The project is funded by the Davis Educational Foundation and is titled "Implementation of Blended Learning for the Improvement of Student Learning," which we refer to as IBIS. Principal investigators Jeannette E. Riley, the campus Academic Director of Online Education and Professor of English and Women's and Gender Studies, and Catherine Villanueva Gardner, Director of the Office of Faculty Development and Associate Professor of Philosophy and Women's and Gender Studies, were early adopters of technology and blended teaching. The project developed from their desire to engage faculty in the development of effective blended courses and

Assessment in Online and Blended Learning Environments, pages 235–251
Copyright © 2015 by Information Age Publishing

to assist faculty in developing effective tools and methods to incorporate a culture of assessment and scholarly teaching into their practices.

This chapter offers a discussion of the faculty development program that was created to support the campus blended learning initiative with a focus on helping faculty develop effective assessment practices and implement effective blended course designs. This discussion is followed by three case studies outlining innovative blended course designs that led to documented improvements in student learning outcomes and behaviors.

The Faculty Development Program

The faculty development program is voluntary. In response to a call for applications, faculty apply to be "faculty fellows" for the program, which runs during the summer months and includes a 2-week online training course, as well as group presentations and discussions in a face-to-face environment. During this time, faculty develop their skills in integrating instructional technologies into their classes and in designing effective assessment practices to gauge the effect of these technologies on student learning.

The training program that was developed had three core elements:

- *Blended Learning:* presents strategies for integrating face-to-face and online sessions and assignments effectively to impact student learning
- *Assessing Your Blended Course:* engages faculty in writing effective student learning objectives, aligning those objectives with course assignments, and then assessing student learning; outlines mentor process
- *IBIS Course Development Process:* outlines grant project next steps and faculty reporting on progress

The blended learning strategies are taught fully online, a process that introduces faculty to the experience of being an online learner. This process facilitates their understanding of the online environment and the frustrations or challenges students might experience. The training course moves faculty through a discussion of what blended learning is by providing different models and examples. Faculty then are provided with various tools to develop a course design for their blended class including design worksheets, model classes to review, and discussion activities with their colleagues. In addition, there are face-to-face meetings where faculty present and share ideas regarding their course designs. The face-to-face sessions are designed to complement the online discussions and activities, thus engaging faculty in a blended-learning experience.

The heart of the training lies in the assessment module that takes participants through all the necessary steps from initial rationales for assessment to understanding the importance of the alignment of assessment measures with course objectives and learning activities. Instead of the online learning module being an accompaniment to the development of each participant's course, the participants use the module as more of a practice site to get feedback as they design their actual course. Thus, for example, they have an asynchronous discussion about how to craft effective student learning objectives using sample learning objectives drawn from other courses. They then discuss their own prospective learning objectives and get feedback from the other participants and the PIs in a face-to-face session, which is followed by the presentation of a revised course plan online in a group wiki site.

It is important to note that the module offers faculty a broad definition of learning ranging from evidence of student improvement in understanding content to evidence of student improvement in applying content knowledge and skills to evidence of changes in student learning behavior (e.g., improved writing processes, more time spent on readings, increased class participation). Terms are also clearly defined for faculty:

- *Assessment*: a quiz or a paper or other assignment that measures student accomplishment of one or more of the course student learning outcomes (SLOs)
- *Learning activity*: an activity that facilitates student achievement of one or more of the course SLOs by actively engaging the students with course content

Suggestions are modeled for possible course strategies. For example, faculty could compare test results of a face-to-face class with a blended class of the same course, or they could compare writing results—using the same rubric—of a face-to-face class with a blended class of the same course. A course could be designed around pre-/post-testing of knowledge by having students respond to a test of knowledge at the beginning of the semester and then having them do the same test at the end. In a similar way, student behavior patterns could be self-assessed by having students complete a pre-/post-survey of their learning behaviors.

Faculty are required to be detailed in their blended course designs. Prior to a course taking place, faculty complete an assessment plan that outlines the course design and the assessment techniques to be implemented. Additionally, faculty assessment plans are reviewed by their colleagues, as well as external reviewers, who provide feedback. Last but not least, all faculty courses are reviewed using the campus-recommended Blended Quality Rubric designed by faculty in 2010. These assessment plans are then used to submit a group IRB application so that any assessment data can be used for presentations and publications in the future. As faculty conduct their course over a semester, they are assisted by a peer mentor and document their students' work as planned. At the end of the semester, faculty submit a final project report that provides overview of their course and what was redesigned for the IBIS project; explains data collected; and provides data analysis and conclusions about the course experience. The central question for these reports: Did the blended course design positively or negatively or not at all affect student learning?

The following case studies provide examples where student learning and student learning behavior is positively impacted by the blended course designs.

Knowledge, Application, and Collaboration: Layering Blended Tools to Foster Student Engagement and Learning

The first case study is drawn from ENL 259: Critical Methods: Theory & Practice, designed and taught by Anupama Arora, Associate Professor of English. Arora's blended course was developed to engage students in difficult content, literary theory, and to facilitate their learning of often complex concepts.

Teaching literary theory and critical methods to undergraduate English majors can be a challenging task as it involves introducing them to dense concepts and sometimes difficult or unwieldy language. Students can also be overwhelmed with the sheer newness of the critical vocabulary and abstract ideas. Arora found the use of some online tools thoughtfully integrated into the face-to-face classroom to be highly effective in meeting the objectives of an introductory Critical Methods course. Specifically, Arora used three tools in tandem—online quizzes, online discussion board topics and postings, and a wiki—to facilitate student learning. This layering of tools functioned to enhance student learning of content as well as skills in a rigorous and supportive environment.

The learning objectives of the courses that were targeted through blending were (a) identify major critical methods, (b) recognize major thinkers associated with each theory, (c) demonstrate an ability to describe and define the characteristics and vocabulary of each theory, and (d) interpret and analyze a variety of texts through utilizing and practicing theoretical vocabulary.

To begin with, Arora created online quizzes with multiple-choice questions on the main terminology offered with each critical literary theory/ critical method. The focus here was on content *knowledge*. The goal was to highlight for the students salient characteristics and concepts associated with each theory, and also to help them wade through the abstract ideas presented in the long chapters of their textbook and lead students to both study and retain material for use in classroom discussion and analysis. Since students were required to take these quizzes online before the face-to-face class, they learned to read carefully, pay attention to detail, and redirect their focus on the main ideas of each theory even before they walked into the classroom. This, in turn, created a classroom environment in which each student was familiar with and able to utilize the conceptual vocabulary of the course.

Students then brought this same conceptual familiarity to a deeper level through discussion boards. The focus here was on *application*. Discussion board topics were designed to help students develop their analytical skills in applying the ideas and vocabulary offered by different theoretical lenses to critically engage cultural texts (TV shows, film, music) and thus also learn to become active "readers" of the world around them. The focus of this activity was on getting students to "practice" applying the abstract ideas to start developing a degree of confidence in articulating their analyses using theoretical vocabulary with some comfort and ease. Carefully considered prompts directed students to specifically explain and then utilize theoretical terminology and ideas. Students were asked to pay attention to how they structured their analysis. Thus, they were asked to state a thesis through a theoretical lens and through utilizing its vocabulary, and list out and explain their supporting arguments.

Moreover, since Arora's goal was to help create an online community of active and engaged learners, Arora asked students to write responses to postings by other students. Through Arora's prompt, students were directed to state what they found valuable in the peers' response, what questions they had (or clarifications that they needed) after reading that response, and also what support they would add to make their peers' argument stronger. Through this process, Arora also sought to inculcate a degree of self-reflection and self-scrutiny by students on their own thought processes, thus highlighting for them the strengths and weaknesses of their own interpretations. In the process of engaging their peers, they also become critical readers of their own work.

In addition, since Arora envisioned the discussion board postings as a space where students made and sustained community, she did not comment on their postings on the group board. This allowed students to feel less self-conscious and also feel a strong sense of independence, responsibility, and freedom in becoming meaning-makers and creators of knowledge. Arora's visible involvement in this space would have run the risk of stifling the free flow of conversation between students as peers or a perception of her desire for a particular analysis as the "correct" analysis. However, while she did not interfere in the online discussion space, Arora did provide each student individually with feedback on their analyses as well as their comments on other students' postings. This also helped her to keep an eye on students' writing skills as they articulated and presented ideas, pushing them to pay attention to the style as well as the content of their writing.

The wiki was designed primarily to facilitate student *collaboration* for their face-to-face group presentations on selected literary theories. The aim was to provide an online space where students could meet and talk to each other about their contribution to the project, report their progress to each other, and organize their PowerPoint presentations. The wiki was an online "working space" especially geared toward providing more flexibility to a student population juggling multiple on- and off-campus commitments. This tool further contributed to community- and rapport-building by providing another online collaboration venue as students did the work of preparing for their face-to-face presentations. Moreover, since their contributions toward the group project were visible for the rest of the class to view, they felt more accountable toward doing their share and working toward a more truly collaborative team effort.

The qualitative and quantitative data Arora collected through anonymous surveys by students conducted at the end of the semester suggests that students responded positively to the online tools. For instance, to the question, "On a scale of 1 to 5, 5 = excellent, 1 = weak), how confident do you feel about being able to use some of the theories to interpret a text (literary or cultural)?" the class average was 4.36. Student responses to the integration of the online tools were positive:

- "The online quizzes were very helpful. After reading a chapter, I don't always remember the key terms. The quizzes picked up the most important terms and concepts in each chapter, which helped me prepare for the class discussion the following day."
- "Enforces the reading that then enforces discussion or even creates them."
- "For me, I doubt myself in classroom discussions even if I have good things to say. The DB [discussion board] was a place to convey my ideas without worrying about the pressures of 'public speaking.'"
- "I liked that [I] could look at what other students posted to understand something that I might have missed."
- "Wiki allowed us to collaborate without actually having to meet when conflicting schedules makes face-to-face meetings impossible."
- "It was great to have a space that made the planning fairly transparent."
- "Wiki was useful because it allowed for a record of all the material the group would need and gave everyone a chance to contribute when they had time."

As these surveys indicated, the online tools infused and impacted face-to-face learning successfully. The careful incorporation of online quizzes, discussion board postings, and the wiki—activities that layered the learning experience—helped to generate and sustain student interest and enthusiasm for the course material to fashion a vibrant community of active learners in the process of meaning- and knowledge-making.

Using Discussion Boards to Build Close Reading Skills, Discover Ideas, and Negotiate Meaning

This second case study offers a discussion of ENL 258: Literary Studies, designed by Shari Evans, Associate Professor of English. Here, Evans discusses how her blended course design focused on building student critical reading and thinking skills.

A critical learning objective of most literature courses is to increase students' skills in critical reading, writing, and thinking while they learn to engage and interpret literature. In the face-to-face classroom this can be modeled through class discussion, small interpretive groups, and the development of literary analysis papers. Yet, students increasingly come to literature courses, particularly at the general education level, with very little training in literary analysis and very little confidence in their ability to understand or interpret literary texts. Many students, in fact, have never come up with their own interpretations, instead relying on either the interpretations they've been given by teachers, or through readily accessible summaries and "analysis" on sites like SparkNotes. Coupled with anxiety about speaking out in front of their peers, or offending their peers with contradictory or conflicting readings, their lack of confidence couples with limited experience and skill to decrease the achievement of important course objectives. This case study examines how a combination of analytical reading and interpretive activities for both the face-to-face and blended learning environment can help students to improve close reading skills, recognize and discover their own individual interpretations of literary texts, and negotiate meaning through respectful and critical interactions with their peers.

Contact, Exchange, and Community in the Blended Multicultural Literature Classroom

The course at the center of this study is a general education literature course in multicultural American literature, which introduces students to writers of varied ethnic and cultural origins within the United States. This particular course focused on short stories, novels, and a graphic novel, and dealt with some very difficult texts such as Leslie Marmon Silko's *Ceremony,* Toni Morrison's *Paradise,* and Maxine Hong Kingston's *The Woman Warrior.* While these can be difficult novels even for advanced English majors, they are also particularly rewarding for students who are developing their skills in literary analysis and close reading. Students gain confidence and skill through collectively grappling with texts they find to be hard to understand. The course began by looking at short stories, leading up to the more complex novels, and prepared students to address the difficulty of the main texts as they developed their interpretive skills.

Designed for students outside of the English major, the course includes students at all levels and multiple majors across the university. This particular section was an honors-designated section, and was limited to 20 students. Students come with varied levels of preparation in close reading, literary analysis and interpretation, and analytical writing, but the vast majority had little experience with literature past high school.

For this case study, Evans chose to examine the effectiveness of the Discussion Board tool as a way to hone students' engagement and interpretation of the literary texts, their development as critical and analytic thinkers, and their interaction with peers in coming to understanding of the texts.

Evans designed Discussion Board (DB) assignments with specific goals and course learning objectives in mind. DBs focused on Learning Objective #1: *Develop critical reading and writing skills*, by developing close reading skills, developing analytical skills, using specific quotes from literature for support, developing interpretive skills for reading literature, and following MLA style. They were designed to meet Learning Objectives #3: *Engage a diversity of perspectives*, and #4: *Understand the complexity of cultural identity*, by directing engagement of complex issues of identity stemming from particular cultural experience and requiring specific engagement of the literary texts, thus encountering and addressing diverse perspectives. Evans designed assignments to increase students' close reading and analysis skills, strengthen their writing, and encourage engagement with their peers while thoughtfully engaging the complex ideas of the course. Discussion Board assignments took the place of one face-to-face class session, and took place on the third or fourth day of five class sessions on a particular novel (Tuesday/Thursday schedule). This scheduling allowed introductory examination and discussion to take place within the face-to-face class before students were expected to engage in serious analysis, and for at least one more face-to-face class session in which the class could engage the novel as a whole, bringing in the discussion threads as well as additional ideas. Students were required to read the DB in its entirety before the following class session.

The requirements for the Discussion Board activity are well defined, and it is directed toward full engagement of the text and ideas at hand. In this thread, students work to focus on specific textual evidence to build their discussions, engage complex ideas in the text, and engage with one another's ideas. The Discussion asks students to do the following:

Respond to one of the following prompts in three to four well-developed paragraphs (four to five sentences each). As in your earlier Discussion Boards, I'm looking for close reading here, so you should make ample use of the text (minimum of two quotations) and really work on developing your analysis of the text as you develop your ideas. Your response should be focused and organized and should develop a close reading and analysis of Silko's text. "Reply to" the prompt you've chosen to answer rather than starting your own thread.

Building Individual Skills

The first part of the assignment builds on classwork, but invites students to develop individual critical reading and analysis through close reading and textual analysis. Students chose one of the four assigned prompts and divided themselves up fairly evenly, with the most (eight) responding to one prompt and the least (four) to another. Evans sometimes assigned students to particular prompts to make sure ideas were equally represented, but here she wanted them to have some control and to be able to focus on something that interested them. Part of interpretation requires a student's investment in the material or the analysis, and being allowed to choose the prompt builds that investment, as the response below demonstrates.

Student A:

The narrative structure I found to be the most closely juxtaposed within Tayo's story was *Sunrise.* The last poem of introduction before Silko delves into the tangled wanderings of Tayo's mind is the simple word "sunrise" (4). Tayo begins his journey as what is described as being "white smoke" (13); however, as his journey throughout his illness progresses and each day begins anew you see his progression from the feeling of smoke back into the reality of the living world.

As each day passes Tayo is able to identify and rectify the feelings of torment he feels within his stomach. Not only does he use the sunrise as a guide, but he also uses the moonlight and the stars as a reference to his Laguna culture. "He stood up. He knew the people had a song for the sunrise.... Father of the clouds / you are beautiful/ at sunrise" (169). This sense of worship toward the sun can also be contrasted by what he refers to as lies of the moon as "he realized how deceptive the moonlight was; exposed root tips and dark rocks waited in deep shaows [sic] cast by the moon. Their lies would destroy this world" (178).

Tayo is constanity [sic] referring to the time of day, and in his strongest, clearest moments the sun is often mentioned. "Sunrise, sunrise." His words made vapor in the cold morning nand [sic] he felt he was living with her this way"

(200). He feels a connection within the sunrise, even as he slips back into his reality where Josiah, Rocky and Old Grandma still exist. "Josiah was driving the wagon, old Grandma was holding him, and Rocky whispered "my brother." They were taking him home.... He crossed the river at sunrise" (236–7). As Ceremony concludes, the final page in the novel ends with another poem "Sunrise, / accept this offering, / Sunrise" (244). Here I believe that Silko created a full circle where she began Tayo's story in the sunrise, and instead of concluding it with a sunset she chose to offer his life, and his struggle to find himself as a new sunrise, and a new beginning.

Works Cited:
Silko, Leslie Marmon. *Ceremony*. New York: Penguin Books, 1977. Print.

Quotes are drawn from throughout the novel as the student considers the internal poem "Sunrise" as a structure in the novel. The student provides analysis rather than summary and suggests the meaning behind the structure she's observed. Student A's response engages the text as it works toward an interpretation of one of the structural elements of the novel, showing the development of important skills in literary analysis.

Building Community

Equally important for this project, though, is encouraging students to work together on their interpretive skills and in negotiating knowledge. The second part of the assignment pushes students to develop ideas together and to willingly challenge and be challenged in their interpretations—something that is sometimes difficult in class, particularly for shy students. Part two is designed to encourage students to negotiate meaning.

> Respond to two of your peers' postings in one to two well-developed paragraphs; choose posts for a prompt other than the one you wrote about in your initial response (you will eventually write about three topics). Your responses to peers should work to extend the discussion: What can you add to what they are saying? What quotes can you find that might be supportive? In contrast, what might you suggest or support that counters what's being argued? You want to do more than say some form of "nice job"—this DB will lead us into our final discussion of the novel (Tuesday) and your second essay (due in draft form next Thursday).

Requiring students to respond to peers' posts on different prompts guarantees that the class as a whole engages with multiple ideas about the novel. Student responses remain grounded in the literary text, but also demonstrate critical engagement with their peers' ideas as they work together to develop an interpretation of the novel.

Response to Student A's posting. Student B:

I agree that Silko's choice to end with sunrise rather than sunset is significant. To end with sunset would not complete the cyclical structure of the story, leaving the novel on the brink of night, darkness, and the influence of the moon. As you suggest, the moon gives way to imagery associated with deception. In closing with sunrise, there is a greater certainty that Tayo is embarking on a new beginning, finding his place of balance after the struggle to transition from illness to health.

I would, however, point out that balance is still essential between sun and moon, day and night. You describe Tayo's "strongest, clearest" moments as those associated with the sun, evidencing a sense of worship for the sun. I think that while these are very strong moments for Tayo, the moment when he recognizes Betonie's stars is just as strong and transformative. The stars appear at night, however, in conjunction with the moon. The stars always appear the same way, unifying all viewers. I see this as evidence of the power of balance in the novel.

Response to Student A's posting. Student C:

The importance of the continuing cycle of the rising and setting sun definitely becomes evident with the conclusion of a sunrise rather than a typical sunset symbolizing the end of the book. In regard to the moon representing the "lie," it makes sense in my mind to make the stars a symbol of the people in the village. The moon then becomes the lie among the people, just a direct image of Tayo's thoughts. I like that you incorporate Tayo feeling like "white smoke" in the beginning of the story, and then progressively becoming more in touch with reality throughout the novel, but after your second paragraph, I lose the direction of that reference. There is definitely a connection between the sunrise and white smoke, tied with other elements of the story and Tayo's feelings, which should be discussed and developed even more (possibly in the classroom?).

In their responses, Students B and C take Student A's ideas seriously as they engage with the original interpretation, but also offer correctives from their own readings of the text. Student B's specific example of Betonie's stars returns Student A to the text itself and a consideration of how Silko's novel itself leads us past an easy closure. Student C similarly offers alternative examples that may support or undermine Student A's interpretation, and suggests that we return to some of the ideas in the classroom. This return to the classroom is essential, as it builds the students' sense of community and their collective engagement with course material.

Results in the Classroom

Assessment for this case study is based on a student survey on the Discussion Board Tool, and a series of face-to-face class observations (before and after DB assignments) and Discussion Board activity review from a peer faculty mentor. Students were asked about the effectiveness of the Discussion Board tool in helping them meet the objectives of the course. One hundred percent agreed that the DB activities met learning objectives. Furthermore, they felt it helped them better articulate their own ideas and bring them to the classroom. One student observed, "[The Discussion Board] helped to get ideas out that may otherwise not have been talked about in class as well as develop some personal development from the text." Similarly, the mentor observed that "Discussion responses allow for a greater degree of contemplation in original posting, as well as a significant depth of insight from the commentary offered by students when commenting on other student postings. The depth (quality) of the engagement in the face-to-face setting following a Discussion Board is significant."

Evans' assessment includes observations about the development of students' interpretive and analytical skills in their written and oral work in the course (daily writing, Discussion Boards, formal essays, and class discussion). Evans noted, and students commented on, marked improvement in students' use of the text and depth of analysis in class and in their written assignments. While in the beginning of the semester students made broad or general statements about the texts, by the end of the semester they never made a claim or observation without passages from the texts for the class to examine. Similarly, the combination of coursework helped students gain confidence in their own ideas and develop productive and respectful dialogue with peers. They learned to specifically engage one another's interpretations, to treat them as seriously as the text. Pulling students' specific DB responses into class discussion increased Evans's engagement with more students on a one-to-one basis and highlighted the broad range of effective student comments, building models throughout the semester. In addition, based on their discussions, Evans could adjust class face-to-face time to push forward and/or clarify students' understanding of the material. Most importantly, students engaged with one another's ideas—challenging, agreeing, building through examples.

Using Wikis for Collaborative Learning

The final case study presented here is drawn from ENL 266: Technical Communication, designed by Karen Gulbrandsen, Assistant Professor of English. Gulbrandsen's blended course design hones in on team projects and the value of wiki sites to facilitate student learning. We often think of collaboration as working in teams, assigning a team project to help students learn to communicate and build consensus around ideas. However, students can find collaboration challenging. Even though they collaborate on many class projects, they may not always collaborate effectively or collaborate to learn from one another. When asked, students often say that managing the team can make collaborative writing difficult—someone doesn't do any work, someone does all the work, or they simply don't have time to meet with each other outside of class. As a result, students tend to use a "patchwork quilt" approach to completing a team project, in which each student writes a section of the document and then all of the sections are pieced together right before the project is due. In doing so, students don't fully engage in a collaborative process.

In this case study, students in a 200-level, blended writing class used a class wiki to manage and write a set of documents for their team project, including a team contract, project proposal, project document, and final report. In this class, students completed a team project to support the learning outcome "to demonstrate effective collaboration strategies." Before blending the course, however, students were largely on their own when it came to writing the documents. In class, students reviewed concepts, brainstormed ideas, and exchanged drafts, but they were also expected to meet and write their drafts outside of class. To better understand how they collaborate in teams, Gulbrandsen incorporated a class wiki into the blend to help students engage with each other in new ways.

First, students were required to post a section of their document before each class meeting. Instead of completing a draft for this assignment, students posted sections of their work to a class wiki before each class period, encouraging all students in a team to be involved in all sections of the document. In class, time was then spent analyzing and discussing student writing projects and recording class discussions on an "Example" wiki page. This approach allowed students to assess the strengths and weaknesses of their work and to get ideas for moving the project forward.

Second, students reviewed each other's documents in the online writing space—both formally and informally. Because the pages on a wiki are open to everyone in the class, students could see the work-in-progress of other teams, which prompted them to ask questions about their own work. Furthermore, students were asked to respond to other teams' drafts, analyzing how concepts from the class were being applied and suggesting ways to revise. As a result, students had an audience other than just the instructor, writing to each other to critically analyze and apply concepts from the course. To enhance this online experience, students brainstormed, wrote, and posted the peer-review questions in the face-to-face classroom. In so doing, they linked the readings and class discussions to their assignment.

In addition, students used the wiki as a virtual meeting place to discuss their projects. The teams' wiki pages included comments about their revisions, links to information they needed, and directions about what needed to be done. In many ways, this discussion was a part of the document, with many teams preserving the comments. Rather than working in isolation, students produced their work in a public classroom space, encouraging all team members to self-assess their progress and success and to deepen their engagement with each other.

Overall, students responded positively to working in the online classroom. In a focus group, students emphasized that "time and flexibility" were two key factors to helping them learn—particularly in relation to the team project. They liked the flexibility of being able to complete team assignments on their own timeline. Student noted, "They can do work early, for example" (focus group). In addition, they liked that they could meet virtually, saying the online tools "helped with the team project because they could 'meet' online" (focus group).

But more than that, when asked in the focus group what they liked about the online elements of this course, "Students stated that it helped them stay engaged" (focus group), giving several reasons: they had to do the class readings, they had access to course materials, and peer reviews were more honest. Results from the focus group included:

- "Students stated that the online elements required them to do the class readings, which then made them ready for class, which then meant they got more out of the class" (focus group).
- "Students stated that it helped them stay engaged. The fact that all the material (including grades) could be found in one place was seen as helping learning."
- "The students felt they learned more from the peer editing because feedback online is more honest and thus more helpful" (focus group).

But students also commented on the integration of the face-to-face and online classrooms, saying that "making it clear how the two components (f2f and online) worked together kept people doing the work" (focus group) and that even when they met online, "class participation was still ongoing" (focus group). These comments suggested that students saw the online classroom as an active learning space, not just a repository for materials or a place to take quizzes.

End-of-semester student evaluations supported the results of the focus group. In the comment section of the evaluations, several students commented on how the blend kept them engaged in the course. Representative comments included:

- "She was able to keep the class's attention. The use of the online really helped to keep the class structured and allowed you to get involved with the class."
- "She introduced a new type of course (blended) and I found it very effective to the subject and class as a whole. Working online every

week always kept me up-to-date with the class, especially the quizzes. I also found online peer editing very beneficial for my papers."
- "The instructor was effective and utilized different methods to explain terms to us. The use of online learning was effective." (Student evaluations, S2010)

In retrospect, Gulbrandsen found the online tools had a positive impact on student learning because it gave students new ways to collaborate with each other in their learning. Rather than envisioning themselves as solitary writers, the online tools created a place in which they could work together. But the online space also opened up a broader audience for their work. Students could see their progress and could comment on its strengths and weaknesses. The wiki in particular encouraged students to see how others were conceptualizing a writing assignment and working as teams. As a result, students interacted with a broader range of voices and, in the process, were encouraged to reflect on their learning.

Finally, the online tools allowed Gulbrandsen to quickly assess their needs on an ongoing basis. Their written discussions and peer reviews documented their learning and helped Gulbrandsen to adjust what she did in the face-to-face classroom to address their needs and to help them collaborate effectively. However, this case study also demonstrates students' need to understand how the online and face-to-face environments work together. Rather than conceptualize the two environments as separate spheres, faculty need to design a cohesive learning environment, using the strengths of both to support self-assessment and responsibility. As shown in this case study, designing an integrated blended classroom experience can motivate students to fully engage in a collaborative learning process.

CONCLUSION

The key to the success of these three projects is purposefully integrated assessment, both formative and summative, into the actual design of the course. Purposefully integrated assessment does not just happen; rather, the IBIS project teaches assessment to faculty and provides peer mentoring to help faculty design effective courses and to integrate productive assessment practices within those courses. The success of the IBIS project in teaching assessment to faculty comes because the co-PIs recognized that assessment as a practice needs to be properly presented and understood. Assessment throughout the training workshops was framed as embedded "reflective practice" in a course. Faculty came to understand this conceptualization of assessment through recognizing that they already embed reflective practices in their courses, through seeing reflective practices modeled in their own training workshop, and through being asked explicitly to reflect on and evaluate their own learning throughout the workshop and at its end.

Using newly learned online assessment practices, faculty were able to see more clearly if students were reaching course objectives or not. The assessment practices they employed led to improved learning outcomes, which, in their turn, led to improved teaching. Improved learning outcomes and improved teaching lead to greater satisfaction with teaching in the short term and greater career satisfaction in the long term, both of which will lead to continued reflective teaching practices by the faculty member.

Not only did the IBIS project benefit individual faculty, but it also benefited the institution, as we now have a faculty cohort who is more aware of assessment strategies and how these strategies can be integrated into a course without significantly increasing the workload of the faculty member. The numbers of faculty who have participated in the IBIS program are now enough of a critical mass to begin to create a culture of self-assessment. A change in culture will support continued reflective teaching practices after the initial stages of the program have ended.

It is clear that the use of online assessment tools—properly integrated—increase student learning. In particular we identified the following: an increase in student preparedness for face-to-face class sessions; more interaction in the face-to-face classroom; enhanced retention and understanding of the course materials; development of analytical skills and writing skills; and greater student responsibility for their own learning.

The question now remains whether we can determine *how* student learning is developed. The project allowed a window into how these online assessment tools actually function to increase student learning: through *peer assessment* and *self-assessment.*

In the first case, it is clear that the design of the course was aimed at producing learning, both content and skill based. Here the online elements of the course helped the instructor reach his or her specific learning objectives. During the specific online task of reading and responding to the work of others, student learners began, as the case study author indicates, a process of self-reflection and self-scrutiny. It is here that a significant shift in formative assessment takes place in an online environment (whether blended or fully online). Instead of a reliance on the feedback of the instructor, the student moves more toward *a process of self-assessment* in order to develop and learn. Learning relationships happen among peers, prompted by student self-assessment. This process was recognized by the instructor, and they deliberately did not intervene in the DB interactions.

In the second case study, the online format allows students to build confidence, both in their interpretations of the texts and in their interaction with their peers. In responding to the posts of their peers, students challenge the ideas of others and are challenged on their own—perhaps dearly held—preconceptions. Through this mutual exchange, students develop a sense of intellectual community and grow to see themselves as deserving of a place in this community. The other element of the process of self-assessment in this course was partially generated by the course material itself. Students reflected on what they had read in the texts and how this had generated personal growth.

In the final case, the online wiki tool allowed students to peer-assess the work of others and also to self-assess their own learning progress in relation to that of others. The process of learning through self-assessment was similar to that of the first case; however, the process was less organic, as the instructor was more involved in directing the use of the specific online tool: the wiki. Directed or undirected, however, the online tools encouraged students to learn through reflection on their own learning. The wiki also functioned as a virtual meeting place, thus creating an intellectual community similar to that of the discussion boards of the second case.

The project will run one final academic year. In addition to collecting further data documenting the perspectives of students in the blended classroom and how the assessment integrated into the course had an impact on their learning experience, the co-PIs will develop student surveys and focus groups to explore further how online assessment tools actually function to increase student learning.

CHAPTER 13

DISCUSSIONS IN ONLINE AND BLENDED LEARNING

A Tool for Peer Assessment

David S. Stein
Ohio State University

Constance E. Wanstreet
Ohio State University

INTRODUCTION

This chapter presents a tool (i.e., a rubric) to assess higher-order thinking in inquiry-based discussions. Although discussion rubrics exist, these tools tend to focus on knowledge acquired by individuals rather than the knowledge generated by the group. Using a knowledge-building process suggested by the authors (Stein, Wanstreet, & Glazer, 2011) and informed by the Community of Inquiry framework (Garrison, Anderson, & Archer, 2000), we propose a formative assessment tool that is designed to be used by students as they engage in online learner-led discussions. The tool, which has not yet been tested, was derived from the literature on discussion and collaborative dialogic approaches to learning as well as from online rubric development and evaluation. The tool was developed to assess synchronous as well as asynchronous discussion postings.

Assessment in Online and Blended Learning Environments, pages 253–267
Copyright © 2015 by Information Age Publishing
253

Providing prompt feedback on how well group members implement discussion strategies can improve on each individual's contribution to the group's collective learning (Stein & Wanstreet, 2013a) and lead to higher-order thinking at the group level (Stein, Wanstreet, Slagle, Trinko, & Lutz, 2013). While instructors typically provide feedback related to course content, it is not always practical for instructors to provide formative assessments immediately following the discussion process, especially when the discussions are learner-led. For that reason, the authors have developed a tool that students can use to assess their efficacy as discussants as they complete learner-led discussions. This approach to peer assessment assists learners in taking ownership of the discussion process and helps them critically assess their contributions to the collective learning of the group.

DISCUSSION AS A TOOL FOR KNOWLEDGE-BUILDING

Discussion is used as a collaborative activity to help learners become critically informed about a topic or issue, take responsibility for their learning, question their assumptions, and gain more insight into themselves as learners (Brookfield & Preskill, 2005). However, we have noted, particularly in asynchronous modes, that postings tend to reflect an initial individual comment and a response post that may offer guidance and critique but might not change the original post or lead to new insights. Even in synchronous chats, students sometimes find that their group's discussion was more painful than productive (Stein & Wanstreet, 2013b). The first step in decreasing the pain of shallow or poorly facilitated chats involves awareness on the part of the instructor about how learners can encourage discussion, coalesce as a group, and synthesize comments to move the group toward shared understanding (Stein et al., 2007).

The content posted in a discussion board is often not really a discussion but an exchange of information in a single direction, typically from the learner to the instructor with others observing the information (Chen & Wang, 2009). What is called discussion might be seen simply as an exchange of individual ideas at best. What we see might be termed *simple talk* or *casual conversation*. Lipman, Bridges, and Dillon (as cited in Brookfield & Preskill, 2005) agree that discussion goes beyond the notion of casual talk or a conversation. In conversation, ideas and feelings are exchanged in a social, cooperative way. In a discussion, the intent is to push participants beyond their everyday thinking, to create a tension and to produce a new and better understanding—a change in the way an issue is thought about. Discussion that produces improved understanding has the characteristics of mutual trust, respect for the members and member contributions, and participants who demonstrate a willingness to listen and who are respectful of challenges to prevailing views. The work of a discussion is to make new meanings in a collective sense involving critical reflection upon the premises of the arguments being formed. Brookfield and Preskill (2005) list four outcomes for a discussion:

- To reach a more critical understanding about a topic
- To become more aware of one's beliefs, values, and meaning schemes
- To develop an appreciation for the diversity of views on a topic
- To provide the energy and motivation to take informed action on the issues raised in the discussion (p. 6)

Discussion can be a transformative experience when conducted in a democratic manner. A democratic discussion is one in which participants feel welcome, are receptive to new ideas and perspectives, participate in ways that are related to the issue under discussion, speak tactfully, express appreciation for thoughtful comments and insights, offer arguments and counterarguments supported by evidence, and are committed to the development of group learning (Brookfield & Preskill, 2005). In a democratic discussion, power relationships are minimized by giving precedence to setting norms for participation, ensuring equal access to speak, recognizing and allowing one's bias to be held in abeyance so that alternative perspectives and voices can be heard, and sharing in a commitment to seek consensus that reflects the best thinking of the community (Brookfield & Preskill, 2005; Mezirow, 1991; Stavredes, 2011). The outcome of a discussion conducted in a democratic manner is new knowledge.

Mezirow (1991), following the work of Habermas, calls discussion an act of communicative competence, meaning that participants logically assess the evidence supporting an argument by testing the validity of claims and negotiating the meanings implied by others, coming to consensual validation and further testing of the assumptions and evidence supporting those assumptions, and allowing for the possibility that agreement reached is temporary and subject to analysis and verification by other groups. Mezirow believes that the ideal discussion is achievable, and he speaks to the very essence of how adults should engage to create an improved understanding:

> [Participants would need to have] accurate and complete information (i.e., read the material and reflect upon its meaning); be able to weigh evidence and assess arguments objectively; be open to alternative perspectives; be able to reflect upon assumptions held by individuals and the group; have equal opportunity to participate; be able to refute, challenge, [and] question the arguments made by others in a safe and respectful manner; and be able to accept an informed, objective, and rational consensus as a legitimate test of validity. (pp. 77–78)

Garrison (2011) defines inquiry-based discussions as those in which learners take responsibility for their learning, create meaning in a group, and learn from the group using the democratic and ideal practices outlined by Brookfield and Preskill (2005) and Mezirow (1991). He characterizes successful discussions as featuring learners engaged in purposeful, critical dialogue to construct individual and group understanding of an issue.

In online environments, Dennen (2008) notes that at the very least discussions may reduce isolation and provide a sense of connection to other learners. Beyond that, however, discussion can help move learners from independent thinking to interdependence, going beyond their present understandings to create new and refined knowledge constructions.

Discussion in an Online Environment

In our course, discussion occurs with multiple groups meeting simultaneously in different chatrooms. This limits the amount of time the instructor can be present in any one chat. Therefore, our learners' facilitation skills are critical to their ability to arrive at a resolution during the chat. In our discussions, resolution is demonstrated by showing a critical understanding of the topic and how that understanding emerges from an integration of diverse views. Individuals should also show how they have become more aware of their own beliefs and values surrounding the topic. Shea, Li, and Pickett (2006) report that students prefer directed facilitation from the instructor and may need to be guided in how to organize and facilitate discussions. This is particularly important in courses such as ours that feature learner-led discussions.

Instructors should not assume that learners have the necessary skills to conduct discussions efficiently, integrate information, and resolve issues under discussion (Garrison & Vaughan, 2007; Wanstreet & Stein, 2011). The artifacts produced from a discussion may not reflect the thoughts expressed in that discussion. This applies to learners in both online and face-to-face environments, who tend to transfer practices from ordinary conversation to their online interactions (Schönfeldt & Golato, 2003).

The idea of an effective discussion in an asynchronous environment was expressed by Chen and Wang (2009) as a discussion that is on task and on time, in which learners express new ideas as well as elaborating their own thoughts. Chen and Wang postulated a relationship in which the artifact produced is based on comments from weekly discussions and in which weekly discussions are related to student experience with the subject matter, data gathering, hypothesis or idea testing, and conclusions. In their model, "Pick-n-Choose," students decide on which "important posts" from which "important threads" will make up the weekly posting (Chen & Wang, 2009, p. 590). This is done on an individual basis and negotiated in a group setting. Social talk, similar to the idea of social presence, helps students negotiate conflict, offer support, and use soft power to improve the performance of nonresponsive group members. When used in a discussion environment, social talk seems to be correlated with more on-task collaborative and reflective posts (Chen & Wang, 2009).

To become more effective discussants, learners in chat environments need time to practice and receive guidance on effective conversational moves made during their discussions. Formative assessment, rather than modeling or direct instruction, may be an appropriate intervention for engaging in democratic, on-time, on-task, synchronous learner-led discussions. Learners who are guided and provided with timely feedback are able to produce improvements in their ability to master the subject matter by better integrating and resolving the issues under discussion (Stein et al., 2013). The question for instructors is how to provide guidance and feedback in educational online environments to help students improve their higher-order thinking skills, such as integration and resolution. If guidance on discussion skills can increase student performance in the discussion, how then might instructors create a safe space for learners to practice and learn the art of discussion in an ongoing discussion-based environment? To address that question, we are proposing a tool (i.e., a rubric) to provide formative assessment on the results of the synchronous discussion process and product.

Critique of Rubrics Assessing Online Discussions

If an online discussion is designed to provoke deep thought, and if participants are using ideal practices for engaging in knowledge construction, then assessment tools should capture the processes as well as the content developed by the group. Assessment tools used mostly for online asynchronous discussion focus on individual contributions rather than group processes and the product generated by the discussants (Aycock, 2008; Churches, 2007). The rubrics tend to focus on presentation and generation of content, member participation, and quality of interaction with other participants. Common factors in the rubrics reviewed by Aycock (2008) and Churches (2007) include:

- Development of ideas (comment shows an understanding of the issue)
- Evidence of critical thinking
- Clarity of the post (writing style, words used)
- Number of responses to other students and the instructor
- Timeliness of the post
- Evidence of reading assignments used to develop the post
- Value added by the post (contributes to further discussion)
- Length of the post
- Respectful communication

Penny and Murphy (2009) reviewed 50 rubrics for asynchronous higher education discussions and concluded that learners were evaluated on the co-construction of knowledge or on how shared understanding was achieved. Rubrics covered four major categories: cognitive core, mechanical core (i.e., writing, grammar), procedural/managerial core, and interactive core. More of the criteria in the rubrics measured the cognitive core and fewer criteria measured the interactive core. Few items were included that measured social presence, defined as "performance criteria and ratings that emphasize interactions with others, particularly the ability to share reflections, insights, information and resources with other members of the group" (Penny & Murphy, 2009, p. 816). Nor was there evidence of the following items in the rubrics reviewed: (a) conflict or negotiation at the group level, (b) assertion, or maintaining and defending ideas, (c) suggestions for new applications of an idea or to applying solutions, (d) ability to apply or test hypotheses, or (e) presenting triggering events (i.e., offering problems, issues, or dilemmas to be solved). Overall, the rubrics Penny and Murphy reviewed did not address how the group generates new knowledge or the processes used to ensure that a democratic discussion takes place.

Lai (2012) used rubrics to improve performance in critical thinking skills. Her study was based on the idea that rubrics addressing content only are ineffective in building process skills. In higher education, rubrics should also address how students arrive at their positions. Focusing on changes in individual students ignores the skills of negotiation, interaction, and evaluating evidence—skills used to produce the content. Lai's work shows that students lack the skills to develop content using critical thinking. However, a rubric showing different levels of performance and an instructor modeling appropriate ways to respond can increase the quality of a response. A weakness in the nine-item critical thinking rubric developed by Lai is that the rubric focuses on individual performance and does not address how a group comes to collective understanding on an issue. Criteria assessed included the following:

- Made relevant comments
- Posed questions to the group
- Responded to criticism
- Sparked discussion and comments from others
- Presented well-structured arguments
- Clearly articulated ideas
- Demonstrated respect for others
- Built on the ideas of others
- Contributed to the learning experience of others. (Lai, 2012)

Nandi, Hamilton, and Harland (2012), researching quality indicators in online asynchronous discussions, suggested that a quality online discussion must have a useable feedback system to allow students and instructors to determine if following the guidance in a rubric about expected levels of performance leads to deep understanding. However, Nandi et al. also suggested that the instructor is the major source of feedback and is primarily responsible for learner satisfaction with the experience. We suggest that in a learner-led online synchronous encounter, the learners are responsible for providing feedback to one another to determine if deep learning is taking place. Feedback guidance would be based on suggestions contained in a peer-assessment rubric.

No rubrics under review considered chats, which differ from asynchronous discussion boards in pace of thought, timing, and outcome. In a knowledge-building discussion, individual contributions build a shared collective understanding of the issue. What occurs in an online course that moves learners from information acquisition or task completion to knowledge building? What might help groups move, as Scardamalia and Bereiter (1994) suggest, from repeating what is known to explaining situations by advancing new ideas, testing those ideas with evidence, subjecting those ideas to public scrutiny, refining the thoughts, and, finally, publishing an idea on the forefront of our understanding with the acceptance of the community to which one belongs? A rubric is needed to assess not individual gain but the product of the group interactions as well as the process used to arrive at the product.

Knowledge-Building as a Chat Outcome

Knowledge-building as a learning activity is an act of creation that stands apart from its creators. Participation and engagement produce a collective understanding of an issue, phenomenon, or situation. Knowledge-building goes beyond sharing of individual thoughts toward new collective thoughts that can emerge only in a community committed to pushing the basis of existing knowledge. In the discussion/chat space, the thoughts that emerge are new to the learners, superior to their previous understandings, and for the good of all (Bereiter, 1996).

Bereiter (1996) described the knowledge-building process as progressive discourse that produces better thinking about content. Progressive discourse involves a commitment to work toward a common understanding that alters individual thoughts and creates new collective thoughts. In addition, progressive discourse involves a commitment to base emerging thoughts on evidence and openness, and to expand the number and scope of thoughts that the group considers valid, whether they agree with them or not. The artifact produced is an external representation of the communal thought and advances the collective understanding of an issue in an intentional way that enhances the intellectual growth of the individual learner and the community of learners to which that learner is now joined (Riel & Polin, 2004). The knowledge produced has meaning to the participants and lives beyond the space in which it was produced. The product of a knowledge-building encounter advances intellectual growth. The product goes beyond the information in an individual mind or a summary of thought from the collective mind. The product offers a better explanation than previously offered by the texts on a subject that is lived by the participants (Bereiter, 1996).

Electronic tools for sharing, recording, and posting emerging thoughts facilitate knowledge-building (Stein et al., 2007). The network for connecting thoughts is provided by online course management systems. On a particular issue or problem, learners can move from reliance on authorities to creating and testing knowledge from collaborative work. The output, or product, of the activity is a knowledge artifact, which is not a summary of individual thoughts but rather a map showing a way to understand or think about an issue that improves on earlier ways of understanding and that can contribute, perhaps, to the learning of another group. In essence, one might think of the output in terms of a creative piece to which others can respond and can reshape as the community continues to learn more about a particular topic. It is not the product alone that counts; rather, it is the commitment to making a contribution that pushes the group's understanding about an issue beyond the existing public knowledge that is the goal (Scardamalia & Bereiter, 1994).

Knowledge-building moves learners to the center of the learning process. In online environments, a knowledge-building approach to learning resembles the way knowledge is created in the real world. The goal is to expand upon the existing canon (i.e., the text and lectures) to solve problems through a collaborative process that improves upon what is known about a subject. The learning involves making a contribution to understanding for all, not just for some or for an individual (McConnell, 2006). New knowledge is generated through collaborative exchanges in which learners explore, test, and refine ideas held in public and private. Knowledge construction is the outcome—not a paper, exam, or project that addresses known content. Indeed, Hewitt (2003) questioned papers, projects, and exams typical in classroom learning communities as artificial contrivances that do not provide meaning outside of the classroom. A knowledge-building approach is appropriate when the subject matter is issue- or problem-focused rather than foundational. A revised Bloom's taxonomy for online learning considers collaboration and publishing knowledge as higher-order thinking skills appropriate for the 21st century (Churches, 2007).

In a knowledge-building discussion, the artifact developed should reflect the best critical and reflective thinking of the group as well as the democratic discussion processes used to create the artifact. A rubric is needed that can be used to trace the development of the artifact from the chat. The assessment is at the group level rather than individual contributions. Text-based discussions have an advantage over face-to-face discussions in that a word-by-word record is produced that allows the instructor to see how the ideas presented in the artifact were developed.

Conventional guidance suggests that a discussion group might have a moderator who is responsible for leading the discussion; a recorder who captures the ideas and who may post a summary of the group discussion;

and participant roles to query, challenge, and advocate for certain positions. However, we have noticed that the moderator or recorder usually feels responsible for taking the raw material—the chat transcripts—and creating a response reflecting the views of the group after the chat has concluded. Even when we have asked for the moderator/recorder to ask for feedback from the group as to the accuracy of the response, the group members generally agree with the statements produced. We note that the artifact produced may not reflect the voices and ideas expressed by the group. In response, we developed guidelines to help correct this situation so that groups produce an artifact that reflects the best thinking of the group and that makes public the private thinking of the group. The artifact becomes part of the community's (i.e., the class's) knowledge base and is submitted for public comment and then refinement by the original group.

To address the effectiveness of group assessment—and keeping in mind Dennen's (2008) admonishment concerning the value of group evaluations—we built and monitored guidelines to better ensure that group chats reflect the ideas and voices of the group members. We provided steps and timelines as to how groups should engage in a collaborative chat. Our guidelines to students include:

1. Determine the intention of the question. What is it that you should have addressed by the end of your discussion?
2. Engage with the content by including your experience and your thoughts within the context of the question.
3. While you are chatting, designate a member to search for relevant material on the Web that might assist with your discussion. Search for documents that would reinforce the points or expand the argument. In addition to interacting with each other and the assigned content, interact with resources both material and human.
4. Consider a two-to-one allocation based on a 60-minute chat, leaving at least 20 minutes to write your collective post. Write at least a one- to two-paragraph group draft response before concluding your chat.
5. Your recorder will need to clean up the text, include relevant links, and post to the whole-class discussion board.
6. Respond to at least one group posting. The purpose of the response post is to challenge, clarify, expand, and illuminate the thinking of the group. Your comments should be informed by questions that might arise from reading the post. If you agree with the thinking, state why. If you challenge, cite evidence for your view. Opinion should be supported with your experiences and with content related to the question we are examining.
7. Each group member should read the responses from other class members regarding your group's original post.

8. Reconvene your chat group, discuss the feedback received, review your original thinking, and repost your new and improved understanding of the issue.

A RUBRIC FOR ASSESSING KNOWLEDGE-BUILDING

A rubric provides input and feedback regarding acceptable performance (Roblyer & Wiencke, 2003). A rubric consists of performance categories, indicators of performance, and ratings. Although a rubric may be daunting for students to use, clear language that describes the expected levels of performance should aid understanding (Palloff & Pratt, 2005). Lai (2012) also recommends that illustrations should be provided to help the learners visualize appropriate levels of responses. A rubric consists of the criteria, a description of acceptable performance, and the assessment scale or level of attainment. More important, a rubric communicates to learners what instructors think is important, how to show that learners have adopted the notions of what is important, and what level of participation is deemed acceptable.

Nandi et al. (2012), investigating qualities of an online asynchronous discussion, suggested criteria generated by learners in a qualitative study of online posts. The rubric generated from the analysis can be used to assess products in terms of how the content is generated as well as the use of interactions to produce content.

Using the rubric generated by Nandi et al. and others (Roblyer & Wiencke, 2003; Lai, 2012; Penny & Murphy, 2009), we modify and expand the ideas expressed and apply the ideas to a synchronous chat environment. We focus on the artifact produced after the conclusion of the chat as the indicator of learning and we trace back from the artifact the processes used to develop the shared understanding. The artifact is assessed by the group according to how content is generated, how interactions help produce content, and evidence of democratic discussion processes and critical reflective thinking. Suggested ratings are based on errors in hundreds of postings we have encountered and commented on in our class for more than a decade.

We are reminded by Dennen (2008) that a rubric should focus on learning rather than merely on participation, number and length of postings, quality of a comment out of context, or looking at only incidences and types of interactions. In our course, the final product is a posting to the discussion board for comment by the community of learners participating in the course. The features of the final product should be traceable to comments made by group members during the live chat. Evidence of learning is in the shared knowledge presented in the final posting as assessed by excellent or good ratings in the rubric (see Table 13.1).

TABLE 13.1   Peer Assessment Rubric for Synchronous Discussions

Element	Evidence in the Chat Transcript	Assessment			
		Excellent	Good	Fair	Poor
Response addresses the issue/problem	In the transcript, the group considers the intent of the question rather than simply its component parts. A draft response in the transcript is on task, integrated, and does not contain comments or thoughts unrelated to the issue.	The document addresses the issue in an integrated fashion. Component parts of the question are answered holistically as one question.	The document addresses most of the question in a holistic manner. A component of the question is addressed separately.	The document addresses each part of the question in a separate fashion but is still on task.	The posted response presents personal opinion and does not address the issue presented. The text wanders from idea to idea.
Response demonstrates use of evidence to support an argument.	The transcript shows comments based on the assigned readings as well as additional resources selected by group members to support and illustrate the answer reached by the group.	The document uses the assigned literature and additional resources to justify a group response and provides an explanation for each of the points expressed.	The document presents a group response using the assigned literature to justify the point of view expressed by the group.	The document contains some unsupported opinions.	The document is based on unsupported opinions.
The response builds new ideas.	Ideas presented in the post can be traced to interim summaries in the chat transcript indicating the development of a new interpretation.	The posted response expands upon the ideas presented in the readings and provides a new interpretation based on the group discussion.	The posted response is based on the ideas presented in the assigned readings and provides examples from the group discussion.	The posted response uses the textbook information as a base to support personal interpretations.	The posted response repeats the textbook information in the form of a summary. New thoughts are not present.

(continued)

TABLE 13.1 Peer Assessment Rubric for Synchronous Discussions (continued)

Element	Evidence in the Chat Transcript	Assessment			
		Excellent	Good	Fair	Poor
The response indicates an awareness of the issue's context in the real world.	The chat transcript shows evidence of questioning one another about the applicability of resources and experiences to the context of the issue.	The response shows application to real-world situations. Readings, additional literature, and personal examples are used to illustrate and describe how the content is relevant in the real world.	A personal connection is made with the issue and supported with evidence from the readings.	A personal connection is made with the issue to illustrate ideas.	No connection is made to the issue outside of the course material.
The response shows mindful engagement among group members.	Each member's ideas related to the content are present in the written document as determined from statements in the chat transcript.	The response contains content-related ideas generated by every member of the group.	The response reflects a single author's ideas with feedback from some of the group members.	The response reflects the ideas of the moderator or recorder and does not acknowledge contributions from other group members.	The response does not reflect the group's thinking and appears not to be based on the chat discussion.
The response is based on an analysis of multiple perspectives.	In the transcript, different views are present and considered by the group for strengths and limitations. A conclusion reflects minority and majority thought.	Majority and minority positions are discussed with strengths and limitations explored before coming to resolution.	Only the majority position is presented with justification for the statement.	A single position is stated as the thinking of the group without justification.	The position is a collection of individual thought statements.

(continued)

TABLE 13.1   Peer Assessment Rubric for Synchronous Discussions (continued)

Element	Evidence in the Chat Transcript	Assessment			
		Excellent	Good	Fair	Poor
The response shows analysis of evidence to arrive at a mutual understanding.	In the transcript statements show negotiation over the evidence presented and integration of ideas from the group members. Positions are questioned to uncover assumptions and biases.	In the post, positions are questioned to uncover assumptions and biases about the assertions. The post shows the progression of ideas used to arrive at a mutual understanding.	In the post some questioning of assumptions and biases is evident. There is general acceptance of the overall conclusions reached by the group.	In the post the statements are based on acceptance of the group's thinking and of authoritative sources without questioning the assumptions behind their assertions.	No critical examination of the issue and personal reactions to the issue is apparent.
The response shows sharing of personal insights and stories to provide a framework for the group's resolution.	In the chat, group members share and incorporate personal insights and stories.	Personal insights and stories are used to help illustrate the overall meaning of the post.	Some personal insights and stories are included.	The response is limited to impersonal examples.	No personal insights or stories included in the final response.

We suggest that instructors review this rubric with students before their first discussion and include examples of excellent, good, fair, and poor postings. Students should also have an opportunity to practice a chat and rate their group's performance individually. Individual assessments should be shared and discussed with other group members so they come to a common understanding of their performance as a group. In that way, the rubric can provide students with concrete, immediate feedback and a path to improving their performance.

REFERENCES

Aycock, A. (2008). Using discussion forums to create online community. In *Sloan certificate program: Faculty development for blended teaching and learning* (pp. 57–66). Milwaukee, WI: The Sloan Consortium and University of Wisconsin–Milwaukee Learning Technology Center.

Bereiter, C. (1996). Implications of postmodernism for science, or, science as progressive discourse. *Educational Psychologist, 29*(1), 3–12.

Brookfield, S. D., & Preskill, S. (2005). *Discussion as a way of teaching: Tools and techniques for democratic classrooms* (2nd ed.). San Francisco, CA: Jossey-Bass.

Chen, F. C., & Wang, T. C. (2009). Social conversation and effective discussion in online group learning. *Educational Technology Research and Development, 57*, 587–612.

Churches, A. (2007). *Bloom's digital taxonomy: Threaded discussion rubric.* Retrieved from http://edorigami.wikispaces.com/file/view/threaded+discussion+rubric.pdf.

Dennen, V. P. (2008). Looking for evidence of learning: Assessment and analysis methods for online discourse. *Computers in Human Behavior, 24*, 205–219.

Garrison, D. R. (2011). *E-learning in the 21st century: A framework for research and practice.* New York, NY: Routledge.

Garrison, D. R., Anderson, T., & Archer, W. (2000). Critical inquiry in a text-based environment: Computer conferencing in higher education. *The Internet and Higher Education, 2*(2–3), 87–105.

Garrison, D. R., & Vaughan, N. D. (2007). *Blended learning in higher education: Frameworks, principles, and guidelines.* San Francisco, CA: Jossey-Bass.

Hewitt, J. (2003). How habitual online practices affect the development of asynchronous discussion threads. *Journal of Educational Computing Research, 28*(1), 31–45.

Lai, K. (2012). Assessing participation skills: Online discussions with peers. *Assessment and Evaluation in Higher Education, 37*(8), 933–947.

McConnell, D. (2006). *E-learning groups and communities.* Berkshire, UK: Open University Press.

Mezirow, J. (1991). *Transformative dimensions of adult learning.* San Francisco, CA: Jossey-Bass.

Nandi, D., Hamilton, M., & Harland, J. (2012). Evaluating the quality of interaction in asynchronous discussion forums in fully online courses. *Distance Education, 33*(1), 5–30.

Palloff, R. M., & Pratt, K. (2005). *Collaborating online: Learning together in community.* San Francisco, CA: Jossey-Bass.

Penny, L., & Murphy, E. (2009). Rubrics for designing and evaluating online asynchronous discussions, *British Journal of Educational Technology, 40*(5), 804–820.

Riel, M., & Polin, L. (2004). Online learning communities: Common ground and critical differences in designing technical environments. In S. Barab, R. Kling, & J. Gray (Eds.), *Designing for virtual communities in the service of learning* (pp. 16–50). New York: Cambridge University Press.

Roblyer, M. D., & Wiencke, W. R. (2003). Design and use of a rubric to assess and encourage interactive qualities in distance courses. *American Journal of Distance Education, 17*(2), 77–98.

Scardamalia, M., & Bereiter, C. (1994). Computer support for knowledge-building communities. *Journal of the Learning Sciences, 3*(3), 265–283.

Schönfeldt, J., & Golato, A. (2003). Repair in chats: A conversation analytic approach. *Research on Language and Social Interaction, 36*(3), 241–284.

Shea, P. J., Li, C. S., & Pickett, A. (2006). A study of teaching presence and student sense of learning community in fully online and Web-enhanced college courses. *The Internet and Higher Education, 9*(3), 175–190.

Stavredes, T. (2011). *Effective online teaching: Foundations and strategies for student success.* San Francisco, CA: Jossey-Bass.

Stein, D. S., & Wanstreet, C. E. (2013a). Coaching for cognitive presence: A model for enhancing online discussions. In D. R. Garrison & Z. Akyol (Eds.), *Educational communities of inquiry: Theoretical framework, research and practice* (pp. 133–147). Hershey, PA: IGI Global.

Stein, D. S., & Wanstreet, C. E. (2013b). e-Coaching success strategies for synchronous discussions. *Distance Learning, 10*(2), 19–24.

Stein, D. S., Wanstreet, C. E., & Glazer, H. R. (2011). Knowledge building online: The promise and the process. In V. Wang (Ed.), *Encyclopedia of information communication technologies and adult education integration* (pp. 985–998). Hershey, PA: IGI Global.

Stein, D. S., Wanstreet, C. E., Glazer, H. R., Engle, C. E., Harris, R. A., Johnston, S. M., . . . Trinko, L. A. (2007). Creating shared understanding through chats in a community of inquiry. *The Internet and Higher Education, 10*(2), 103–115.

Stein, D. S., Wanstreet, C. E., Slagle, P., Trinko, L. A., & Lutz, M. (2013). From "hello" to higher-order thinking: The effect of coaching and feedback on online chats. *The Internet and Higher Education, 16*(1), 78–84.

Wanstreet, C. E., & Stein, D. S. (2011). Presence over time in synchronous communities of inquiry. *The American Journal of Distance Education, 25,* 1–16.

CHAPTER 14

CRITERION-REFERENCED LANGUAGE ASSESSMENT IN BLENDED ENVIRONMENTS

Wojciech Malec
John Paul II Catholic University of Lublin, Poland

CRITERION-REFERENCED ASSESSMENT

One of the primary considerations in language testing is the frame of reference (or type of score interpretation), according to which tests are divided into norm-referenced tests (NRTs) and criterion-referenced tests (CRTs). In the case of NRTs, each student's performance is compared to the performances of the other students taking the test, as well as to the performances of the norm group (the group representing the population). The purpose of norm-referenced testing is to see whether or not a given student's performance is close to what is typical of the entire population of similar students. An ideal NRT produces a set of scores that are normally distributed around a mean (see Figure 14.1a), which results in placing students in rank order of educational achievement. In the case of CRTs, on the other hand, a student's performance is compared to a predetermined criterion (a standard specifying a minimally acceptable performance at a given level). The purpose of criterion-referenced testing is to see whether, and to what extent,

Assessment in Online and Blended Learning Environments, pages 269–288
Copyright © 2015 by Information Age Publishing

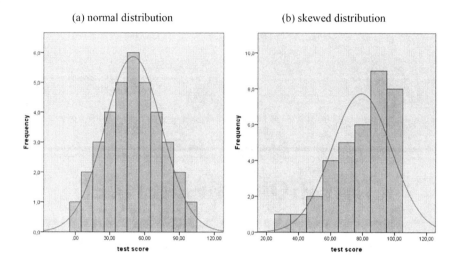

(a) normal distribution   (b) skewed distribution

Figure 14.1 Distribution of test scores (normal vs. skewed).

the student has attained mastery of the specified domain. If most of the students taking a test have indeed mastered the domain of content, the scores will be left-tailed, as in Figure 14.1b (for more on the differences between NRTs and CRTs, see, e.g., Bachman, 1990; Miller, Linn, & Gronlund, 2009; Urbina, 2004).

These two approaches to language testing have different uses and serve different purposes. CRTs are particularly suitable as classroom tests conducted with the aim of measuring students' progress and achievement because they are "specifically designed to assess how much of the content in a course or program is being learned by the students" (Brown & Hudson, 2002, p. xiv). Such tests measure a specific domain (rather than general abilities), and they are administered with a view to finding out whether the students have attained the learning objectives (rather than in order to see who is better/worse in relation to the other students). In classroom settings, NRTs would usually be considered "inappropriately competitive, and discouraging for the 'average' student" (McNamara, 2000, p. 64). This is because NRTs pay little attention to how much progress a student has made. CRTs, by contrast, may facilitate individual learners' progress toward predefined performance goals at their own pace. "In this way, motivation is maintained, and the striving is for a 'personal best' rather than against other learners" (McNamara, 2000, p. 64). On the other hand, NRTs are more appropriate than CRTs whenever differences in ability between students need to be brought out. For example, a placement test with a distribution of scores similar to that shown in Figure 14.1b would be of little value, and in an extreme case, when all of the students get the same score, its results would be completely useless.

The distinction between NRTs and CRTs is important not only for interpreting test scores, but also for the entire process of test development, whether traditional or Web based, because some of the statistical procedures that we use when evaluating the quality of tests and individual items only apply to one or the other approach. The teacher's awareness of the differences between the two approaches to measurement is also important in the context of formative assessment because, as observed by Fulcher (2010), "it is not useful in [this type of] assessment to compare learners with one another" (p. 68). The examples given in this chapter are all taken from criterion-referenced language tests, administered for the purpose of assessing students' progress. However, they were also used to help diagnose learners' strengths and weaknesses, and to give them useful feedback on their achievement of the learning objectives.

ASSESSMENT FOR LEARNING

Since Black and Wiliam (1998) demonstrated the effectiveness of formative assessment in enhancing student achievement, there has been a growing interest in assessment *for* learning, defined by Black, Harrison, Lee, Marshall, and Wiliam (2004), as "any assessment for which the first priority in its design and practice is to serve the purpose of promoting students' learning" (p. 10). It stands in marked contrast to assessment *of* learning, which is designed for grading students' progress and achievement (e.g., Chappuis & Chappuis, 2002). While some researchers equate assessment *for* learning with formative assessment (e.g., Hargreaves, 2005), others point out that the distinction between assessment *for* learning and assessment *of* learning is related to the *purpose* of assessment, whereas the formative–summative distinction pertains to assessment *functions* (see Wiliam, 2011, p. 10, for more on this).

Classroom practices that can be viewed as touchstones of assessment for learning include providing clear learning objectives (and helping students understand them), continually revising and adjusting instruction on the basis of information obtained from tests and pretests, providing regular constructive feedback on students' progress toward the learning objectives, matching better students with weaker ones to facilitate peer tutoring, and encouraging students to engage in peer and self-assessment (cf. Cauley & McMillan, 2010; Chappuis & Stiggins, 2002; Department for Education and Skills, 2004; for more on self-assessment, see Gardner, 2000; Little, 2005).

In her article about assessment for learning, Brown (2004–05) goes as far as to state that "[a]ssessment is probably the most important thing we can do to help our students learn" (p. 81). She argues that assessment must be "fit-for-purpose" and that it should make extensive use of feedback. She also recommends alternative forms of assessment, such as portfolios, reflective commentaries, reviews, role plays, etc. However, such assessments should supplement rather than replace traditional tests. The usefulness of tests consisting of selected-response and limited-production items is widely recognized, for example, in assessments of grammar and vocabulary (e.g., Purpura, 2004; Read, 2000).

The provision of constructive feedback is at the center of assessment for learning. Its purpose is to show students where they stand in relation to the learning objectives and to help them understand what precisely needs to be done to close the gap (cf. Sadler, in Taras, 2002, on conditions for effective feedback). Several types of feedback can be distinguished, for example, oral and written, immediate (directly after submitting a response) and delayed, simple (knowledge of correct response) and elaborated (further comments on student performance), and general (irrespective of the response given) and answer-specific. Studies such as Ellery (2008) indicate that feedback can have a positive effect on learning outcomes. Moreover, students often consider elaborated feedback to be quite useful (see van der Kleij, Eggen, Timmers, & Veldkamp, 2012, on the usefulness of written feedback in computer-based assessments).

WEBCLASS

WebClass (Malec, 2012) is a homegrown learning content management system (LCMS) whose architecture is based on a MySQL database backend and server-side PHP scripts generating HTML code. In addition to these, the system implements such Web technologies as CSS, Javascript, Ajax, and Flash-based video and audio streaming. Among other things, WebClass can be used to manage learners, create and publish learning content, and conduct assessments.

The system's core features are directly accessible from the menu, as seen in Figure 14.2. In student accounts, they include basic user settings, a file uploader, a messaging system, learning objectives (teacher-defined and students' own learning aims), self-assessment, and access to learning materials, tests, and assessment reports. Learners have the option of editing the available materials using an HTML editor and (optionally) sharing them with other students within the same class. Apart from formatted text, WebClass documents can contain links, images, audio, video, flash objects, glosses (with optional audio), as well as file attachments.

Several additional features are available for WebClass teachers (see Figure 14.3). Among these are registering and managing classes/students,

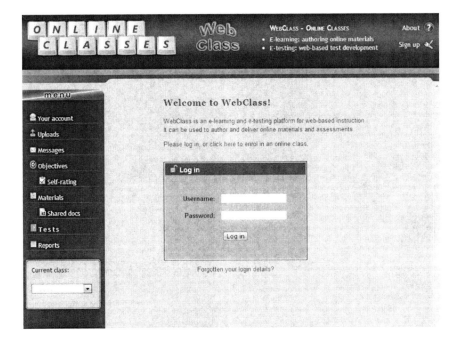

Figure 14.2 WebClass login page.

grouping classes into courses, creating attendance grids, viewing student activity logs, and authoring and managing materials (and sharing them with other teachers). Moreover, instructor accounts contain a number of options for creating and administering (both online and traditional) assessments, such as a test creator wizard, text-to-items converter, item banks, quantitative analysis, downloading scores through Excel, and so on. The system can also generate tabulated reports for a given class as a whole, with the results of all assessments, total mean scores, and final grades (see an example of such a report in Figure 14.12).

The WebClass system has been under development since 2010. It was first launched as an online testing application (*e-testing.net*). As new elements were gradually added, most notably Materials and Messages, the domain name was changed to *webclass.co* (in 2012) to reflect the fact that the platform was no longer exclusively for testing. It is currently available to students of English Philology at the John Paul II Catholic University of Lublin (KUL) and the State School of Higher Professional Education (PWSZ) in Zamość, Poland. At the time of this writing the number of all student accounts has exceeded 1,900. Although there are 43 instructor accounts, most of them are temporary ones created for colleagues and BA seminar students. The system is still mainly used by its developer, the author of this

Figure 14.3   WebClass instructor account.

chapter. However, there are plans to make use of its repository of test items in the next academic year. With the help of the system's test generator wizard, teachers of practical English at KUL will be able to create lexical and grammatical tests, either to be administered online or to be printed out and given as traditional paper-and-pencil tests.

Blended Testing

This section provides a review of the stages of language test development, with a special focus on what the entire process looks like on WebClass. The way in which online tests are constructed, administered, and analyzed with the help of this system is a strong case for using the term *blended testing* rather than simply *Web-based testing* (Malec, 2013a). To start with, although the tests are delivered via the World Wide Web, most of them are actually taken in the classroom with the instructor monitoring the entire assessment procedure. Moreover, even though the scoring is largely automated, human judgment may be necessary (e.g., in the case of limited-production items). Finally, students receive feedback on test performance, both individual and collective, either online or by being addressed face to face.

Test Development

Test development is an ongoing process. A language test should be continually improved through various kinds of analysis, rather than being used repeatedly without any modifications, like a ready-made product. By the same token, there is no such thing as a single "best" test for any language testing situation. A test that is good for one situation may be useless for another.

In Bachman and Palmer's (1996) framework, the cycle of language test development consists of three stages: design, operationalization, and administration (see also, e.g., Fulcher, 2010; Hughes, 2003). In the design stage, we define the construct and decide what the test will be used for, what kind of domain will be measured, what task types will be included, and who exactly will be tested. The outcome of the second stage is the operational definition of the construct. During this stage, we develop test task specifications and a blueprint that specifies the structure and organization of the whole test. We also develop the test tasks themselves, write instructions, and establish the scoring procedure. Test specifications can be very detailed and lengthy. However, for low-stakes classroom assessment, they can be reduced to the necessary minimum and "contain just a general description and a sample item" (Fulcher, 2010, p. 147). In the final stage of test development, the test is administered to a group of test-takers, first in order to gather information about its qualities (tryout), and then for its primary purpose, such as assigning grades (operational testing).

Language test development is not necessarily a linear process. Even though at certain stages we progress from one activity to the next in a sequential fashion, the whole cycle is essentially of a dynamic and iterative nature. Most importantly, in the course of analyzing prototype tests, the original items should be revised or even removed. The overall aim throughout the entire test development process is to make sure that the test adheres to the fundamental principles of assessment.

Language assessment principles, including practicality, reliability, validity, authenticity, and washback (Brown, 2004), serve as a basis for determining the usefulness of an existing assessment tool. Even more importantly, they also provide guidelines for language testers to follow throughout the entire test development cycle, at each step of test construction, administration, and analysis we need to make sure that the test is practical, free from errors of measurement, that it simulates real-world tasks and offers beneficial washback, and, above all, that scores obtained from it are valid indicators of whatever the test is designed to measure. In order to maximize the validity of score interpretations, the test constructor should ensure, among other things, that each learning objective is adequately represented in the test content and that the test is not based on a single item format (e.g., Hughes, 2003; Morgan & O'Reilly, 2006; Read, 2000). Guidelines such as these apply in equal measure to both online and paper-and-pencil testing. This is because, conceptually, Web-based tests do not constitute a major departure from traditional measurement: online test development should follow the same well-established principles of assessment. The real difference that online technology makes is in the area of test practicality: time saving (with respect to test construction and statistical analysis), easy delivery of tests and feedback, and scoring efficiency (see also the following sections; cf. Malec, 2013b, on the application of assessment principles to Web-based language testing).

Construction

With WebClass, tests can be constructed either by writing each question from scratch or by importing items from an item bank or from another test. It is also possible to speed up the process of item writing by using the built-in text-to-items converter. Teachers have a number of item formats to choose from. Some of the most common ones include multiple choice, multiple correct, true–false, matching, cloze, multiple-choice cloze, gap-filling, transformations, error correction, and short answer. In addition to these, it is possible to create tasks that elicit extended production responses (which can be submitted as text or in the form of recorded audio).

When retrieving items from a bank, teachers can decide to import only those items that meet certain psychometric criteria (i.e., have some desired [mean] value of item facility, and/or item discrimination, and/or B-index), either at random or by means of manual selection (Figure 14.4).

Furthermore, the text-to-items converter is capable of transforming text into test items. For example, the following sentences can be easily imported as multiple-choice items:

- She racked her [brains/memory/head], trying to remember what David had said.
- They [charge/spend/price] $20 for bed and breakfast at this hotel.
- He kept [paying/telling/handing] me compliments on my cooking.

The converter replaces the square brackets with gaps, and the words inside them are stored as options, of which the first one is saved as the key. If students send such preformatted sentences in a message, the teacher can quickly turn them into a quiz.

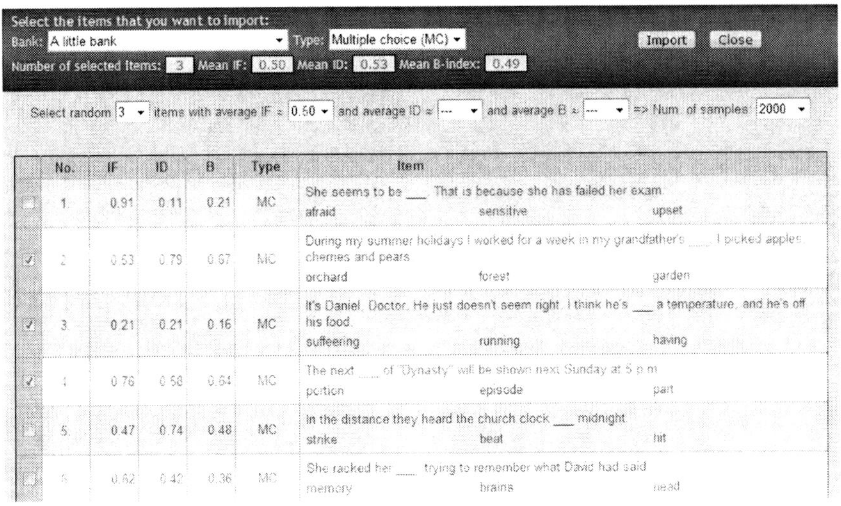

Figure 14.4 Importing three items from a bank by means of random selection.

Administration, Marking, and Feedback

Students can take tests after logging in to their accounts. The items can be displayed either all on one page or just one at a time, with a navigation menu at the top (as in Figure 14.5). Moreover, the order of items (and sets

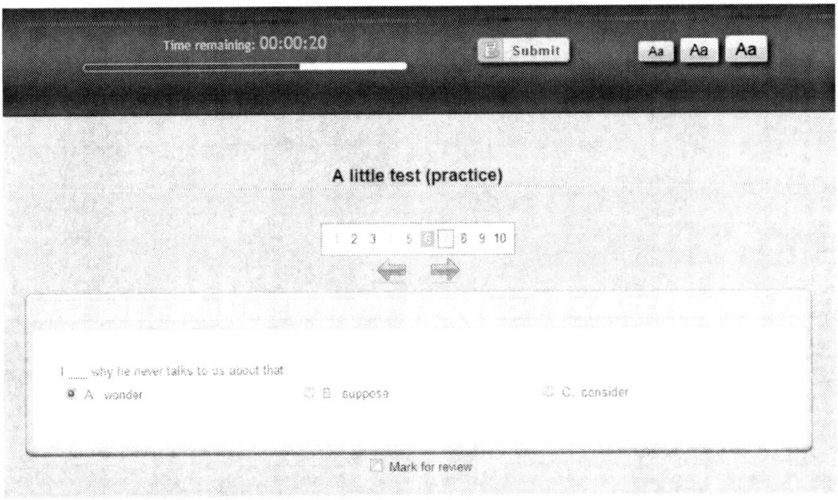

Figure 14.5 Student taking a multiple-choice test.

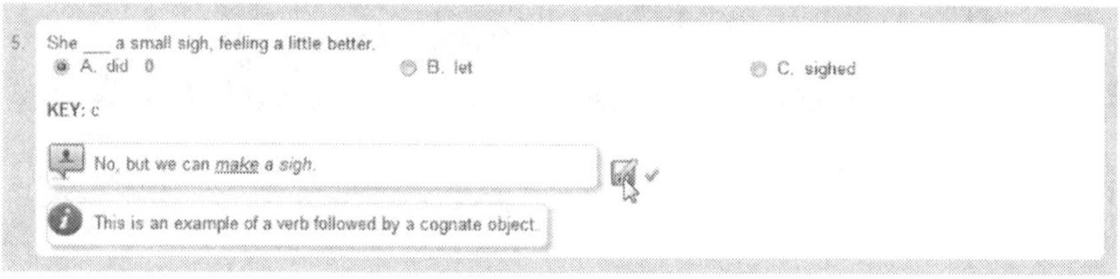

Figure 14.6 Instructor saving answer-specific feedback.

of items) can be automatically randomized, which creates the impression that the students are each taking a different test.

When the answers are submitted to the database, depending on the settings selected by the teacher, the marking (and optionally the key with feedback) can be viewed immediately afterward. In addition to this, for each student a tabulated report is created, containing the results of all of the tests, followed by arithmetic and weighted means of all scores, as well as the final grade. The reports are not stored in the database, they are dynamically generated upon access. Thanks to this, they are always up-to-date, even if the instructor makes changes to the automatic scoring.

Changes to the scoring may be necessary at times, for example, when a student inadvertently types an extra word that is not a language error but a mere oversight. If this happens, the teacher can override the system's automatic scoring and award a point (or a half point). If there are more students with an identical answer, the change will apply to all of them.

The teacher can provide feedback on student performance, which can be either general (the same for all students) or answer-specific. Although both types of feedback can be saved when test items are created, it is usually more convenient to do so when students' responses have already been submitted (see Figure 14.6). Further (and more detailed) feedback can be given using the messaging system.

ANALYSIS

Test analysis is a key element of test development. It can be either qualitative or quantitative. Item quality analysis is essential for valid interpretations of classroom test scores: it reveals whether the items measure what they are supposed to measure. This type of analysis can be carried out by another teacher who is familiar with the objectives of the syllabus that we are teaching. It consists in considering the content of individual test items with a view to answering the following basic questions (see also, e.g., Hughes, 2003, p. 64, for a checklist that can be used for moderating grammar items): Does this item target the content of the syllabus? Does it do so in an appropriate way? Isn't it tricky, perhaps? For example, if a multiple-choice item that is supposed to test collocational knowledge contains options that are all lexically correct but only one is spelled in the right way, the item is tricky and unsuitable for its intended purpose (Malec, 2010).

Quantitative analysis can only be done on the basis of test scores (i.e., when the test has been tried out on a representative sample of test-takers). It consists of calculating and interpreting item statistics such as item facility and cut-score indices. It also involves statistical estimation of various aspects of test reliability, referred to as dependability in the context of CRTs (for more on quantitative analysis, see Bachman, 2004; Brown & Hudson, 2002).

We often shun quantitative analysis because it is time-consuming and, as implied by Popham (2001), "while perhaps not as complex as rocket science, [it] is well beyond our comfort zone" (p. 27). However, the usefulness of this kind of analysis for classroom assessment is unquestionable. For example, the B-index is a simple statistic that indicates the extent to which a given item separates masters (those who passed the test) from non-masters (those who failed the test). In an ideal world, students who answer a given item correctly also pass the test as a whole, and those who answer it incorrectly fail the test. Accordingly, an item that does not target the same content as the other items can be expected to have a low value of this statistic.

In an attempt to determine the usefulness of the B-index, the following question was once included in a multiple-choice vocabulary quiz: *It was Pythagoras/Socrates/Tales who discovered that $a^2 + b^2 = c^2$.* Indeed, item analysis revealed that in terms of the B-index this was the worst-performing item of all, though not by a large margin, perhaps due to the fact that it appeared to be very easy. On another occasion, quantitative analysis of a paper-and-pencil test helped in the identification of the following faulty item: *How long... (you stay) in Canada last year?* The problem was that the instruction required the *present perfect simple* or *continuous* form of the verb in brackets, while the context demanded *past simple.* Some of the students supplied the correct answer (*did you stay*) but received no credit because the teacher who (hastily) did the marking was not aware of the inconsistency in the construction of the item.

The greatest merit of the B-index is arguably the fact that it can provide valuable feedback on our teaching practices. A test item may be perfect, and yet its B-index may be quite low. This can happen when the content domain measured by the item has been given inadequate instructional time or, quite simply, as a result of ineffective learning/teaching. For example, on a "nouns and articles" test that was delivered to a group of EFL learners, the test-takers were asked to supply the plural forms of several English nouns. The item targeting *pianos* had a very low value of the

B-index (0.05). On closer inspection, it turned out that one of the students who passed the test supplied **pianoes*, while quite a few of those who failed the test supplied the correct form. Interestingly, the latter group included a student whose response to another item was **tomatos*. Something was definitely wrong with the students' knowledge of how nouns ending in *o* form their plural forms. The fact that a number of weaker students gave the correct form does not necessarily mean that they actually *knew* the answer. Rather, they might have simply added the default *-s* ending to the singular form, without being bothered by the final *o*. The better student was aware that such nouns were "special" in this respect, but her knowledge was patchy. In short, rather than being an indication of a badly constructed item, a low value of the statistic in question can stimulate reflection on the effectiveness of our teaching practices.

Conducting quantitative analysis can be quite an effort: when a paper-and-pencil test has been marked, every single item score (usually one or zero) must be entered for each test-taker into an Excel spreadsheet (e.g., Malec, 2011) or some test analysis program (e.g., Brooks & Johanson, 2003). In the case of a test consisting of 50 items and a class of 30 students, it is necessary to enter 1,500 values. However, with the help of online technology, the amount of time required for quantitative analysis can be minimized. In fact, the case described in the previous paragraph has been analyzed online using WebClass.

Arguably, the greatest advantage of developing tests using a system like WebClass is the ready availability of automatically calculated test and item statistics. An example of the results of quantitative analysis is given in Figure 14.7. The statistics indicate a relatively low degree of dependability of the test scores (the values of the phi coefficient, phi lambda and kappa squared are nowhere near 1.00). This means that we should exercise caution in making mastery/non-mastery decisions on the basis of scores obtained from this test because many of them would be incorrect.

Following test statistics, the system displays each test item with the results of item analysis. Figure 14.8 shows an example of such analysis carried out for three multiple-choice test items. It includes item facility, item discrimination, *B*-index, and omission rate, as well as the results of a basic distractor analysis.

It must be stressed that although the statistics can help in the identification of faulty items, the ultimate decision as to whether or not to retain a given criterion-referenced test item lies with the test constructor, who is often guided more by common sense than by statistics. On the other hand, item statistics can provide teachers and curriculum developers with useful feedback on the degree of learners' mastery of specific areas of the syllabus and the program's objectives. In this way, important information can be gained as to what precisely should be given more emphasis in the

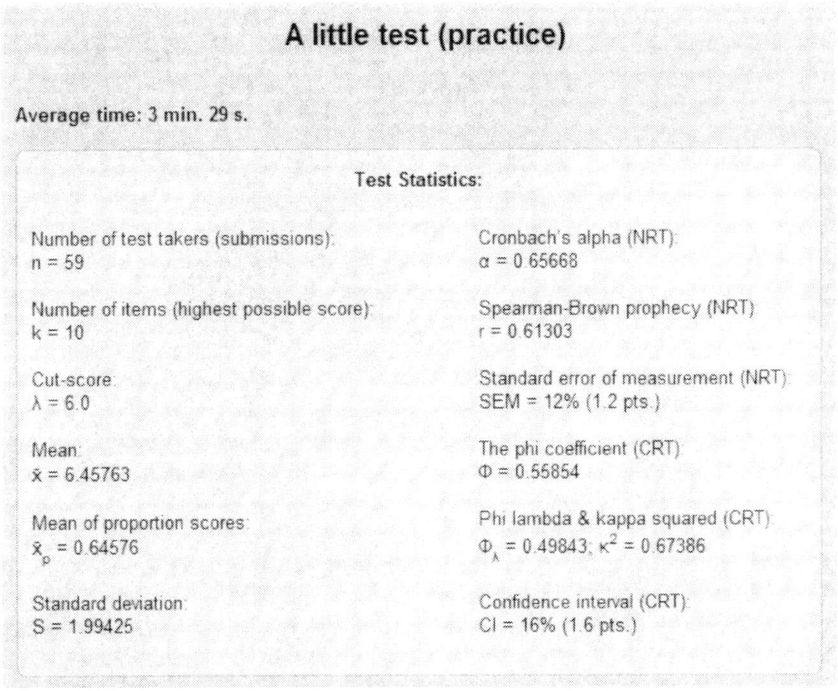

A little test (practice)

Average time: 3 min. 29 s.

Test Statistics:

Number of test takers (submissions):
n = 59

Number of items (highest possible score):
k = 10

Cut-score:
λ = 6.0

Mean:
x̄ = 6.45763

Mean of proportion scores:
x̄$_p$ = 0.64576

Standard deviation:
S = 1.99425

Cronbach's alpha (NRT):
α = 0.65668

Spearman-Brown prophecy (NRT):
r = 0.61303

Standard error of measurement (NRT):
SEM = 12% (1.2 pts.)

The phi coefficient (CRT):
Φ = 0.55854

Phi lambda & kappa squared (CRT):
Φ$_\lambda$ = 0.49843; κ^2 = 0.67386

Confidence interval (CRT):
CI = 16% (1.6 pts.)

Figure 14.7   Results of quantitative analysis.

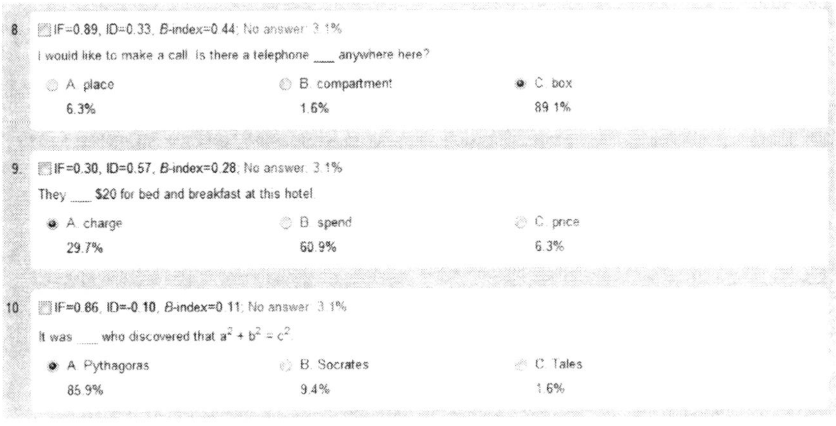

8.   IF=0.89, ID=0.33, *B*-index=0.44; No answer: 3.1%

i would like to make a call. Is there a telephone ____ anywhere here?

○ A. place
6.3%

○ B. compartment
1.6%

◉ C. box
89.1%

9.   IF=0.30, ID=0.57, *B*-index=0.28; No answer: 3.1%

They ____ $20 for bed and breakfast at this hotel.

◉ A. charge
29.7%

○ B. spend
60.9%

○ C. price
6.3%

10.   IF=0.86, ID=-0.10, *B*-index=0.11; No answer: 3.1%

It was ____ who discovered that $a^2 + b^2 = c^2$.

◉ A. Pythagoras
85.9%

○ B. Socrates
9.4%

○ C. Tales
1.6%

Figure 14.8   Multiple-choice item analysis.

classroom. Moreover, the information provided by item statistics (specifically, item facility values) can help in constructing language tests that are at the appropriate level of difficulty.

IMPLICATIONS OF USING AN ONLINE TESTING SYSTEM FOR LANGUAGE ASSESSMENT

A test is considered to be practical as long as it "is not excessively expensive, stays within appropriate time constraints, is relatively easy to administer, and has a scoring/evaluation procedure that is specific and time-efficient" (Brown, 2004, p. 19). Online and blended assessments such as those on WebClass have arguably more to offer in terms of practicality than traditional paper-and-pencil tests. Benefits for the teacher include easy test construction (e.g., thanks to the test generator wizard, which retrieves random items from an item bank), easy delivery (a standard browser is all that is needed to conduct assessments), and scoring efficiency and accuracy (humans can make errors, even when marking multiple-choice items), as well as automated quantitative analysis. Benefits for the student include easy access to tests, feedback, and assessment reports (which include the results of self-evaluation).

In addition to the above, students can contact each other using the messaging system and engage in peer correction. Figure 14.9 shows part of a composition written by a student during a writing class and sent over to another student as a WebClass message. When users reply to a message, they are directed to a window containing an HTML editor, in which they can, for example, mark errors (by highlighting words/phrases), insert corrections and comments, suggest a grade, etc. Messages edited in this way can then be forwarded to selected recipients (including the sender, other students, and the teacher), and the entire procedure can be repeated.

When extended responses such as the one given in Figure 14.9 are submitted as tests (rather than, simply, as messages), they can be marked manually by the instructor in a window containing a simplified HTML editor. Feedback on an extended response can contain the following:

- Marked errors (lexical, grammatical, other)
- Insertions (missing words/phrases)
- Comments/alternatives
- Links to webpages
- Bold, italic, underlined, and strikeout text

Figure 14.10 shows an example of how the feedback is displayed for the student. The features that can potentially contribute to test practicality

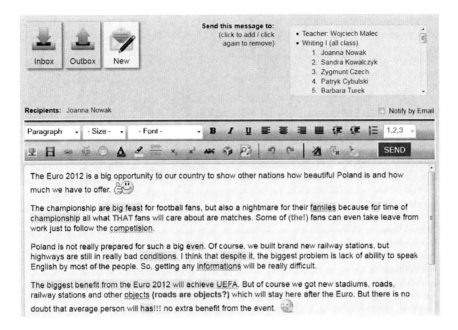

Figure 14.9 One student correcting another's composition.

include the possibility of looking up mouse-selected text in the BNC (British National Corpus) or in Google Books as well as a plagiarism detection script (see Malec, 2014, for more on this).

One of the most recent extensions to WebClass is a voice recorder, which allows students to submit audio responses. For example, students can respond to a prompt orally, record a short speech, and send it over to the database. The instructor can then play the audio in the browser and offer comments.

WebClass students can also self-assess their progress relative to the learning objectives. At the beginning of a course of study, students are informed about the teacher-defined learning goals, to which they can add their own specific aims (they can also do so later). Then, at any time during the term or semester, students can indicate how well they think they have done on each objective on a teacher-defined scale. This is simply done by moving sliders such as those in Figure 14.11 right and left with the mouse. The results of student self-assessment can be viewed by the instructor, providing useful information on areas that are in need of revision. These results can also be automatically included in the calculation of final semester grades; if this is the case, some specific (predefined) weighting is applied to teacher-administered assessments and student self-assessment.

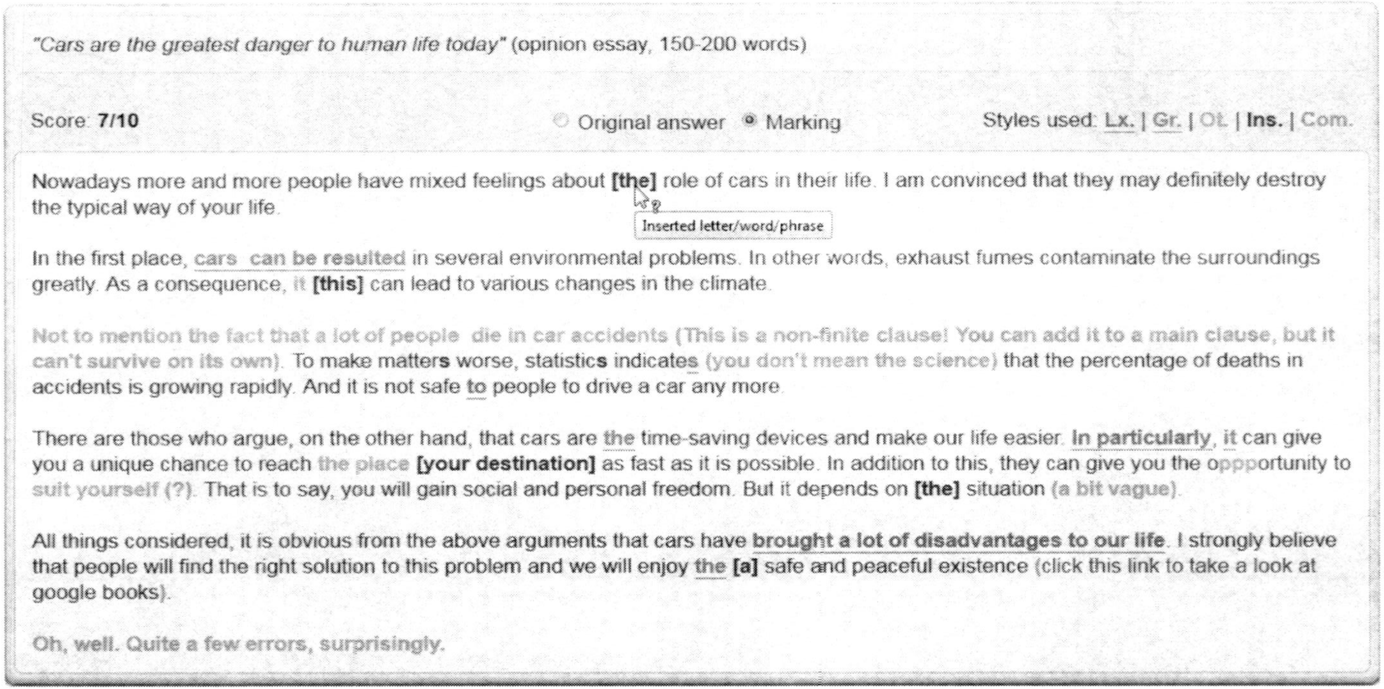

"*Cars are the greatest danger to human life today*" (opinion essay, 150-200 words)

Score: **7/10**

○ Original answer ● Marking

Styles used: Lx. | Gr. | Ot. | **Ins.** | Com.

Nowadays more and more people have mixed feelings about **[the]** role of cars in their life. I am convinced that they may definitely destroy the typical way of your life.

In the first place, cars can be resulted in several environmental problems. In other words, exhaust fumes contaminate the surroundings greatly. As a consequence, it **[this]** can lead to various changes in the climate.

[Inserted letter/word/phrase]

Not to mention the fact that a lot of people die in car accidents (This is a non-finite clause! You can add it to a main clause, but it can't survive on its own). To make matters worse, statistics indicates (you don't mean the science) that the percentage of deaths in accidents is growing rapidly. And it is not safe to people to drive a car any more.

There are those who argue, on the other hand, that cars are the time-saving devices and make our life easier. In particularly, it can give you a unique chance to reach the place **[your destination]** as fast as it is possible. In addition to this, they can give you the opportunity to suit yourself (?). That is to say, you will gain social and personal freedom. But it depends on **[the]** situation (a bit vague).

All things considered, it is obvious from the above arguments that cars have brought a lot of disadvantages to our life. I strongly believe that people will find the right solution to this problem and we will enjoy the **[a]** safe and peaceful existence (click this link to take a look at google books).

Oh, well. Quite a few errors, surprisingly.

Figure 14.10 Extended response feedback (student view).

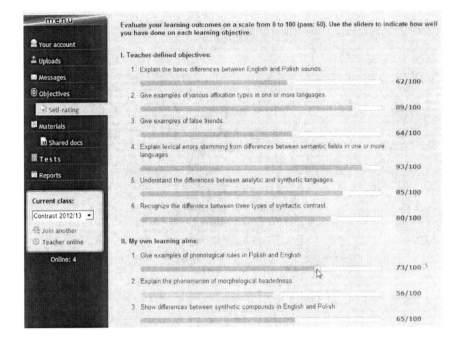

Figure 14.11 Student self-assessment (contrastive grammar course.).

It is also worth mentioning that the system can generate summary assessment reports for a class as a whole (an example is given in Figure 14.12). From one compact table the instructor can access all students' test results, including the marking itself, by clicking a table cell containing a numerical score. The reports include the results of student self-assessment and final grades.

CONCLUSION

This chapter started with a discussion of the basic differences between norm-referenced and criterion-referenced language testing. It was pointed out that the latter approach is most appropriate for classroom testing and much more in line with the requirements of assessment for learning than the former. Using the WebClass system as an example, it was argued that online technology can enhance the development of high-quality language tests, benefitting both teachers and students, particularly in the area of test practicality. In addition to this, online and blended environments have the potential for promoting peer correction and self-assessment, as well as for facilitating the provision of feedback.

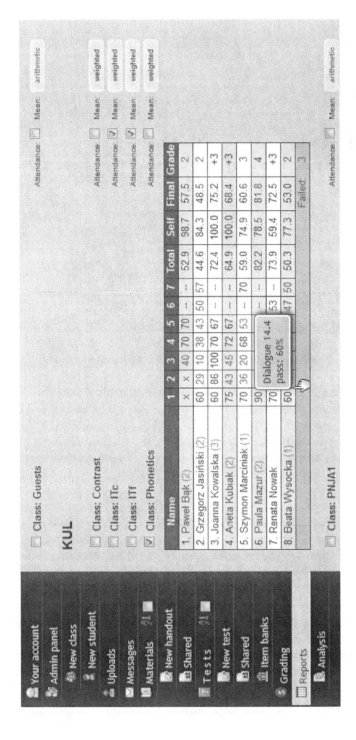

Figure 14.12 WebClass assessment report generated for a whole class.

REFERENCES

Bachman, L. F. (1990). *Fundamental considerations in language testing.* Oxford, UK: Oxford University Press.

Bachman, L. F. (2004). *Statistical analyses for language assessment.* Cambridge, UK: Cambridge University Press.

Bachman, L. F., & Palmer, A. S. (1996). *Language testing in practice: Designing and developing useful language tests.* Oxford, UK: Oxford University Press.

Black, P., Harrison, C., Lee, C., Marshall, B., & Wiliam, D. (2004). Working inside the black box: Assessment for learning in the classroom. *Phi Delta Kappan, 86*(1), 9–21.

Black, P., & Wiliam, D. (1998). Assessment and classroom learning. *Assessment in Education, 5*(1), 7–74.

Brooks, G. P., & Johanson, G. A. (2003). Test analysis program. *Applied Psychological Measurement, 27,* 305–306.

Brown, H. D. (2004). *Language assessment: Principles and classroom practices.* White Plains, NY: Pearson Education.

Brown, J. D., & Hudson, T. (2002). *Criterion-referenced language testing.* Cambridge, UK: Cambridge University Press.

Brown, S. (2004–05). Assessment for learning. *Learning and Teaching in Higher Education, 1,* 81–89.

Cauley, K. M., & McMillan, K. H. (2010). Formative assessment techniques to support student motivation and achievement. *The Clearing House, 83*(1), 1–6.

Chappuis, J., & Chappuis, S. (2002). *Understanding school assessment: A parent and community guide to helping students learn.* Portland, OR: Assessment Training Institute.

Chappuis, S., & Stiggins, R. J. (2002). Classroom assessment for learning. *Educational Leadership, 60*(1), 40–43.

Department for Education and Skills. (2004). *Pedagogy and practice: Teaching and learning in secondary schools (Unit 12: Assessment for learning).* Norwich, UK: HMSO.

Ellery, K. (2008). Assessment for learning: A case study using feedback effectively in an essay-style test. *Assessment and Evaluation in Higher Education, 33*(4), 421–429.

Fulcher, G. (2010). *Practical language testing.* London, UK: Hodder Education.

Gardner, D. (2000). Self-assessment for autonomous language learners. *Links and Letters, 7,* 49–60.

Hargreaves, E. (2005). Assessment for learning?: Thinking outside the (black) box. *Cambridge Journal of Education, 35*(2), 213–224.

Hughes, A. (2003). *Testing for language teachers* (2nd ed.). Cambridge, UK: Cambridge University Press.

Little, D. (2005). The Common European Framework and the European Language Portfolio: Involving learners and their judgements in the assessment process. *Language Testing, 22*(3), 321–336.

Malec, W. (2010, Summer). Multiple-choice test items: Some tips on writing good distractors. *TESOL-Ukraine Newsletter,* pp. 22–25.

Malec, W. (2011). *Excel spreadsheets for item and test analysis.* Available from http://webclass.co/info/analysis.php.

Malec, W. (2012). *WebClass (online learning management system).* Available from http://webclass.co.

Malec, W. (2013a, November). *Combining traditional and Web-based language testing: A case for blended assessment.* Paper presented at the International Linguistics Conference "Linguistics Beyond And Within," Lublin, Poland.

Malec, W. (2013b). Implementing language assessment principles in an online testing system. In E. Smyrnova-Trybulska (Ed.), *E-Learning and lifelong learning* (pp. 387–396). Katowice-Cieszyn, Poland: University of Silesia, Studio Noa.

Malec, W. (2013c). Towards Web-based language test development for classroom assessments. In M. Kleban & E. Willim (Eds.), *PASE Papers in Linguistics* (pp. 213–234). Kraków, Poland: Jagiellonian University Press.

Malec, W. (2014). On the potential of Web-based assessment of language skills. In H. Chodkiewicz & M. Trepczyńska (Eds.), *Language skills: Traditions, transitions and ways forward* (pp. 432–455). Newcastle upon Tyne, UK: Cambridge Scholars Publishing.

McNamara, T. (2000). *Language testing.* Oxford, UK: Oxford University Press.

Miller, M. D., Linn, R. L., & Gronlund, N. E. (2009). *Measurement and assessment in teaching* (10th ed.). Upper Saddle River, NJ: Pearson Education.

Morgan, C., & O'Reilly, M. (2006). Ten key qualities of assessment online. In M. Hricko & S. L. Howell (Eds.), *Online assessment and measurement: Foundations and challenges* (pp. 86–101). Hershey, PA: Information Science Publishing.

Popham, W. J. (2001). *The truth about testing: An educator's call to action.* Alexandria, VA: Association for Supervision and Curriculum Development.

Purpura, J. (2004). *Assessing grammar.* Cambridge, UK: Cambridge University Press.

Read, J. (2000). *Assessing vocabulary.* Cambridge, UK: Cambridge University Press.

Taras, M. (2002). Using assessment for learning and learning from assessment. *Assessment and Evaluation in Higher Education, 27*(6), 501–510.

Urbina, S. (2004). *Essentials of psychological testing.* Hoboken, NJ: Wiley.

van der Kleij, F. M., Eggen, T. J. H. M., Timmers, C. F., & Veldkamp, B. P. (2012). Effects of feedback in a computer-based assessment for learning. *Computers and Education, 58*(1), 263–272.

Wiliam, D. (2011). What is assessment for learning? *Studies in Educational Evaluation, 37*(1), 3–14.

CHAPTER 15

FRAMEWORK FOR ASSESSMENT FROM AN INSTITUTIONAL PERSPECTIVE

Jean-Marc Wise and Tami Im
Florida State University

INTRODUCTION

The role of assessment in higher education is changing. Economic pressures, political leadership, technological advances, and global competition increasingly demand the use of data to drive strategic decision making. Traditionally, student performance has been at the center of assessment in education, measured by test scores, graduation rates, and job placements. However, while a focus on student-centered outcomes may serve as an indicator of overall institutional effectiveness, additional data are needed in order to identify specific areas of improvement in case student performance targets are not met. Furthermore, students, faculty, and administrators each use different sets of indicators to drive their decisions, and the outcome of one typically depends on the assessment of another. If we also consider external factors such as university rankings, accreditation, local economies, or the political climate that impact student enrollment and faculty turnover, assessment emerges as a web of interrelated variables.

Assessment in Online and Blended Learning Environments, pages 289–306

289

The introduction of blended and online modes of instruction not only opened the field for institutions to compete globally for students and professors, but also introduced additional layers of complexity in assessment. For example, traditional learning assessments administered in classroom-based situations quickly prove impossible when students participate at a distance and live in different time zones. These situations require faculty and support staff to implement decentralized, asynchronous exams and use specialized technology such as lock-down browsers, screen captures, and webcams to ensure integrity and prevent cheating. The context of distance learning also requires institutions to adjust to new requirements and change the nature of their assessments to account for regional and cultural differences, language barriers, and local laws. Appropriate assessments must be put in place to measure new definitions of success and effectiveness in a global context and guide strategic decisions of the institution.

The key stakeholders in higher education are constantly using data to drive decisions that impact the institution—and they each have an interest to ensure that the data they and others use are accurate and up-to-date. Ideally, stakeholders should all have access to shared data that were collected through reliable and valid assessment instruments, and it is in the interest of each institution to provide appropriate access to these data.

In this chapter, we introduce a framework for guiding the design of assessments that address the needs of the core stakeholders in higher education at various levels of impact. Along with introducing the components of the framework and referring to relevant literature, we present methods to assess critical success factors and illustrate how each depends on and impacts the other in the context of online and blended learning. We conclude with comments about the general application of the framework, a discussion of its current limitations, and an outlook on further development.

OVERVIEW OF THE INSTITUTIONAL
ASSESSMENT FRAMEWORK

The Institutional Assessment Framework (see Figure 15.1) defines six core dimensions of assessment, each forming the intersection of an agent with an area of performance. At the macro level, the model distinguishes three primary areas of performance: education, academia, and economy. Education represents the realm where instructors and students interact with the aim of increasing literacy, promoting critical thinking, and ultimately preparing the student for citizenship (Georg, 2009). Academia is the environment in which institutions employ faculty in order to contribute to the advancement of knowledge through inquiry with a responsibility to apply new knowledge ethically (Benjamin, 2008). Economy is the target domain

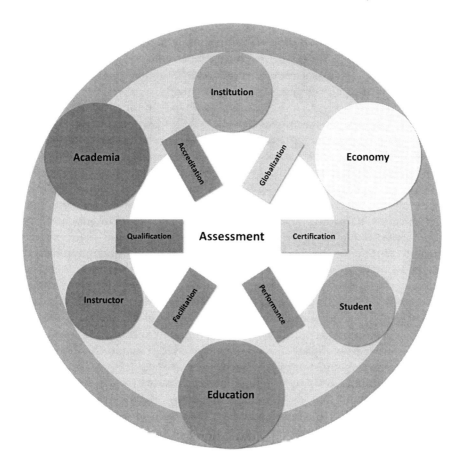

Figure 15.1 A framework for assessment from an institutional perspective.

in which institutions compete globally to prepare students for employment, competition, and cooperation (Shriberg, 2002). Success of an institution can be assessed by comparing its performance on these major goals to relevant standards as well as the performance of similar institutions.

The agents represented in the model are student, instructor, and institution. Students enroll in programs offered by the institution in order to enhance scholarship as a basis for academic success, to increase professionalism to ensure skills are successfully applied in the job market, and to develop membership in groups and organizations (Yarime & Tanaka, 2012). Instructors contribute to the success of the institution and the student through conducting research, developing and implementing effective methods of teaching, and providing service to the institution, organizations, and the community at large (Brignall & Modell, 2000; Wilson & Scalise, 2006; Yorke,

2003). Institutions serve as a conduit for enabling academic success by providing adequate administration and contributing to advancement of knowledge (Karp, 2011). Similar to measuring institutional effectiveness within the areas of performance as outlined above, institutional assessment can be based on the indicators listed for each of its agents.

At the micro level, the model distinguishes six core dimensions that can be used to measure institutional success: certification, performance, facilitation, qualification, accreditation, and globalization. Certification addresses the outcome for students as they leave the institution in terms of degree completion, acquisition of competencies, and establishment of character leading to appropriate choices (Bailey, Alfonso, Scott, & Leinbach, 2004; Bers, 2008). *Performance* targets assessment in the traditional sense, including learning, transfer of knowledge and skills, and adequate judgment in their application (Bers, 2008). *Facilitation* of learning includes planning, design, development, and implementation of effective teaching methods and materials; approaches to coaching students to scaffold their success; and advising them in their choices in education, academics, and professional careers (Yorke, 2003). *Qualification* refers to the need for institutions to ensure that their faculty and staff have appropriate levels of education and experience, support their professional development, and provide incentives for them to actively engage in research and service (Capano, 2010). *Accreditation* encompasses institutional effectiveness as measured by appropriate strategic planning and implementation, which is determined by means of assessing academic and programmatic outcomes (Moosai, Walker, & Deborah, 2011). Finally, *globalization* addresses the effectiveness of an institution to provide educational and academic services to a global audience, manage global outreach to remote and underserved populations, and facilitate the respectful exchange of ideas among a wide range of cultures (Altbach & Knight, 2007; Vaira, 2004).

In analogy to the assessment mentioned above for agents and areas of performance, the criteria described for each of the six dimensions can be used to complete a comprehensive strategy for the assessment of institutional effectiveness and success. In the following, we first discuss the opportunities and challenges of each agent and area of performance in the context of online and blended learning. This sets the stage for a comprehensive look at assessment from an institutional point of view, which is presented for each of the micro components of the framework.

AGENTS IN THEIR AREAS OF PERFORMANCE

Comprehensive assessment from an institutional perspective requires the inclusion of data from multiple sources documenting the activities of agents in their respective areas of performance. The institution sets standards for effective performance against which these data are measured in order to identify any needs for improvement. In this section, we first introduce the three areas of performance identified in the framework and discuss their opportunities and challenges in the context of online and blended learning. Next, we describe the three agents and characterize them with respect to their role in online and blended learning as well as particular challenges they might face in nontraditional teaching and learning.

Areas of Performance

Education

At the heart of the triad of performance areas in the framework is *education*, representing all aspects of teaching and learning. Online and blended learning technologies offer the opportunity to expand access to education by reaching populations for whom access was limited in the past (Moloney & Oakley, 2010). For example, educational materials and activities can be customized to meet the needs of individual learners by offering various levels of support, alternative languages, an array of examples, multiple modes of delivery to account for disabilities, and adaptive release technology to ensure that materials are made accessible to the learner at an appropriate pace. Assessments can be built into the learning environment to provide continuous, nonintrusive feedback on a learner's individual performance, offering early warnings in case a student falls behind or is at risk of dropping out (Gaytan & Mcewen, 2007). Education can also take advantage of new teaching and learning technologies to ensure that students have the opportunity to learn relevant skills and gain expertise in the use of technologies needed for successful job performance.

On the other hand, online and blended learning environments present unique educational challenges that must be considered by institutions that offer such programs (Reeves, 2000). In particular, care must be taken to include motivational strategies into the design of online and blended learning activities in order to engage students and prevent them from feeling disconnected. The success of virtual learning communities depends on creative approaches to provide students the opportunity to collaborate, share their experiences, and offer each other support (Swan & Hiltz, 2006). Tracking of student participation and progress throughout the curriculum is critical for early detection of problems that may jeopardize course or program completion. Learning management systems can be configured to collect relevant statistics and most offer dashboards and communication tools to support instructors and mentors in their effort to help students stay on track. For example, a mentor might run a weekly report that shows students' log-in times and pages they accessed. She might contact students who didn't participate at the expected level via email to encourage them, give them pointers, or offer her help. These assessment strategies help instructors and mentors address the unique challenges of delivering online and blended courses.

Academia

The second area of performance that the framework covers is *academia*, the realm where academics create and share knowledge, skills, and technologies. The advent of online and blended learning technologies has opened new possibilities for academia, allowing researchers and scholars to collaborate at a global level without the need for travel. Rich virtual communication channels, high-speed transmissions of files, and cloud-based collaborative platforms transcend geographic boundaries and level the playing field for students and academics to contribute and share their knowledge and experience. Furthermore, online and blended learning environments offer new avenues for conducting research into the effectiveness of strategies, technologies, and media (Cooper, 2013; Dale, Newman, & Ling, 2010).

Although the opportunities are numerous, online and blended learning also presents challenges for academia. Staying abreast of the wave of innovation in technology and information is a significant challenge (Spector, 2013). Furthermore, as is frequently the case with new technologies, the international community is slow in adopting shared definitions and standards, which causes complications for the development of related tools (Spector, 2013). Members of academia do not share a common vision and goals for the use of these new technologies. For example, while some institutions offer free access to online materials and massively open online courses without the possibility of earning a degree, others include online and blended courses in their regular curriculum, including complete online degree programs, and charge additional fees on top of regular tuition to cover the expenses of online development and delivery (Cusumano, 2013; Vardi, 2012).

Economy

The third area of performance in the institutional assessment framework is *economy*, the space in which institutions interface with the world by preparing their students for entry into the job market, competing for talent in the recruitment of faculty, and collaborating with businesses and governments in the research and development of new products and technologies. Online and blended learning technologies have changed the game for educational institutions by making their curricula globally accessible, increasing competition to new levels, and offering greater opportunities for collaboration. Institutions that adopt these technologies provide greater diversity in their employment options and more flexibility for faculty. Enrollments have the potential for significant increase by attracting students whose lives would prevent them from completing a higher education degree in a traditional format. Online and blended programs can also help institutions leverage resources and facilities, avoiding the need for additional classrooms while simultaneously increasing the potential for individualized learner support.

Institutions that adopt online and blended technologies, however, also face particular economic challenges (White, 2007). These programs require a significant investment in technology infrastructure, resources, and know-how (Garrison & Kanuka, 2004). Hardware and software needs to be purchased and maintained, providing for stability, speed, and scalability. Staff and faculty need to be trained to utilize new technologies, and their skills and knowledge is subject to constant update. Faculty and staff need to be carefully balanced in order to effectively facilitate learning in courses with potentially massive enrollments. New support services need to be created in order to handle the needs of online and blended learning students. Furthermore, institutions are faced with questions of how and whether to charge for their online courses and programs, and how to compete with new revenue models of openly accessible courses and curricula.

Agents

Student

The first of the three key stakeholders identified in the institutional assessment framework is the *student* and, indeed, students should be the main focus of institutions of higher education. Online and blended learning environments have the potential to offer tremendous advantages to students, including accessibility, flexibility, adaptability, and customization. Because of these technologies, students no longer have to choose between attending a local institution and moving away; between pursuing higher education and a full-time professional career; between completing course assignments and spending time with their family. Online and blended learning experiences can be customized to the student's needs, providing additional, personalized support, more time or acceleration, and catering to learner preferences. For example, students with learning disabilities or language barriers can be offered alternative or supplemental materials, receive just-in-time help, and work at their own pace according to their preferred schedule and in an environment that meets their particular needs.

One should, however, also consider that students in online and blended learning environments might face additional challenges (Thorpe, 2002). Since students frequently have family and job responsibilities that compete with their academic efforts, they must effectively manage their time and find the motivation to persist in the face of obstacles even more so than traditional students. The fact that communication happens in mediated form (via email, video or text chat, for example) and is frequently asynchronous can present challenges for students who are used to communicating face to face. This is especially true for group collaboration, where logistics and project management tasks become much more critical to the success of a group project than in traditional courses where students meet once a week to collaborate (McNeil, Robin, & Miller, 2000; Swan & Hiltz, 2006).

Instructor

Another integral agent in the institutional assessment framework is the *instructor*. Whether a tenured or tenure-track faculty member, adjunct, or teaching or lab assistant, the instructor provides educational experiences to students and typically represents the institution in academia through research contributions. In the context of online and blended learning, the instructor has greater flexibility in terms of providing course materials in a variety of formats. This allows for the inclusion of optional readings, audio and visual material, and customization to accommodate for special needs and preferences. These new technologies also allow for greater control and monitoring of student participation and progress, since learning management systems typically include the ability to collect statistics on materials accessed and time spent on task.

On the other hand, instructors are also faced with the challenges of constantly finding and learning new technologies to keep up with industry advances and meet the demands of students who are used to taking advantage of the latest technologies (Easton, 2003; Fein, Logan, & Holmes, 2003). Dealing with logistical and technical problems that are unique to online and blended learning can be time-consuming for the instructor unless the institution provides additional support. Furthermore, instructors who are new to online and blended learning must spend time developing new strategies for effective online course design and delivery in order to be fully prepared for the challenges of teaching in these new formats. Handling individual emails, reading and replying to discussion threads, monitoring student access, coordinating remote proctoring for high-stakes exams, and managing mentors are tasks that emerge above and beyond the usual responsibilities of delivering lectures and grading assignments in online and blended learning.

Institution

The third and final agent featured in the institutional assessment framework is the *institution* itself. Unlike student and instructor, the institution embodies multiple levels of administration, groups of individuals working together to establish and implement the organizational vision, mission, and structure; set goals; monitor progress; and make adjustments as necessary. Effectiveness is vital to the survival and success of an institution, and also a core requirement for accreditation.

Institutions that offer online and blended programs have the opportunity to extend their mission to include both nontraditional students and faculty (Thorpe, 2002; White, 2007). This strategy can help to attract the best and brightest candidates who may not consider applying to traditional degree programs or faculty positions that require relocation. Online and blended programs provide institutions with options for sustainable growth, since increasing enrollments do not have as critical an impact on facilities as they might have with traditional students. Finally, the inclusion of online and blended learning allows an institution to offer courses and programs that meet the expectations of students who are used to adopting current technologies and integrating them in their everyday lives.

Nevertheless, institutions face significant challenges with the inclusion of online and blended learning in their curriculum. In order to effectively implement the major technological changes across academic units, centralized change management is essential. Similarly, in order to track progress toward an institutional goal of this magnitude, comprehensive and consistent assessment across academic units is required. However, these strategies might find opposition in a culture that is rooted in academic freedom and administrative independence.

CORE DIMENSIONS OF INSTITUTIONAL ASSESSMENT

Recall that Figure 15.1 included circles representing agents and areas of performance, and tiles representing core dimensions of institutional assessment. In the previous section we presented the three areas of performance and the three agents, discussing their opportunities and challenges with respect to online and blended learning environments. The stage is now set to introduce the six core dimensions of the institutional assessment framework. For each dimension we discuss critical indicators of success along with examples of how they can be assessed in an institutional context and references to relevant publications.

Student Dimensions

Certification: The Student in the Economy

Arguably one of the most important goals of an institution of higher education is to provide graduates with *certification* of the knowledge and skills they acquired throughout their course of study (Bailey et al., 2004;

Bers, 2008). Certification typically takes the form of a diploma along with a transcript detailing specific coursework accomplished. Some institutions also provide certificates in particular areas of specialization, which offer potential employers additional credentials to distinguish job applicants. In the context of online and blended learning, institutional assessment of certification is particularly important since these types of program tend to be under a great deal of additional scrutiny and are sometimes suspected of demanding less rigor.

Assessment for the purpose of certification typically takes the form of comprehensive exams or capstone projects. These assessments tend to cover a significant amount of knowledge and skills, and students are frequently asked to demonstrate mastery by solving complex problems, applying theoretical concepts, and evaluating alternatives. Responses are frequently provided in essay form or involve the creation of some artifact such as a lesson plan, research paper, or composition. Due to the critical nature of these assessments, they tend to be administered under proctored conditions and institutions increasingly use sophisticated software to detect plagiarism and other forms of cheating. Students who do not have to physically attend class may be tempted to take credit for someone else's work; in fact, services like WeTakeYourClass.com promote a sense that online degrees are purchased rather than earned (Tilsley, 2012).

The value of a diploma or certificate depends greatly on the perceived amount of effort and academic rigor that is required to obtain it. Online programs in particular sometimes attract students who expect to get a diploma for less effort than a traditional program; they may hope to be able to get academic credit for years of working experience or have the opportunity to take an exam instead of doing coursework. Institutions can assess the perceived value of their nontraditional programs by conducting surveys with prospective, current, and past students, and by participating in national surveys that provide comparative data and rankings that are frequently used by prospective students in their decision-making process.

Performance: The Student in Education

Student *performance* in the educational setting is perhaps the most common association with the term "assessment." It includes knowledge-based exams of various formats (e.g., multiple choice, short answer, matching, etc.), essays, research reports, artifacts, performances, presentations, and many more. The constructs that are being measured align with the course and program objectives, which should be defined in terms of observable actions. Competencies typically consist of collections of related objectives and tend to be assessed indirectly through the accomplishment of these objectives (Berdrow & Evers, 2010; Bowden & Masters, 1993; Serban, 2004).

In addition to course-level student performance, institutions can assess success in terms of course and degree completion, participation, communication, and collaboration (Peterson & Augustine, 2000; Serban, 2004). Many of these metrics can be collected automatically by mining the logs of learning management systems, which are critical to the efficient administration of online and blended courses. Ideally, institutions should use centralized systems that share a common organizational structure to manage courses and programs; otherwise, it may be difficult to collate, summarize, and compare data across academic units.

Assessment of student performance could also include data on the effectiveness of new technologies and educational strategies, such as the use of multimedia and adaptive release of course materials. Institutions are interested in validating the use of resources and technologies by measuring their effect on student learning outcomes. This type of assessment is critical to justify expenses and ensure the continuation of grants and other funding. Online and blended learning environments lend themselves to the collection of massive amounts of data in support of such efforts that can easily be tabulated and analyzed.

From an institutional perspective, student performance is ultimately measured in terms of course and program completion (Alexander, 2000; Peterson & Augustine, 2000; Serban, 2004). In addition to comparing admission to graduation figures, tabulating dropout rates, and calculating completion time, institutions can take advantage of new technologies to investigate causes for delays and even implement early warning systems that are based on usage statistics gathered within the learning management system. One of the advantages of online and blended learning is the fact that students leave electronic footprints that are evidence of their effort, for example in reading texts, viewing videos, and contributing to discussion boards (Hershkovitz & Nachmias, 2011; Morris, Finnegan, & Wu, 2005). The instructor can define custom rules or adopt departmental rules to filter out or flag students who fail to meet the criteria for reasonable progress. These early warning systems are a critical tool to prevent students from falling too far behind in learning environments that require them to manage their own time rather than participate in weekly classroom meetings.

Instructor Dimensions

Facilitation: The Instructor in Education
A core function of the instructor is the *facilitation* of learning. In online and blended environments, this typically involves the use of mediated communication, which adds a layer of abstraction and thus introduces additional challenges not typically faced in the traditional classroom (Garrison,

Anderson, & Archer, 2001; McNeil et al., 2000; Thorpe, 2002). Nevertheless, core indicators of facilitation are universal and should be considered equivalently, regardless of mode of instruction.

Instructors should be assessed with respect to their effectiveness in course design and delivery, including feedback, communication, student support, presence, and mentor management. Comprehensive assessments should include multiple sources of data such as student perceptions, review of course syllabi, and peer assessment. The data for these assessments are typically collected through surveys, interviews, document reviews, and observations. Many institutions that offer online and blended courses have adopted one of several available systematic course review and assessment methods, such as MarylandOnline's *Quality Matters* (MarylandOnline, 2013) or SLOAN-C's *Quality Scorecard* (SLOAN-C, 2013). These methodologies include standardized checklists along with training materials and certification for reviewers. The quality reviews focus on aspects of course design, including alignment of objectives, assessments, and instruction; use of media; motivational design; learning activities; communication protocols; and collaboration.

Also included in this area of performance are services such as libraries, writing centers, technology support, learning management systems, advising, and field experience coordination, to name but a few (Benjamin, 2008; Rogers & Gentemann, 1989; Serban, 2004). The quality of these services is typically assessed by means of interviews or surveys, along with stratified usage counts (Chism & Banta, 2007). For example, the effectiveness of a writing center might be assessed by counting the number of students—categorized by year in school and other properties of interest—and comparing their scores on writing assignments before and after receiving help at the center. The effectiveness of the center might be assessed overall in addition to assessing the performance of individual staff members.

Qualification: The Instructor in Academia

A second critical dimension of the instructor is *qualification* (Brennan & Shah, 2000; Rogers & Gentemann, 1989). Decisions of students to enroll in a program are often driven by the qualifications and specializations of the teaching faculty, especially at advanced levels of higher education. Given the relative novelty of online and blended teaching, faculty qualifications must include appropriate expertise and experience in related technologies beyond the subject matter at hand.

Assessment of an instructor's readiness to teach online and blended learning courses may take the form of an online quiz with scenario-type questions, or may be built into a series of tutorials or workshops. The aim of such training programs is to ensure that faculty who are new to teaching this type of course have an opportunity to fill any gaps in knowledge about the learning management system as well as pedagogical and administrative aspects that are unique to online and blended learning. An effective way of combining training with assessment is to use real course components. For example, an instructor preparing for her first online course might be asked to submit a draft version of her syllabus as an assignment during a training workshop. The document could then be improved and the final version would serve as evidence of mastery and could be used in the new online course.

In addition to academic credentials, subject-matter expertise, and teaching experience, institutions may also assess an applicant's research activities, publications, and grants with respect to online and blended learning. This applies in particular to fields such as communication and education, as well as subjects that have seen an increase in online and blended programs, including business, nursing, and social work. Hiring new faculty who are engaged in this type of research contributes toward an institutional base of expertise, which is useful for collaborative, interdisciplinary development of new courses as well as peer teaching evaluation and improvement programs.

Institutional Dimensions

Accreditation: The Institution in the Academia

The first institutional dimension that deserves attention in the context of assessment is *accreditation* (Peterson & Augustine, 2000; Welsh & Metcalf, 2003). Particularly where online and blended learning are concerned, accreditation is an important indicator of legitimacy and quality, helping students interested in getting their education online to select an institution whose diplomas are valued and respected.

The main focus of assessment for accreditation is to ensure that the institution meets the accrediting agency's standards, which tend to be stated in rather general terms in order to account for differences among candidate institutions. It is the institution's responsibility to interpret and apply these standards to its organization, to assess its own effectiveness, and to provide documentation and supporting evidence for the agency's review panel. Assessment for accreditation covers every aspect of the institution, including mission, governance, administration, educational programs, faculty, resources, services, and compliance with policies. Each standard requires the collection of relevant data, analysis, interpretation, and explanation of how the institution currently meets the standard. For example, the institution might provide copies of procedures and technical specifications for systems that are used in order to ensure the identity of its online students; copies of program and course-level outcomes, along with course syllabi and instructional materials, are submitted to document effectiveness with respect to equivalency of online courses as compared to classroom courses; and lists of faculty credentials and specialized training matched to teaching assignments are produced in order to provide evidence of instructor qualifications for teaching online and blended courses.

Contribution to the advancement of online and blended learning may be included in an institution's mission, especially if the leadership envisions the university to become a leader and global competitor in these new educational directions. Since an accrediting agency will assess the alignment between the institutional mission and its implementation, it would be important to provide appropriate data in support of the institution's effort in this respect, including faculty engagement in online and blended learning through teaching and research, production of relevant publications, and hosting of virtual or traditional conferences and educational events. Assessment of the effectiveness of such activities and engagement might include participant surveys that could be correlated with admissions, enrollment, graduation, alumni success, faculty promotion, and new faculty hiring data.

Globalization: The Institution in the Economy

The final core dimension of the institutional assessment framework is *globalization* (Clugston & Calder, 1999; Cortese, 2003; Vaira, 2004). We selected this dimension because it effectively captures an essential ingredient that determines the success of institutions of higher education in the 21st century. Without addressing globalization, institutions will likely be left behind as students increasingly follow new paths of education that fit their needs and promise their success after graduation. Students are no longer bound by geographical, economic, and even political boundaries in their choice of higher education. While the success of institutions depends on a multitude of factors, the following stand out as particularly important.

In order to ascertain global competitiveness, institutions must continuingly assess their effectiveness with respect to capitalizing on online and blended learning opportunities. Ongoing research of alumni, prospective students, employers, global job markets, and competitors is essential in this respect. Savvy institutions will maximize the benefits of Web technologies by creating a seamless virtual presence in social and educational media, having faculty contribute to forums, publish their academic work in a variety of formats, and present at and even host international conferences. Such events present the opportunity to build contact lists, get input and feedback, promote events and programs, and hold the potential for increasing exposure through virtual referrals. Institutions should monitor demand and develop flexibility to adjust course and program offerings to meet it. They should strive for diversity in all aspects of their organization, including student population, faculty and staff, as well as curriculum and services, because diversity enables both resilience and stability of the institution overall. Cultural diversity of faculty and staff is essential in order to develop the necessary sensitivity and cultural intelligence needed to cater to an increasingly international audience.

Institutions must also assess their effectiveness in meeting the particular challenges of online and blended learning, including technologies, communication, and learning management. In order to stay globally competitive it is necessary to constantly assess the effectiveness of current methods and solutions; look for improvement opportunities; identify new developments that could affect student needs and expectations; address deficiencies and limitations; and increase the institution's competitiveness through new opportunities. Openness to change and effective change management is a prerequisite for success in this respect. Institutions should include critical assessments of the their internal procedures that govern innovation and the implementation of change to ensure that the corresponding policies and procedures do not present a bottleneck that may prove to be a disadvantage in the global marketplace of online and blended learning.

CONCLUSION

The institutional assessment framework presented in this chapter provided an overview of the breadth and depth of applications related to assessment in higher education. While there is significant overlap with the traditional classroom, online and blended learning environments do present unique challenges that require creative solutions and an open mind toward change. Effective assessment in this context is especially important, since this information is needed in order to determine whether the institution is on the right track and what areas need improvement. The elements of the framework provide a solid point of reference for administrators to develop the necessary tools and methods that will allow them to assess the performance of their institution as it relates to its vision and mission. Particular goals and objectives likely vary among different organizations, and with them each institution needs to develop appropriate indicators of success. The examples provided in this chapter were selected in order to illustrate the complexity of the task and should not be considered exhaustive or even necessarily applicable to all organizations. Due to space constraints, this chapter does not include a detailed discussion of methods and instruments needed to conduct the various types of assessment included in the framework. Future publications are planned to address this need, including specific examples, case studies, and guidelines for conducting these assessments. Nevertheless, exposure to the concepts introduced in this chapter may help individuals approach assessment with a fresh mind, consider new connections and dependencies among existing measures, and perhaps expand on current means of assessment to include additional perspectives.

REFERENCES

Alexander, F. K. (2000). The changing face of accountability: Monitoring and assessing institutional performance in higher education. *Journal of Higher Education, 71*(4), 411–431.

Altbach, P. G., & Knight, J. (2007). The internationalization of higher education: Motivations and realities. *Journal of Studies in International Education, 11*(3–4), 290–305.

Bailey, T., Alfonso, M., Scott, M., & Leinbach, T. (2004). *Educational outcomes of occupational postsecondary students.* Washington, DC: U.S. Department of Education, National Assessment of Vocational Education.

Benjamin, R. (2008). The case for comparative institutional assessment of higher-order thinking skills. *Magazine of Higher Learning, 40*(6), 50–55.

Berdrow, I., & Evers, F. T. (2010). Bases of competence: An instrument for self and institutional assessment. *Assessment and Evaluation in Higher Education, 35*(4), 419–434.

Bers, T. H. (2008). The role of institutional assessment in assessing student learning outcomes. *New Directions for Higher Education, 141*, 31–39.

Bowden, J. A., & Masters, G. N. (1993). *Implications for higher education of a competency-based approach to education and training.* Canberra: Australian Government Publishing Service.

Brennan, J., & Shah, T. (2000). Quality assessment and institutional change: Experiences from 14 countries. *Higher Education, 40*(3), 331–349.

Brignall, S., & Modell, S. (2000). An institutional perspective on performance measurement and management in the "new public sector." *Management Accounting Research, 11*(3), 281–306.

Capano, G. (2010). A Sisyphean task: Evaluation and institutional accountability in Italian higher education. *Higher Education Policy, 23*(1), 39–62.

Chism, N. V. N., & Banta, T. W. (2007). Enhancing institutional assessment efforts through qualitative methods. In S. R. Harper & S. D. Museus (Eds.), Using qualitative methods in institutional assessment. *New Directions for Institutional Research, 136*, 15–28.

Clugston, R. M., & Calder, W. (1999). Critical Dimensions of Sustainability in Higher Education. In W. Leal Filho (Ed.), *Sustainability and university life* (pp. 31–46). Frankfurt: Peter Lang.

Cooper, L. (2013). Trends in online academic publishing. *Metaphilosophy, 44*(3), 327–334.

Cortese, A. D. (2003). The critical role of higher education in creating a sustainable future. *Planing Higher Education, 31*(3), 15–22.

Cusumano, M. A. (2013). Are the costs of "free" too high in online education? *Communications of the ACM, 56*(4), 26.

Dale, A., Newman, L., & Ling, C. (2010). Facilitating transdisciplinary sustainable development research teams through online collaboration. *International Journal of Sustainability in Higher Education, 11*(1), 36–48.

Easton, S. S. (2003). Clarifying the instructor's role in online distance learning. *Communication Education, 52*(2), 87–105.

Fein, A. D., Logan, M. C., & Holmes, O. W. (2003). Preparing Instructors for online instruction. *New Directions for Adult and Continuing Education, 100*, 45–55.

Garrison, D. R., Anderson, T., & Archer, W. (2001). Critical thinking, cognitive presence, and computer conferencing in distance education. *American Journal of Distance Education, 15*(1), 7–23.

Garrison, D. R., & Kanuka, H. (2004). Blended learning: Uncovering its transformative potential in higher education. *The Internet and Higher Education, 7*(2), 95–105.

Gaytan, J., & Mcewen, B. C. (2007). Effective online instructional and assessment strategies. *American Journal of Distance Education, 21*(3), 117–132.

Georg, W. (2009). Individual and institutional factors in the tendency to drop out of higher education: A multilevel analysis using data from the Konstanz Student Survey. *Studies in Higher Education, 34*(6), 647–661.

Hershkovitz, A., & Nachmias, R. (2011). Online persistence in higher education web-supported courses. *The Internet and Higher Education, 14*(2), 98–106.

Karp, M. M. (2011). How non-academic supports work: Four mechanisms for improving student outcomes. *Community College Research Center Brief*, pp. 1–4.

MarylandOnline. (2013). *Quality matters.* Retrieved from http://www.qualitymatters.org.

McNeil, S. G., Robin, B. R., & Miller, R. M. (2000). Facilitating interaction, communication and collaboration in online courses. *Computers and Geosciences, 26*(6), 699–708.

Moloney, J. F., & Oakley, B., I. (2010). Scaling online education: Increasing access to higher education. *Journal of Asynchronous Learning Networks, 14*(1), 55–70.

Moosai, S., Walker, D. A., & Deborah, L. (2011). Using student and institutional characteristics to predict graduation rates at community colleges: New developments in performance measures and institutional effectiveness. *Community College Journal of Research and Practice, 35*(10), 802–816.

Morris, L. V., Finnegan, C., & Wu, S.-S. (2005). Tracking student behavior, persistence, and achievement in online courses. *The Internet and Higher Education, 8*(3), 221–231.

Peterson, M. W., & Augustine, C. H. (2000). External and internal influences on institutional approaches to student assessment: Accountability or Improvement. *Research in Higher Education, 41*(4), 443–479.

Reeves, T. C. (2000). Alternative assessment approaches for online learning environments in higher education. *Journal of Educational Computing Research, 23*(1), 101–111.

Rogers, B. H., & Gentemann, K. M. (1989). The value of institutional research in the assessment of institutional effectiveness. *Research in Higher Education, 30*(3), 345–355.

Serban, A. M. (2004). Assessment of student learning outcomes at the institutional level. *New Directions for Community Colleges,* (126), 17–27.

Shriberg, M. (2002). Institutional assessment tools for sustainability in higher education: Strengths, weaknesses, and implications for practice and theory. *International Journal of Sustainability in Higher Education, 3*(3), 254–270.

SLOAN-C. (2013). *Quality scorecard.* Retrieved from http://sloanconsortium.org/quality_scorecard_online_program.

Spector, J. M. (2013). Emerging educational technologies and research directions. *Educational Technology and Society, 16*(2), 21–30.

Swan, K., & Hiltz, S. R. (2006). Assessment and Collaboration in Online Learning. *Journal of Asynchronous Learning Networks, 10*(1), 45–62.

Thorpe, M. (2002). Rethinking learner support: The challenge of collaborative online learning. *Journal of Open, Distance and e-Learning, 17*(2), 105–119.

Tilsley, A. (2012). Sites offering to take courses for a fee pose risk to online ed. *Inside Higher Ed.* Retrieved from http://www.insidehighered.com/news/2012/09/21/sites-offering-take-courses-fee-pose-risk-online-ed.

Vaira, M. (2004). Globalization and higher education organizational change: A framework for analysis. *Higher Education, 48*(4), 483–510.

Vardi, M. Y. (2012). Will MOOCs destroy academia? *Communications of the ACM, 55*(11), 5.

Welsh, J. F., & Metcalf, J. (2003). Faculty and administrative support for institutional effectiveness activities: A bridge across the chasm? *Journal of Higher Education, 74*(4), 445–468.

White, S. (2007). Critical success factors for e-learning and institutional change?: Some organisational perspectives on campus-wide e-learning. *British Journal of Educational Technology, 38*(5), 840–850.

Wilson, M., & Scalise, K. (2006). Assessment to improve learning in higher education: The BEAR assessment system. *Higher Education, 52*(4), 635–663.

Yarime, M., & Tanaka, Y. (2012). The issues and methodologies in sustainability assessment tools for higher education institutions: A review of recent trends and future challenges. *Journal of Education for Sustainable Development, 6*(1), 63–77.

Yorke, M. (2003). Formative assessment in higher education: Moves towards theory and the enhancement of pedagogic practice. *Higher Education, 45*(4), 477–501.

ABOUT THE EDITORS

Dr. Selma Koç is an associate professor of education. She currently serves as the coordinator of the Master's Degree Program in Educational Technology at Cleveland State University. Her teaching experience includes teaching face-to-face, videoconferencing, and online courses in educational technology, educational psychology, and gifted education. One recent course she has designed and taught is "Designing Online Instruction." Her research interests are: online/blended learning and assessment, web 2.0, technology planning and integration in K–12 and higher education. She currently serves as a member of the Editorial Review Board of the Journal of Research on Technology in Education.

Dr. Xiongyi Liu attended graduate school and earned her PhD in Educational Psychology from University of Nebraska–Lincoln after two years of teaching college English in China. During 2006–2008, she worked as research assistant professor at the Center for Research and Evaluation, University of Maine. She joined the Cleveland State University faculty in 2008 and has taught undergraduate and graduate students educational psychology. Dr. Liu has worked as co-PI and program evaluator for multiple research projects funded by Department of Education, National Science Foundation, etc. Her research interests include: computer-supported collaborative learning, peer assessment, motivation, and self-regulated learning strategies.

Assessment in Online and Blended Learning Environments, pages 307–308
Copyright © 2015 by Information Age Publishing
All rights of reproduction in any form reserved.

Dr. Patrick Wachira is an Associate Professor of Mathematics Education. He holds a joint appointment in the departments of Mathematics and Teacher Education. His teaching experience includes teaching mathematics content and education courses both face-to-face and online. His main research interest is in the appropriate integration of technology in mathematics teaching and learning.

CPSIA information can be obtained
at www.ICGtesting.com
Printed in the USA
FFOW01n2151160717
37819FF